TEXTILE ART

TEXTILE ART

by

MICHEL THOMAS

Editor of the periodical *Textile/Art*, Paris
and Director of the International Centre
of Textile Art, Paris

CHRISTINE MAINGUY

Research Assistant at the National Centre
of Scientific Research, Paris

SOPHIE POMMIER

Egyptologist and graduate of the
School of Oriental Languages, Paris

SKIRA

RIZZOLI
NEW YORK

© 1985 by Editions d'Art Albert Skira S.A., Geneva

Reproduction rights reserved by A.D.A.G.P. and
S.P.A.D.E.M., Paris, and Cosmopress, Geneva

Published in the United States of America in 1985 by

Rizzoli INTERNATIONAL PUBLICATIONS, INC.
597 Fifth Avenue/New York 10017

Translated from the French by André Marling

Printed in Switzerland

Library of Congress Cataloging-in-Publication Data

Thomas, Michel.
    Textile art.

    Translation of: Histoire d'un art.
    Bibliography: p.
    Includes index.
    1. Textile fabrics–History.   2. Tapestry–
History.   3. Wall hangings–History.   4. Soft sculpture
–History.   I. Pommier, Sophie.   II. Title.
NK8806.T4813   1985   746   85-42942
ISBN 0-8478-0640-5 (Rizzoli)

CONTENTS

PREFACE

Every two years since 1962, the Fine Arts Museum in Lausanne, Switzerland, has housed an exhibition known as the Tapestry Biennial. In preparing more than ten of these exhibitions, the selection committees have chosen several hundred out of several thousand works submitted, all of them considered, with the implicit assent of the artists, to be covered by the term tapestry.

At the same time, the selection committees have on several occasions stated that the definition of the term tapestry cannot be established *a priori* but must emerge *a posteriori* from the exhibited works. Nevertheless, by comparing the regulations of the successive exhibitions, it is possible to follow recent trends in this branch of the arts as it has, little by little, built up its own image as one of the contemporary visual arts, whose scope and specific features it has, moreover, been the aim of this and other exhibitions to identify.

Thus the booklet published in 1975 by the International Centre for Ancient and Modern Tapestry, the body organizing the Lausanne Biennial, reads: "Under the regulations for the First Biennial Exhibition, only works woven on high- or low-warp looms were accepted, although provision was made for the inclusion of other techniques in subsequent exhibitions. The Second Biennial did in fact admit embroidery and appliqué. Still more flexible, the regulations for the third exhibition created a section for research without any other stipulation."

◁ JAGODA BUIC (1930)
FIREBIRD
Homage to Stravinsky (detail), 1977
High warp
Overall size: 6′7″ × 8′4″

▷ GERHARDT KNODEL (1940)
GRAND EXCHANGE, 1981
Hand-woven wool, mylar,
wire and nylon rope

MAGDALENA ABAKANOWICZ (1930)
LARGE RITUAL SPACE, 1977
Black and red ropes, wood and hemp
Konsthall, Malmö, Sweden

8

Peter Jacobi (1935)
and
Ritzi Jacobi (1941)
Variable Environment, 1970
Woven wool, wood, metal
Venice Biennale

The regulations for the tenth exhibition, in 1981, began: "The Tenth Biennial purports to review the evolution of textile art as a whole, in its forms and applications (techniques, modes of expression, research, uses, situations, etc.)."

This definition implicitly recognized that in abandoning the initial privilege accorded to one technique, loom tapestry, in order to admit other techniques using fibres, threads and fabrics, the presence of new artistic modalities changed the very nature of the exhibition. Besides tapestries based on painters' cartoons, which were essentially the translation of a painting, model or design, familiar to the public, the exhibition included autonomous forms of artistic expression based on the specific foundations, properties, application and functioning of textile writing.

The strong emphasis placed from the start on a question of definition may seem surprising, but the Lausanne Biennial has shown that in comparison with other contemporary arts, painting, sculpture and drawing, the very concept of textile art is more recent. Its definition was established in the first place in relation to that of tapestry.

As traditionally defined, the term tapestry is applied to a particular kind of plain weave material in which the weft covers the entire warp and is itself the means of creating the design and expressing complex themes.

This definition fits most Coptic fabrics, Chinese *k'o-ssu*, Japanese *tsuzure-ore*, some pre-Inca fabrics, Western hangings such as the *Angers Apocalypse* and, needless to say, tapestries woven on high- or low-warp looms after painters' cartoons. All the works shown at the first exhibition were comprised in this category.

In the light of this definition, it is easy to see the significance of the extended scope of the second exhibition. Tapestry has been only one of the traditional means of artistic expression in fabrics. Embroidery and, in particular, needlework tapestry and appliqué have lent themselves just as well to the presentation of complex designs and subjects.

Furthermore, new modalities have made the technical methods of tapestry making much more apparent by using, as means of artistic expression, all the structural elements that tapestry makers since the Renaissance, required to make tapestry resemble painting as closely as possible, had deliberately concealed or kept in the background. Coptic or pre-Columbian tapestry makers, on the other hand, knew very well how to use these same elements as an integral part of textile design. Similar methods, specific to textiles, have likewise been rediscovered by artists not only in weaving techniques in general, but also in sewing, embroidery, knitting or spinning where the scriptory elements have often been developed on a monumental scale. Similarly, handicraft techniques have benefited from recent discoveries in industrial techniques, which have added to the range of possibilities open to them.

In short, there has been a vast rediscovery of means of expression in textile materials, many of them thousands of years old and stemming from different civilizations some of which still uphold their original traditions.

The Lausanne Biennial, which has done so much to make this rediscovery known, has at the same time promoted more widespread appreciation of textile art. Following the lead it has given, other exhibitions have been held at regular intervals in all parts of the world.

Some, such as the London Minitextiles Biennial, organized by the British Crafts Centre, cover a different area from that of the Lausanne exhibition. Whereas the Lausanne Biennial requires artists to submit very large works, London sets a maximum limit of 20 centimetres (8 inches) for the length of the works it accepts. The aim of the organizers is to encourage research in the expression of ideas on a minimal scale.

Countries from the Eastern bloc have likewise initiated regular events of the same kind. Lodz, the chief town of the Polish textile industry, intends to hold a triennial exhibition. In Hungary, at Szombathely, a Biennial held since 1970 has been accompanied since 1974 by another for minitextiles.

In the United States, although the idea of regular exhibitions has not been taken up, some public events have reflected official recognition of trends in international textile art. One of these was the "Fiberworks" exhibition, held in 1977 at the Cleveland Museum of Art. "The Dyer's Art," prepared in 1977 by Jack Lenor Larsen, brought together in a highly significant manner pieces of archaeological and ethnographic textiles typical of the main dyeing techniques, together with others produced by contemporary artists applying the same methods in new contexts.

VERENA SIEBER-FUCHS (1943)
HAT, 1984
Black wire, black and
red beads, and crochet
Diameter 13½″, height 2¾″

SYMBOLIC TREE
FROM A GRAVE
AT CHANCAY, PERU
1100-1400
Woollen thread over straw
and reed frame,
bearing woven fruit,
flowers and birds
Height 26½″

Jack Lenor Larsen is also the author of two basic publications written in collaboration with Mildred Constantine: *Beyond Craft: the Art Fabric* (1973) and *The Art Fabric: Mainstream* (1980). The latter work was published for an exhibition which toured ten American museums in 1981 and 1982.

Some European museums have reviewed artistic creation in the textiles area. At the Stedelijk Museum, Amsterdam, Will Berteux and later Lisbeth Crommelin surveyed the general situation in "Perspectief in Textiel," 1969, and "Structuur in Textiel," 1976, to give two examples. In Paris, in 1973, François Mathey took stock of current developments in "Tapisseries Nouvelles" at the Musée des Arts Décoratifs. Since 1981, under the heading of "Art et Création Textile," Danielle Molinari has held exhibitions of the works of individual artists at the Musée d'Art Moderne de la Ville de Paris. Finally, twice a year since 1982, Jean Coural, administrator of the Mobilier National, in association with the magazine *Textile/Art*, has organized exhibitions of artists under the title "Identités Textiles."

Likewise, international symposiums bringing together creative artists, museum curators, art critics, researchers and directors of art galleries afford useful occasions for regular stock-taking.

Meetings and exhibitions of this kind could not have been held and become a permanent institution if they had not been a means of discovering artists of genius who have won recognition outside the limits of professional circles and specialized exhibitions.

Through other international biennial exhibitions, such as those held at Venice or São Paulo, an even wider public has become familiar with the names of Magdalena Abakanowicz, Jagoda Buic, Patrice Hugues, and Peter and Ritzi Jacobi.

The monumental works of some of these artists have attracted the attention of architects in the same way as those of Soto, Dubuffet or Serra.

Orders for the environmental textile creations of Magdalena Abakanowicz, Daniel Graffin, Sheila Hicks, Barbara Shawcroft, Lenore Tawney or Susan Watson have drawn attention to the peculiar gentleness and magic luminosity characteristic of their works, in striking contrast to the rigidity of contemporary architecture.

More generally, after a period during which these new forms of expression in textiles caught the public eye above all on account of their radical difference from the classical conception of tapestry–an aspect examined in depth by the Lausanne art critic André Kuenzi in 1974 in his book *La Nouvelle Tapisserie*–art critics and museum curators have turned their attention to the investigation of textile creation, considered in particular in its relations with contemporary trends in sculpture and painting.

Mildred Constantine described the nature of this research very well in 1980 in her book *The Art Fabric: Mainstream*. "Working directly with cloth and other 'non-art' materials, some artists have broken the barriers and changed the definition of what constitutes art. This can be seen in the work of Eva Hesse, Sam Gilliam, Man Ray, Robert Rauschenberg, Colette and Christo."

Textile fibre is essentially a supple element, belonging to a family of materials called by André Leroi-Gourhan "supple solids." Works created with it lend themselves quite naturally to varied kinds of display giving them a sculptural dimension: they can be spread out on the ground, hung from the ceiling, tensed between several points, attached to a mast or wire like banners, or–why not?–in a more ephemeral manner, supported by the wind like a kite.

It is even possible to conceive their arrangement in the form of penetrable structures.

Finally, some creators design their works as an original garment, adorned with artistry, a kind of living sculpture, a genre classified by the Anglo-Saxons under the term "wearable."

ROBERT MORRIS (1931)
FELT, 1976
White industrial felt and eyelets
8′ × 12′4″ × 8″

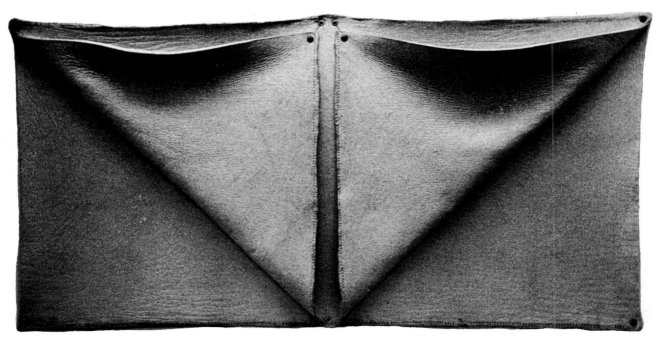

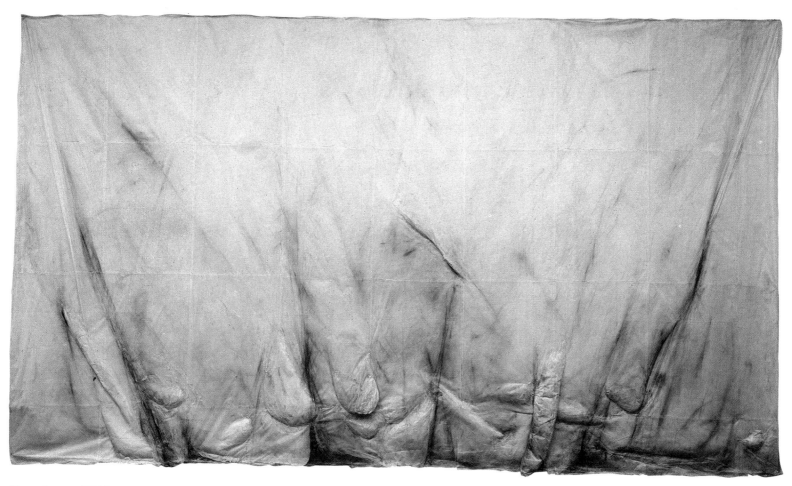

RITZI JACOBI (1941)
STUDY XV No. 2, 1976
Graphite on rice paper,
mounted on rice paper
8'2" × 13'9" × 4"

More rigid fibres, such as those traditionally used for basketry, can be given fixed sculptural form, which some artists have shaped along the lines of the human figure.

It is not surprising therefore that textiles should be considered today as a basically supple art, which shares to some extent the problems of those visual art works known as Soft Art.

At the end of 1979, Erika Billeter, in an exhibition entitled "Weich und plastisch, Soft Art," at the Kunsthaus, Zurich, showed the works of artists who used materials expressing notions of flexibility, gentleness and softness in order to create forms to be touched, or forms that changed on being touched. There the *objets trouvés* of Marcel Duchamp, Man Ray and Meret Oppenheim could be seen beside the works of Pop Art and the New Realists, the soft furniture of Salvador Dali and the soft objects of Claes Oldenburg, together with the conceptual or minimal works of Pedro Manzoni, Ruthenbeck, Robert Morris, Richard Serra, Eva Hesse or Klaus Rinke, who explored the use of materials as messages, structures and forms. It was significant that the compressed jeans and jutes of César should be placed opposite the large black costumes of Magdalena Abakanowicz, or Ritzi Jacobi's rice paper covered with graphite facing the paper sculptures of Anne and Patrick Poirier.

This Zurich exhibition, like the Harry Szeeman exhibition at Berne in 1969, "Wenn Attituden Form werden" (When Attitudes become Form), or "Material wird Kunst" (Material becomes Art) in Berlin in 1982, supply the proof that the codes of sculpture have changed in the same way as those of painting, tapestry making, drawing on paper, and that these changes in codes have entailed such deep interpenetration that traditional vocabularies no longer serve to express the precise nature of the works.

For example, the supple nature of textiles and the nomadic character of fabrics are elements taken into account by sculptors and painters as well as by the artists of the "New Tapestry."

13

Consequently, the relations of textile artists with painting now feature cross-checking of a different kind from that which was typical of tapestry making based on painters' cartoons.

To grasp the significance of this new relationship, it is enough to evoke the American artist, Morris Louis, whose work has been described by Clement Greenberg in terms that emphasize the role of fabric: "Imbued with paint instead of being covered by it, the fabric itself becomes paint and color, like a dyed cloth. The warp and weave are in the color."

Within the trends in French painting that developed in the 1960s round the notion of "Support Surface," the canvas came to be recognized as a subject in its own right owing to its qualities of flexibility, porosity, texture.

Claude Viallat, for example, chose the most varied kinds of textile supports: "From tarpaulins to parasols, from old curtains to sheets with openwork borders, or even dresses, the painting covers the everyday surface of the fabric, sometimes leaving the writing of the latter bare, as in the case of floral print or striped material when the painting only adds punctuation." Marcel Alocco who since 1962 has called all his canvases "Patchwork Fragment" is a typical example of this trend.

The Erika Billeter exhibition in Zurich, in 1979, also replaced this inter-penetration of artistic disciplines in the retrospective light of ethnographical objects. The presence of feathered headdresses of the Indians of Brazil, Australian objects made with hair, objects of religious cults forming part of the ritual and myths of non-Western societies, was a clear indication that behind this new art there lay a historical process: the rediscovery of the fundamental role of these materials in traditional societies.

In turning their attention to archaeological and ethnographical fabrics, these artists have not only revived the use of materials and techniques forgotten by creative artists for many centuries, they have also transferred their interest from the specific structural and plastic features of textiles to the problems of their social integration.

This transfer can be compared with the attitude of Western artists to African sculpture.

Just as the Cubists became interested in the fact that masks and totems raised the problems of representation on bases involving radically different notions of perspective and proportion from those current in the West since the Renaissance, so contemporary artists of the Land Art school, or those developing individual mythologies, are rediscovering a mythological and cosmological dimension.

The interest of textile artists in fabrics is characterized by the recovery of a language.

This language is the language of art, long forgotten by the traditional disciplines, but also an everyday language.

It is a language that is still living, written into the structure of some societies in rites that are often only a repetition of primal myths, and living also in our societies, as close as it is possible to be to each of us, indeed right next to the skin.

A language inscribed in fabrics which our hands touch, fabrics with which we come into physical contact.

Patrice Hugues describes this revival in general terms, insisting on the fact that "the fabric, a carrier of signs, does not run counter to thought, nor confine itself to being only 'for living.' The communication it conveys keeps more closely to both than we may think: like speech and the tongue. It is never more than partly subject to the threat of imposition. This silent communication through textiles offsets in its own way many one-way ruptures of the kind that make up so much of life today."

In artistic matters, artists guide art critics and not the contrary.

In the specific area of textile art, the artists' reflections have prompted reconsideration of fabric values.

It is hoped therefore that this book will contribute to the rediscovery of the diversity of textile art in the different centres where it has flourished in the past and help to give tapestry, which has for so long been the only synonym for art fabric, its proper place once again in the full range of approaches to the artistic use of cloth.

The privileges accorded to tapestry in the West have certainly helped to spread the notion that art fabrics were necessarily a projection of painting. The rediscovery by contemporary creators of methods specific to tapestry has not only entailed the freeing of tapestry from the unique pictorial approach to fabrics, but has also made it possible to take a new look at the textile world as a whole.

Textiles have once more won recognition as an art material with its own values, a medium comprising language and meaning.

Textiles are, moreover, now losing in the West their futile daily connotations and reacquiring a nobler cultural status.

The artists who have once again taken account of the language of textiles will have been the precursors of a more general social phenomenon.

This recovery has been obtained through research in origins and history.

Claude Viallat, referring to painting and art in general, has given admirable expression to this linguistic reapprenticeship: "We find ourselves today in search of infantile babblings, of our origins. Taking our languages and techniques to pieces, we put them all to the challenge. The world is learning to know itself again as it becomes known, as it questions itself, divests itself of its inventions by looking back into its inmost self."

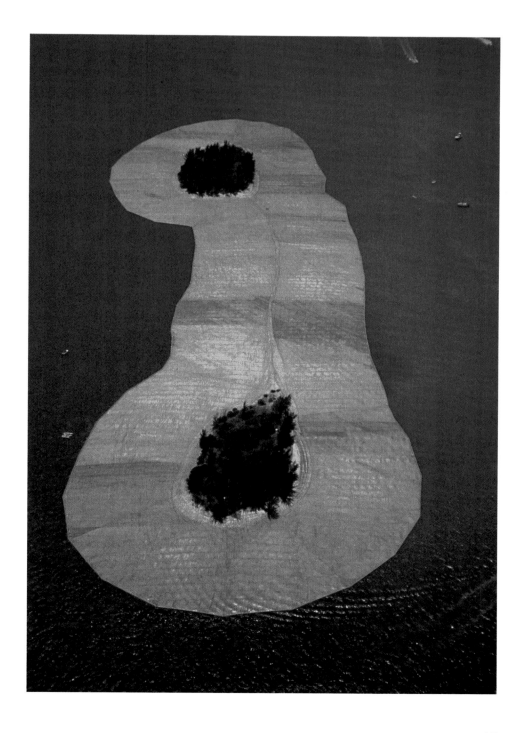

CHRISTO (1935)
SURROUNDED ISLANDS, 1980-1983
Biscayne Bay, Greater Miami, Florida

WORLD CENTRES OF TEXTILE ART

ARCHAEOLOGY

MAN'S TUNIC, CLOAK AND CAP
from Muldbjerg, West Jutland, Denmark
Early Bronze Age (1500-800 B.C.)

The question of the origin of man's utilization of textiles would not be so difficult to answer if fibres were a less perishable form of matter. The preservation of fabrics is, indeed, only possible under special conditions of extreme dryness or extreme humidity. Owing to the very limited number of textile remains, very few chronological accounts of prehistoric times give any place to technological or aesthetic inventions concerning textiles, unlike those in the evolution of figurative painting or sculpture, ceramics, agriculture or writing. André Leroi-Gourhan, writing in 1971 in *L'homme et la matière*, states: "It is clear that if we try to visualize the invention, that is to say the origin of weaving, we have nothing to go on apart from often contradictory records giving the general impression of a development starting from relatively simple forms and proceeding towards technical forms yielding better (not necessarily more complex) results as the outcome of a succession of often minimal improvements." Some indications are obtained from what Leroi-Gourhan calls "negative evidence": encrusted impressions on weapons, metallic buttons, adornments of dress, clay pottery, plaster coating. Evidence is also provided by written documents. The Louvre papyrus deciphered by Gaston Maspero describes the organization of work in a cloth mill, and there are pertinent references in the *Iliad* and the *Odyssey*.

Proofs of the cultivation of textile plants such as flax or cotton and the breeding of camelids are another element to be taken into consideration. Needless to say, however, only excavations can afford positive proof of hypotheses and fix dates.

Ideal conditions as regards dryness have obtained in Egyptian tombs and the sandy regions along the arid coast of Peru. On the other hand, some damp places also provide excellent conditions for the preservation of textiles: the Bronze Age lake settlements in the Italian, Swiss and French Alps (Charavines and Lake Paladru), the earthen dykes in Holland, the ferruginous Bronze Age tumuli in Germany which form an impermeable crust and hold the water as in a cloche, the peat bogs and funereal barrows in Denmark in which fabrics are preserved by the very high acidity of the water or the tannins produced by oak coffins.

In Europe and the Mediterranean basin, fabrics and tools found in Neolithic lake dwellings are direct proof of weaving between the fourth and second millennium B.C. Plain weave fabrics, like those from Irgenhausen (canton of Zurich) decorated with stripes, squares and herringbone patterns, are already significant of technical mastery.

Earlier still, "Clear impressions of fabrics on plaster coatings found at El Kown in Syria (dating from 5800 B.C.) take us back several thousand years... Older still (going back to about 7000 B.C.) are long, flat and pointed objects which, held together by the middle, would be identical with the Swiss Neolithic carding combs, and other objects quite like shuttles. The origins of weaving can therefore, without great risk of error, be dated back to the seventh millennium B.C." (Danielle Stordeur).

In South America, Ecuador and Northern Peru are the countries where remains of Neolithic agricultural communities producing ceramics and woven cloth have been discovered. Marion Rembur of the American Department of the Musée de l'Homme, Paris, draws attention to the fact that "soft texture" cloths woven more than five thousand years ago have been found at different sites along the coast and in the northern Andes, and adds: "The cruder and more ungainly pieces can be given an even earlier date. At Guitarrero, in a cave in the northern Sierra of Peru, many cords and three fragments of basket-work made of vegetable fibres were found. This site formed part of a hunters' settlement of the pre-ceramic period. It was occupied from 8600 to 8000 B.C."

Going still further back, as concerns textile activities such as the sewing of skins, bone needles similar to our Neolithic needles but dating from 20,000 B.C. have also been found. All these datings go to show the antiquity of weaving and textile activities in relation to other basic activities such as ceramics, metallurgy and writing.

As regards ceramics, there is good reason to believe that in the beginning textile decoration was the model for the decoration of pottery, and not vice versa.

More fundamentally still, textiles would appear to have assumed a priority role in relation to other human activities.

Apart from their mythological relations with speech, the lines of woven yarn have, without any doubt, a relation to lines of writing.

As has often been pointed out, the words text, textile, texture and architecture have a common root. All supple materials, the "supple solids" as Leroi-Gourhan calls them (animal and vegetable fibres, stems of trees, leather thongs, metallic wires), have properties in common and therefore a common manufacture.

Basketry, weaving and building may therefore have a mingled origin.

Many theories have been put forward to account for the invention of weaving. Some models appear indeed to be derived from nature: the criss-cross fibres of the palm tree, the felted fibres of bark, spiders' webs, birds' nests. Others are based on psychoanalytical explanations. Thus for Sigmund Freud, the wife must have contributed to the invention of weaving because "Nature herself supplied the model for a copy of the kind by making hair grow to mask the genital organs. The progress that remained to be made

GREEK VASE PAINTING OF THE FIFTH CENTURY B.C. WITH PENELOPE AT HER LOOM BESIDE TELEMACHUS
Attributed to the Penelope Painter
Vase found in Attica, now in the Museo Etrusco, Chiusi, Italy
Height 8''

Besides the impressions of cords, basket-work, fabrics or tools such as carding combs, found on Chinese pottery as well as on that of the Mediterranean basin, it is tempting to follow Henri Stierlin when he states that the orthogonal designs on gourds found at the same time as fabrics by Junius Bird at Huaca Prieta in Peru in 1946–1947 are the product of a transposition of textile motifs: "These facts evidence the permanence of forms despite changes in their support. It would seem that the transfer from a perishable material to a more resistant support may have been made in a desire to give greater durability to designs symbolizing the human face."

was a matter of intertwining the fibres planted in the skin and forming only a kind of felting."

But the most obvious theories stem from the will of man to delimit a space around him, whether that of the body in the form of clothing, or that of a nomadic territory (by a tent).

Along these lines, Jean-François Pirson, commenting on theories of primitive architecture, was led to write: "Before being form, architecture was an attitude, a response to the need to recreate and inscribe the myths and structures of the group on everything constituting a body: the skin, its coverings and the territory."

Poncho with Bird, Puma and Fish Designs,
surrounded by a Geometric Border
Height 31″
Featherwork
Peru
Chimu culture (1200–1462)

THE FABRICS OF ANCIENT PERU

CEREMONIAL CLOAK FOUND ON A MUMMY
Embroidery
Peru, southern coast
Paracas period (700–100 B.C.)

Weaving made its appearance very early in this part of the world, well before the production of the first ceramics. The oldest textiles brought to light so far, on the sites of Guitarrero and Callejon de Huaylas in the north of Peru, date back to about the year 8500 B.C. Woven of vegetable fibres and still quite stiff, they preceded the first known supple fabrics, which date from 5700 B.C. onwards.

The most instructive region as regards textile art in Pre-Columbian America is unquestionably the zone along the thousand miles of coast between the frontier of Chile with Peru in the south and the environs of Trujillo in the north. Thousands of fabrics have been unearthed in this area where, owing to the particularly dry climate, they have been preserved in the sandy soil in which they lay buried with the dead of the different cultures that succeeded each other in the region. Traces of human occupation along these Pacific coasts barely go back beyond the second millennium, a period much later than the settlement of the upper valleys of the Cordillera, which were peopled as long ago as the eighth millennium. The first inhabitants of the coast did not have looms, but they spun agave and cotton fibres with which to make pre-fabrics using the principle of the riddle; although rudimentary, this system enabled them to produce geometric designs brightened by spots of coloured powder. After this initial phase, there followed an eclipse of more than ten centuries correspond-ing probably to a movement of the population and tem-porary exodus from the coast lands. By the time the presence of man is again evidenced, substantial changes have taken place: ceramics are known, maize is cultivated and not only cotton but also wool are woven on looms which are primitive but none the less rich in technical possibilities. Fabrics produced by a wide range of man-ufacturing processes have been discovered but with little or no indication of the stages in the elaboration and final development of the processes used in making them. This is due to the interruption in the archaeological evidence and the fact that the weavers learnt their art in other re-gions, where conditions were less favourable for the preservation of their work and have left few indications relating to these origins of weaving. Specialists are therefore obliged to be content to list the productions of an art that is already fully mature.

An art that was adult, certainly, but not static, since from then on successive civilizations, although they did not introduce basic innovations of their own, none the less developed their own textile language, favouring this or that technique, giving special significance to decorative themes, or creating designs and rhythms reflecting new forms of sensibility. The Chavin culture (1200–400 B.C.) established on the north coast, produced cottons that were tie-dyed or decorated with painted plants or animals, in-cluding stylized felidae. Similar felines are found as well (fabrics travel) on embroidered material from the Paracas

peninsula where, between 700 and 100 B.C., there flourished a community that must have attached great importance to military feats, judging by the many trophy heads included among the portraits of fantastic beings with enormous bulging eyes and divers complicated appendages. At Nazca (100 B.C.–700 A.D.) artists used all techniques with equal success, but showed a certain preference for tapestries with geometric designs, while in the region of Lake Titicaca, the Tiahuanaco civilization (600–900 A.D.), besides reversible cloths and wonderful fabrics enhanced by feathers, made fine tapestries adorned with Grecian weave and enlivened by figures representing human and animal themes. The coast peoples of Chimu, Chancay and Ica (1100–1400 A.D.) opted for designs representing the birds and fish that peopled their everyday world, whereas the Inca textiles (1438–1530) with their intelligently planned chequerboard weave reflected the structure of the strictly ordered and rigidly hierarchical society in which they were conceived.

Before considering further the techniques used by the weavers of Peru, it will be as well to recall the basic materials that were available to them. Besides agave fibre, which was strong but not very flexible and reserved for coarse materials, there was in the first place cotton—cul-

tivated in the valleys from as early as 2500 B.C.—which was braided and then woven in its two forms, brown and white, the former being the most highly valued because it spared the worker the task of dyeing, a particularly delicate operation in the case of this fibre. For the coloured parts, wool proved to be the most suitable material. Wool was obtained from the Andean camelids: the llama, which provided the wool for everyday materials for domestic use, and the alpaca and vicuña whose finer and softer fur was reserved for better quality materials. The workers learnt very early to produce mixed wool and cotton fabrics, and the oldest of these mixed fabrics, dating from about 1000 B.C., are evidence of the close interdependence, already in those distant times, of the pastoral populations in the mountains and the agricultural folk in the valleys.

For spinning, the workers had a primitive implement of a kind still in use today; many of these have been found in ancient tombs where, as a symbol of woman's work, they were placed to accompany their user into the Beyond. The spindles were wooden rods sharpened at one end, with a carved whorl in the middle, usually made of pottery, around which the thread wound itself as the spinner rotated it. In this connection it should be recalled that since the

wheel was unknown to Pre-Columbian peoples, they could not possibly have invented the spinning wheel. This did not, however, prevent them from producing yarn that was not only even but also astonishingly fine; yarns were used singly or composed of several ends, the most common form being double-ended, perhaps because the excessive twist of some yarns had to be counterbalanced by the addition of another end plied in the contrary direction.

As soon as it was spun, the fibre was dyed. The range of colours was very rich, but the nature of the colouring materials is often difficult to determine, apart from those of the basic colours: the blues, whose subtle shades reveal detailed knowledge of indigo dyeing techniques; the carmine reds produced with cochineal, and finally, the yellow obtained from the bark of the pepper tree.

Paintings on agave paper or pottery representing weavers at work and their looms, which have been found in tombs, show that Pre-Columbian fabrics were made on a very simple machine, of a kind still used in the Andes today. The warp was plied between two parallel bars one of which was attached to a fixed point while the other was tied to a strap passing behind the waist of the weaver, whose movements adjusted the greater or lesser tension of the threads. Starting from this modest and manageable

support, all kinds of combinations were possible; the worker could choose from a great variety of techniques and even change from one to another in the course of the work. The only disadvantage was that he could only weave small pieces (2½ feet wide, 7 to 10 feet long) with four lists. To produce larger pieces, several fabrics had to be sewn end to end using needles of various sizes ranging from the thickest, made of copper or precious metal, to the finest, of fishbone, wood or cactus thorn.

Pre-Columbian weavers knew how to do all kinds of work from the most complicated to the simplest. Besides ordinary cloth or repp, which were very common, they made tapestries with remarkably fine weft, often using warmly coloured vicuña wool. Unlike the Copts, the Peruvians seldom, except for the edging, drew oblique or curved lines with these weft yarns, which gives their creations an angular appearance in marked contrast to the flowing curves of Egyptian fabrics. Where the colours changed, the passage from one pick to the next could leave openings, which were liable to weaken the fabric and did not always produce a very happy aesthetic effect. The weavers sought to remedy this defect in various ways, either by arranging the decoration diagonally so as to minimize the risk of breaking by better distribution of the

23

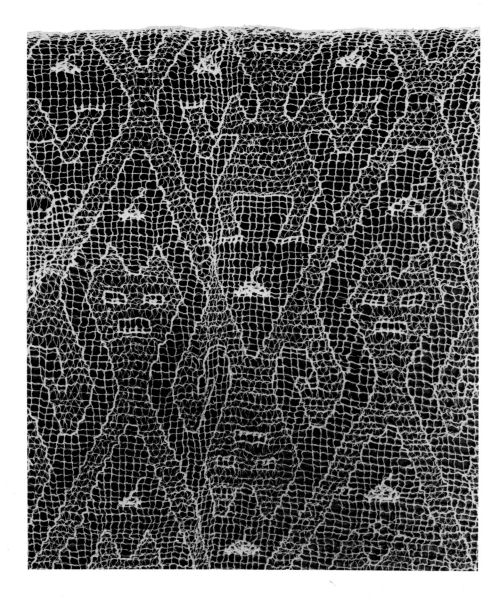

GAUZE (DETAIL)
White cotton
Embroidered openwork net gauze
Peru, central coast (Lima department)
Ancón civilization (1000 B.C.-early Christian era)

weak zones, or by tying the picks together directly or by an extra weft yarn, or finally by using the openings as a decorative element or even enlarging them and making them serve a useful purpose.

Like the Copts, the Pre-Columbians produced the kind of tapestry known as "bouclé," the result of an arrangement of loops made by twining the weft yarn round little rods which were withdrawn when the picks were bunched up closely enough to ensure that the loops held. The use of this technique was confined to parts of the fabric where a particular effect was sought, for example where it was desired to represent a fleece. The choice of a technique was always made advisedly, and the possibilities afforded by each of them were exploited to the full.

Besides simple weave fabrics, the weaver could opt for more complex processes: serges, particularly suited to polychrome designs, figured fabrics, open-work fabrics and light gauzes sometimes ending in a fringe of needlework embroidery. The worker knew also how to weave simultaneously two superimposed pieces in different colours by crossing the yarns of the two wefts and the two warps in such a way that the designs stood out coloured inversely on either side. Repetition of small identical themes gave these "double cloths" a rhythmic positive/negative play of contrasting colours, which was especially successful with simple alternations of white and brown cotton.

Fabrics were decorated by all kinds of methods in addition to those already described, which were an integral part of the weaving process. The first solution consisted in preparing the theme by treating the yarn by the *ikat* technique or rolling it up partially in a yarn of coloured wool by a technique of which examples were found at Nazca.

Once woven, the fabric could be treated by local dyeing operations, but the Peruvians did not exploit all the possibilities of the *plangi* method. They limited their use of it to pieces of supple cotton and did not take advantage of it for polychrome designs. In that respect, their experiments in painting on fabric were barely more satisfactory.

On the other hand, the art of embroidery was very highly developed by the Peruvians, particularly at Paracas and Nazca. The stitches most frequently used were loop-stitch, stem-stitch and chain-stitch, the last less often. The chief beauty of the designs lay in their rich colours dyed in the wool.

Coloured wools were likewise the material that gave all its beauty to the imitation velvet cloth reserved in the Nazca region for making headbands and four-pointed bonnets. This material was a network of knots enclosing –imprisoning–within them coloured wool yarns curled in the form of little loops, which the maker cuts a second time at the top so as to create a special effect of relief and thickness.

DOUBLE CLOTH (DETAIL)
Figured double cloth taffeta
Peru
Inca period (1438–1530)

IMITATION VELVET BONNET
Wool
Peru, southern coast
Nazca period (100 B.C.–700 A.D.)

FABRIC WITH DOLL DESIGNS (FRAGMENT)
Length with fringes 39½″
Cotton and wool, probably alpaca wool
Tapestry-work tunic
Peru
Chimu culture (1200–1462)

FEATHERWORK
29⅞″ × 23¼″
Peru, southern coast
Pre-Inca period (9th–14th century)

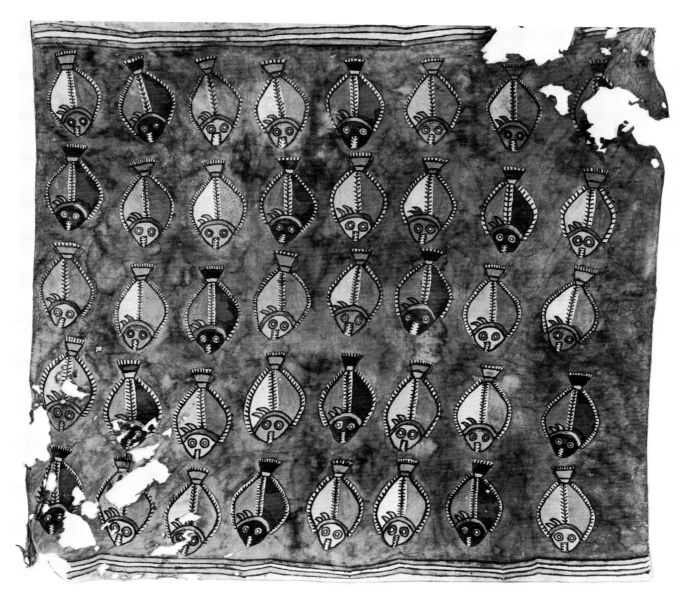

FABRIC WITH FISH DESIGNS
55″ × 52″
Painting on cotton akin to repp
Peru, central coast (Lima department)
Nazca period (100 B.C.–700 A.D.)

FEATHERWORK WITH SMALL METAL PLATES
Peru, central coast, Ancón Bay
Ancón civilization (1000 B.C.–early Christian era)

It would take too long to list all the techniques the Peruvians used to embellish their fabrics. Pompoms, tassels or groups of veritable dolls, braid, facings of small scales of silver or gold sewn on the cloth–the most surprising kinds of adornment were invented, including the feathered headdresses, highly prized by the Incas, which were made from ancient times with the plumage of the most beautiful birds of the Amazon.

The wealth of techniques was matched by the multiplicity of forms and ideas inspiring the arrangement of the adornments. Each culture had its favourite images drawn from its own pantheon or based on the local fauna, fish, birds, jaguars, and more rarely the flora. In geometric compositions, the key pattern theme predominated.

In view of the many and varied means of expression at the disposal of the weaver, Patrice Hugues does not hesitate, in his book *Le langage du tissu*, to draw a parallel between this art and writing: "By contrary directions, spacings and countings, a complete system of signs and coherent implied meanings was brought into operation. Never, perhaps, was weaving nearer to being itself a form of writing.

"This fact should no doubt be considered in relation to the absence of any real writing among the Quetchuas of ancient Peru, for whom everything was above all a matter of counting, everything came 'before writing'."

These obvious links between weaving and mathematics appear to have taken practical shape in the invention of the *quipu* (literally "knot"). This calculating machine functioned by means of a system of little cords coloured according to the objects to be counted (crops, gold, silver or soldiers), and with knots along them assumed to have represented units, tens, hundreds and thousands. It is not impossible that this instrument, which was especially widespread in the time of the Incas, had been invented much earlier by weavers. Wishing to have the assistance of a mnemotechnical device when weaving complex designs, they would naturally have made such an instrument with the materials to hand.

Garments were not waisted. According to the belief of some Bolivian Indians even today that "to cut a cloth is to kill it," this shape must be attributed to an ancient belief that fabrics were actually living beings. The pieces coming from the loom were therefore ready to be worn, or sewn together to make the different parts of costume: breeches, loincloth, tunic and coat for men, and for women a simple dress with a belt tied round it and covered with an often richly ornamented cloak secured in front by a thick needle called a *tupu*. Besides these garments, there were the many bags used to hold coca or the personal effects of their owner, as well as mural hangings and shrouds. The size of some of the funereal fabrics discovered at Paracas is impressive (up to 2750 square feet), requiring for their manufacture unbroken warp yarns from 60 to 110 miles long.

It may well be asked how the weavers were able to make these cloths, since the tools they are known to have possessed could not have served for such work. Recently, Henri Stierlin, in his book *Nazca, la clé du mystère*, has suggested an answer to this riddle that is the more attractive in that it solves at the same time the question of the famous "tracks" observed from the air when flying over Nazca, and about which so much ink has already flowed. According to Stierlin, the big geometric figures appearing in one place and another were made when the land was cleared to facilitate the storage of enormous quantities of yarn, which was wound round small pickets in order to make it possible to warp such gigantic yarns. On this hypothesis, the animal designs appearing on these sites (figures of monkeys, dogs, pelicans, etc.) would have had a magic function, placing under the best auspices the sacred operation of manufacturing immense pieces of fabric for funereal usage.

Generally speaking, it has to be recognized that fabrics had a place apart in Pre-Columbian society, especially during the Inca period.

"Quipu" (literally "knot")
11" × 64½"
Cotton
Peru, Andes region
Inca period (1438-1530)

SHROUD PAINTED WITH ANTHROPOMORPHIC MOTIFS:
PRISONERS WITH ROPES AROUND THEIR NECK
73″ × 53¼″
Cotton
Peru, northern coast
Chimu culture (1200–1462)

First of all fabrics had an obvious economic value. To establish the State warehouses that so astonished the Spaniards at the time of the conquest, the Inca Empire had a strictly organized system. The population had to pay a tax called *mi'ta* by working up fibres supplied by the authorities in order to produce cloths which were subsequently collected and stored by the State. The inhabitants thus obtained the right to the wool and cotton supplied to them and even to the fabrics they needed for their personal use; this arrangement made it possible in particular to cover the enormous needs of the army and its commissariat.

Secondly, fabrics had a social function: their quality indicated the rank of the user, and gifts of clothes were a means of promoting good diplomatic relations as well as of rewarding soldiers who had distinguished themselves in battle, or securing the desired loyalty of others. Conversely, enemies, dead or alive, were stripped of their clothes. Gifts of cloth accompanied all the important events of life: birth, initiation rites, marriage. Fabrics, again, always accompanied men in death. Besides shrouds, tombs contained changes of clothes which had to be regularly renewed lest the deceased should return to obtain from the living the things he lacked in the other world.

Often invested with sacred significance, fabrics had their place in all religious ceremonies where, together with llamas, they were the principal offerings destined to be burnt.

That, very briefly, was the situation that existed before the Spaniards set the native population to work to meet their own needs in cloth. They organized workshops in each town of the Viceroyalty of Peru and taught the local weavers the use of sheep's wool, linen, silk and metallic wire in the manufacture of cloth, furnishing materials or liturgical vestments made to Spanish taste and adorned with new decorative motifs: coats of arms, the Hapsburg two-headed eagle, crowns and Christian symbols. At the technical level, they introduced the treadle loom and favoured certain processes, such as tapestry making and embroidery, at the expense of others.

In the eighteenth century, Chinese influence was added to that of the West. Silks, landed from Spanish ships sailing between Mexico and the Philippines, were clearly a source of oriental themes in Peruvian tapestries.

Peruvian traditions as regards both techniques and beliefs connected with weaving have, however, survived to the present day. In Bolivia, garments made of parallel longitudinal strips, alternately decorated and plain, still woven by the ancient method for plain repp with the warp showing and the weft hidden, contain many elements directly inherited from Pre-Columbian times. Needless to say, the decorative motifs are different from those of the Pre-Columbian era, and new designs have been developed with their own stylistic conventions, for example the person of the village priest. An interesting detail is worth noting. In some places, the decorated strips are broken by patch of vague colour exactly similar to those that appear on some ancient fabrics, although there is no technical need to account for this strange practice. It is therefore a genuine survival corresponding to more or less consciously expressed motives whose signficance is no longer clearly perceived. An old Indian asked the reason for the custom replied simply: "It is done so that the fabric should not be perfect."

BOLIVIAN FABRIC WITH PARALLEL BANDS (DETAIL)
Sheep's wool dyed with
anilines and vegetable products
Bolivia, La Paz department
Quetchua craft-work

THE MEDITERRANEAN BASIN

The Mediterranean basin can rightly be regarded as one of the major centres of textile art, if only on account of the wealth of Egyptian and Sumerian archaeological discoveries.

The lands surrounding the Mediterranean will indeed be the setting for local installation and radial dissemination of textile activities, the most famous being those of the Copts on account of their special application to tapestry and their capacity for assimilating and synthesizing varied influences.

It will also be characterized by intensive exchanges with the East, exchanges in both directions, following the famous silk routes.

In the midst of this profusion of techniques and styles, pride of place has been given to weaving and tapestry, and to a lesser degree to embroidery, without forgetting, however, that carpets form a diversified textile world of their own—a subject deserving a book to itself.

Examination of Syrian, Byzantine, Coptic, Moslem, Italian and French fabrics reveals the immense capacity of textile materials as a medium for the synthesis of the influences corresponding to different civilizations. In this respect, the observation of Patrice Hugues is most pertinent: "It is quite possible that in this 'zone of encounter,' Syria, Mesopotamia, Persia—our Near and Middle East today—some initial, original definitions took shape, certain basic options in the language of textiles. Setting out from these, more often than not the trends followed diverged towards the East and towards the West, and the criteria were contrary."

SYRIAN FABRICS

The Near East region, particularly the part occupied by Syria, has played an essential role in the history of textile art, first in the elaboration and subsequently in the dissemination of techniques and manufactured products. Already in ancient Egypt oriental craftsmen were held in high esteem, and after a number of them had settled in the valley of the Nile during the reign of Tuthmosis III (1504–1450 B.C.), the name "Syrian" became for the Egyptians synonymous with "weaver."

The Syrian fabrics discovered at the beginning of the century by Pfister in the tombs at Palmyra and Doura Europos have provided valuable information about these techniques admired by the ancients.

The Syrian tunic, which inspired the Egyptians for their costume, was woven in a single piece and extensively decorated. The plain weave cloth was brightened by strips of wool usually dyed murex purple and made with tapestry weave. Everything seems to indicate that the origins of this technique must be sought in the Near East, since the oldest known piece of the kind, dating from about 2500 B.C., was unearthed near Troy. Besides tapestries and repp, fabrics with very close weft behind which the warp threads were hidden, the Syrian weavers were perhaps the first to produce twill weaves by fitting more than two heddles to their horizontal looms.

Exchanges with China played an important part in the history of Syrian fabrics, although it is often difficult to tell how their influence made itself felt. Antioch and Palmyra were stages on the Silk Route along which raw material and silks made up in China were traded, as is evidenced by the many fragments dating from this period discovered in the ruins of Palmyra. Some of the silks were unpicked there and worked up again in the local taste, using the process called "unravelling." As for the raw silk, the Syrian weavers used it at first to reinforce the wool or cotton threads, by which it was completely hidden, and later for the production of their own silk damask. It would seem indeed to have been these silks imported from the Far East that first gave Syrian and Iranian weavers the desire to manufacture mechanically cloths with repeat pattern decoration, whereas tapestry weave had previously been the only means of introducing decorative motifs.

Antioch, capital of Syria, was also the first town of the country for the production of these silk materials. It competed with its Egyptian rival, Alexandria, producing fabrics decorated in a style strongly reminiscent of Sassanian cloths (with combinations of circles, for example). In 636, however, the Arabs captured Antioch, and communications with China were interrupted for several centuries, leading to the eclipse of Syrian textile production.

Archaeological discoveries in Syria, however interesting, have in reality only brought to light fragments of not particularly striking fabric, which are indeed quite disappointing considered in the light of the impact of Syrian textile art on the neighbouring Egyptian and Byzantine civilizations (taste for cloths decorated by the use of tapestry technique; cut and design of costume...). Nothing, for example, comparable with the magnificent tunics portrayed on the funerary sculptures found at Palmyra.

Sassanian fabrics

Conquered by Alexander in 331 B.C., then occupied by the Parthians (250 B.C.-226 A.D.), the Persian Empire was restored to the full height of its power at the beginning of the third century A.D. by the Zoroastrian Sassanian monarchs, who ruled the country until the Islamic conquest.

Profiting from the pivotal position of Iran between East and West, the Persians controlled the trade in Chinese silks and made fabulous profits out of their services as middlemen. With the silk they had known how to produce since the beginning of the Christian era and the quantities they levied on Chinese exports transiting their country, they supplied their own industry for the manufacture of fine fabrics in a general context of striking cultural progress evoked even today by the famous names of Persepolis and Ctesiphon.

The sovereigns took a keen interest in the production of luxury materials, in which they and the Court were the parties mainly concerned. Following victorious military campaigns, they took Syrian weavers to Iran in order to promote instructive comparison of Syrian techniques with those of the craftsmen of their own kingdom. Shapur I (241–272 A.D.) was moved by the same desire when he took advantage of the improvement in relations between his Empire and that of the famous Zenobia to arrange for weavers from Palmyra to settle in Iran. Later, when the State took over the silk workshops in the Byzantine Empire by closing down private centres, Syrian workers again left for Persia where conditions for the industry were less restrictive.

It was doubtless these workers from Syria who taught the Iranians the samite technique, which was used for all the Sassanian silk materials known to have survived. In this connection, it should be emphasized that the fabrics held to be Sassanian, their origin being deduced from their relation to other modes of artistic expression typical of Sassanian culture, have all been found outside Iranian territory. The dearth of textile remains from archaeological sites in Iran is due partly to the ravages suffered by the region, and partly to unfavourable funerary customs, according to which the bodies of the dead had to be burnt or exposed to birds of prey. The only pieces remaining in existence are therefore exported fabrics discovered in countries where conditions were more propitious for their preservation.

In some cases, the Sassanian origin of fabrics is self-evident as, for example, the silk piece from Antinoë featuring a repeat pattern absolutely contrary to Coptic textile practice, which favoured tapestry with its unitary language. Unfortunately, it is sometimes much more difficult to distinguish a Sassanian exported fabric from a local product inspired by Sassanian models. It has to be remembered that some themes or compositions favoured by Persian weavers enjoyed considerable success abroad and are also found on Coptic, Chinese, Byzantine or Moslem fab-

Fragment of a Hanging with Cocks and Peacocks
17¾″ × 25¼″
Silk tapestry, samite
Antinoë, Egypt
5th century A.D.

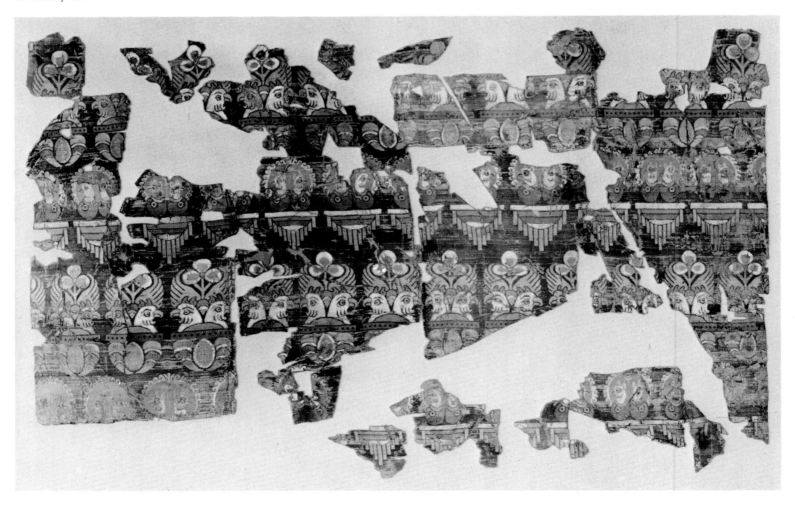

ANIMALS AMONG PLANT DESIGNS
30″ × 21¼″
Red silk with damask ground, heightened with gold thread
Italy, 15th century

FABRIC WITH CONFRONTED LIONS (FRAGMENT)
Red ground silk ("lampas")
Spain, Mudéjar art, 15th-16th century

IMITATION OF ANCIENT CLOTH: MODEL WITH CONFRONTED LIONS
12¼″ × 11″
Embroidered silk
19th century

rics as well as on Italian and Spanish twelfth, fourteenth and fifteenth century products, and surprisingly recur on early medieval sculptures and stained glass.

Sassanian fabrics are characterized first of all by a very special arrangement of the decoration, which was most often composed of rows of isolated or tangential circular compartments inscribed with symmetrically ordered motifs sometimes separated by a median axis. The most frequent subjects are those common to all Sassanian arts: hunting scenes, fabulous animals such as winged horses or griffins, lions devouring each other, or in more peaceful vein, birds such as cocks, ducks, thrushes or peacocks. In the centre of the composition the Assyrian *hom*, or Tree of Life, sign of eternal rebirth, alternates with the Altar of Fire, the Pyraeum, symbolical evocation of the towers on top of which burned the sacred fire kept alive by the Magi.

These subjects are limited in number and the elaboration of an iconography for each of them, fixed permanently in its least details, led to the creation of veritable stereotypes. From the floating scarves adorning the neck of the king or of sacred animals to the rows of pearls edging

HORSEMAN WITH HOUND BASED ON SASSANIAN MODELS
10″ × 8½″
Decorated part of a tunic
Wool and linen
Coptic tapestry
7th-8th century

medallions, each element seems to have had its own particular meaning. It may even be that the primacy accorded to the circle, which was singularly exacting in so far as its reproduction was not facilitated by the medium of tapestry or brocade, also had symbolic significance and should be interpreted in accordance with astrological values.

In their adaptation to the support fabric, however, the motifs became less exotic, took on a less stylized form, which made them more easily transmissible to other civilizations. This happened with the theme of the king laying low the lion, an allusion to the great Mazdean principle of the victory of Good over Evil. In its woven version, the person of the king became less clearly identifiable: while he kept his floating scarf, he generally lost one of his other attributes, the tiara, either winged or adorned with horns, the *kymbolos* which, where it subsists, is barely distinguishable from an ordinary diadem. What remains is the more neutral idea of the huntsman prince, which the master weavers of foreign countries could take over more easily by giving him a new significance, as the Copts did, seeing in him the image of St George or the Archangel Michael triumphing over the Dragon.

BYZANTINE FABRICS

What is a "Byzantine" fabric?

A good number of pieces woven in the provinces under Byzantine domination fall outside this denomination because they stem from local traditions and owe nothing to the official art of Byzantium. This is the case, for example, with many Coptic fabrics.

At the same time, however, these same provinces made faithful copies of works from the metropolis and sometimes mixed national elements with others borrowed from the dominant culture. As, on their side, the workers of Constantinople were not insensible to the charm of the provincial productions and in their turn underwent their influence, it is obviously no simple matter to discover the exact origin of a cloth and above all to determine what constitutes an original Byzantine textile creation. The task is the more arduous since Byzantine weavers also drew inspiration from outside the Empire, particularly from their Sassanian neighbours.

The interest shown by the Byzantine authorities in textile production goes back to the origins of Byzantium itself, since it was the Emperor Constantine who by an edict dated 333 A.D. prescribed the regulations for the workshops of his new capital. From the end of the fourth century, the gynaeceum of the Great Palace housed craftsmen specializing in the weaving of raw silk obtained from the

VIRGIN AND CHILD
Tapestry
6th century

VICTORIOUS CHARIOTEER
29½″ × 28¼″
Silk, figured samite
Byzantium, 8th century

Far East via Persia. But the exorbitant transit dues which the Byzantines had to pay the Sassanians restricted the production of silk materials for some time, despite the creation of provincial workshops in Syria and Egypt.

The historian Procopius of Caesarea (late fifth century–565) relates how, tired of depending on the good will of the Iranians, the Byzantines sent two monks to Asia with instructions to discover the secrets of silk making. On their return, towards 552, these industrial spies brought back mulberry seeds, hidden in their pilgrim's staffs, and introduced sericulture to the West.

While this development gave new impetus to the silk industry, the Emperor Justinian (527–565) strengthened State control of the sector as regards both manufacture, which was a monopoly of the imperial workshops or gynaecea, and the use of these luxury cloths, which was reserved for the Emperor and members of the Court. The precious fabrics were also offered as gifts to foreign princes, although their export, properly speaking was strictly limited.

In the imperial entourage, the white tunic with a purple and gold band was replaced by heavy, richly decorated silk garments. The Ravenna mosaics, which provide information on fabrics of the period that is the more valuable on account of the scarcity of archaeological remains, reveal

FABRIC FROM MOZAC
28¾″ × 27″
Silk, samite
Found in the Abbey of Mozac
(Puy-de-Dôme), France

the existence of cloths illustrated with stories, such as the cloak of Theodora (527–548) at San Vitale, Ravenna, which is decorated with the Adoration of the Magi. A century earlier, Theodoret of Cyrrhus related already that he had seen the whole life of Christ depicted in scenes woven and embroidered on the toga of a senator.

As this evidence shows, the fabrics of the first centuries of the Empire, during which its Christian character was being affirmed, often treat religious subjects. This was true of many woollen tapestries produced in Coptic workshops or in Asia Minor, at Cyzicus and Heraclea Perinthus. The subjects in this vein that appear most often are the lives of the saints or the Holy Virgin, as in the piece from the Cleveland Museum reproduced here.

Fabrics were, besides, a by no means negligible element of the decoration of churches, where heavy hangings were suspended between the pillars and draped round the episcopal throne.

Constant contacts with Persia in war or trade led to the migration of workmen with consequent artistic exchanges that were particularly evident in the area of iconography. The Sassanian bestiary invaded the Byzantine repertory, peopling it with lions, elephants and griffins.

In the course of the eighth century, concurrently with this assimilation of a language of foreign origin, a Byzan-

tine iconography proper came into being inspired mainly by the circus and the amphitheatre, as can be seen from the silk fabric of the victorious charioteer (quadriga), in the Musée de Cluny, Paris.

From this period date the rare pieces whose attribution to the Constantinople workshops, evinced by valuable woven inscriptions, is almost certain. From the Macedonian period (867–1036) onwards, Sassanian influence increased, and even if the designs of the Byzantine pieces were more stylized than those of their Iranian models, the difference between the two is often difficult to discern. Both feature the same animals inscribed in circles, and the Sassanian eagle sets its seal henceforth on the products of the gynaecea.

The Macedonian dynasty, by authorizing the use of silk for the dress of all classes, initiated a revival of production. New workshops were opened at Tyre and Berytus (Beirut) in Syria. Technical improvements in the processes inherited from previous periods and the expansion of freer and less conformist handicraft weaving contributed to the preparation of a golden age of textile art covering the tenth, eleventh and twelfth centuries, a development favoured at the commercial level by relations with Venice and by the Crusades, which also promoted the dissemination of manufactured silks.

When the Moslems captured Syria, the silk industry was transferred to Greece. From then on, the workshops of the capital had to face keen competition from the provincial centres in Sparta, Patras, Corinth, Thebes, and Cyprus, famous for the gold brocades it exported to Italy.

Under the reign of the Palaeologues (1261–1453), the sumptuary arts as a whole and weaving in particular suffered an eclipse. Only the embroiderers prospered, placing their talents at the service of religion and concerned mainly with the decoration of different parts of priestly vestments and the embellishment of liturgical veils. From the thirteenth to the fourteenth century the number of embroidered pieces increased, and it was not by chance that they improved in quality since they were probably executed after cartoons by the great masters of painting of their day when pictorial art was passing through a particularly brilliant period.

The capture of Constantinople by the Arabs in 1453 was followed by the reorganization of the system of production. Byzantine textile traditions were perpetuated from then on in the framework of Turkish manufactures, where they acquired fresh vitality. Some weavers, however, preferred to place their art at the exclusive service of their faith and left the official workshops for the monasteries where, as at Mount Athos, they dedicated their entire output to the representation of biblical themes.

BYZANTINE COPE KNOWN AS THE "DALMATIC OF CHARLEMAGNE"
Embroidered silk
14th century

COPTIC FABRICS

PORTRAIT OF A WOMAN IN A SQUARE
8¼″ × 7½″
Linen warp, weft of coloured wool, and raw linen
Tapestry
9th century

Taking their cue from the Pharaohs, who called the town of Memphis "Het-ka-ptah" (sanctuary of the *ka* of Ptah), the Greeks had created the word "Aigyptos," from which the Arab conquerors in turn coined the term "Copts" to designate the populations of the Nile valley. Since then, the tendency has been to assimilate Copt to Christian, forgetting that the spread of Christianity only began in the second century so that the word Copt covers for quite a long period elements that remained pagan.

Before they were brought under Moslem rule, the Copts had been subject to many other overlords. The Greeks with the Ptolemies (306–30 B.C.), the Romans (30 B.C.–395 A.D.), the Byzantines (395–619) and the Persians (619–629), each in turn left their mark on this country, which was none the less able to create out of such diverse influences an original art, as can be seen from the fabrics discovered since the end of the nineteenth century in the necropolises at Akhmim and Antinoë. These very numerous cloths (hundreds of thousands of pieces have been unearthed) owe their remarkable state of preservation to a happy combination of circumstances including, in the first instance, the practice originated under the Pharaohs of siting cemeteries in desert zones, a practice resumed later in order to economize arable land too valuable for such use. The dryness of the climate together with the care taken over the inhumation contributed to the preservation of archaeological material, whose value is further explained by the length of the period during which the cemeteries remained in service. It should also be remembered that after the period of the Pharaohs, the dead were no longer buried wrapped in bandages but dressed in the clothes they had used when they were alive.

As well as the articles of Roman costume adopted by the Copts (tunic, toga and cloak), there were hangings in which the body was swathed and funerary cushions on which the head and feet rested. These cushions were made of reversible tapestry reproducing the same design on either side, an allusion perhaps to the two-way regard of the dead: towards the world above and the world below.

The spinning techniques practised in Egypt remained for a long time rudimentary. The oldest spindles discovered in the Mediterranean basin date back to about 5000 B.C., but manual spinning seems to have persisted concurrently with their use. The distaff only appeared fairly late, probably in the Roman era.

Spinning was followed by dyeing. After the fibres had been washed, a mordant, usually an alum-based compound, was applied to them to fix the colour. Analysis of cloths has provided valuable information on the colouring materials employed. For red, the root of madder, which grows in Egypt, was used alternately with imported dyes produced from kermes or cochineal and even, in the most recent period, by a third insect, the lac-dye or Indian aphis. Blue was obtained either from a local product cultivated in Fayum, or from the indigo plant, whose leaves were imported. Other dyes were made by combining these reds and blues and adding browns and yellows whose composition has not been discovered.

It is known that the Egyptians after weaving linen on horizontal looms under the Pharaohs, adopted in the time of the New Kingdom the high-warp loom, probably invented in the Near East, and naturally inherited by their successors.

In reality, Coptic weavers used two kinds of vertical loom. In the first, the warp was held between two bars and the weft pressed downwards, the cloth being rolled up on the lower bar as it was made. This loom is sometimes called a tapestry loom. However, the discovery of weights of stone or baked clay, the oldest of which date back to the New Kingdom, indicates the existence of another tool called precisely the weight loom, or Greek loom, on account of the representations of this kind of loom found on Greek vases of the sixth to fourth century B.C. These weights are pierced in the centre so that they can be attached to the warp threads they have to tense.

In spite of the preponderance of vertical looms, the use of horizontal looms was not abandoned, and it should also be noted that in the third century, the draw loom, a variant held to have been invented by the Chinese, made its appearance in Egypt having reached the Copts via Persia.

For the manufacture of the braids that adorned tunics in particular, the Copts had a special tool, the card loom.

VINE LEAF SHAWL
50½″ × 28½″
Linen warp, weft of linen and coloured wools
Tapestry, using the flying shuttle
3rd-4th century

CHILD'S TUNIC WITH HOOD
15¾″ × 19″. Hood 8⅝″ × 5½″. Sleeve 6¾″ × 2⅜″
Wool
Tapestry and woollen cloth
11th century

40

It is not clear whether Egyptian weavers produced their designs directly on the loom, giving free rein to their inspiration as they worked, or whether they followed cartoons on which the decoration was more or less simply outlined. Two papyri, one in Turin and the other in Berlin, present motifs curiously similar to those of certain fabrics and might have been models for weavers. Their role as cartoons has still, however, to be proved, and it is too early to draw general conclusions from them regarding the working methods of Coptic craftsmen.

The garments found in tombs are only partly decorated, the decoration comprising three main elements: long narrow bands called *paragaudes*, square or oval motifs or *tabulae*, and finally *clavi* or nailheads, circular roundels arranged usually at the bottom of the tunic. These designs were either sewn on or woven at the same time as the rest

of the piece. In the latter case, the decoration was produced by the introduction of coloured wool-weft picks at given points of the cloth, which formed the background. The *Vine Leaf* shawl in the Louvre shows quite clearly the resulting increased density of the cloth. The decorative bands in this case cover only part of the fabric, but the tapestry/fabric ratio was to develop in favour of the second, which took up an ever larger area of the cloth.

While the main lines of the history of Coptic textile art can be traced, the attribution of even an approximate date to a particular fabric is hazardous owing to the lack of any scientific method in prospection at the time the first official excavations were made, not to speak of the "methods" of clandestine prospectors. Furthermore owing to the length of time during which sites served as burial grounds, pagans, Christians and Moslems who lived at different epochs being buried side by side, historians are naturally hesitant to give specific dates even for the limits of the period covered by Coptic art. After having decided that original Coptic production ended in the seventh, then in the ninth, century A.D., researchers now seem agreed to advance the date to the twelfth century. Between the second and twelfth centuries, the classification of fabrics is made as well as can be by the comparison of examples with the products of other better known artistic areas, particularly mosaics, and by grouping pieces according to their style, decoration or manufacturing techniques. Most of the dates advanced are not, however, unanimously agreed and remain unconfirmed.

The works that are considered to be the oldest seem to show genuine interest in the naturalistic style favoured by the Greeks. Examples of this realistic trend are the *Hanging with Fish*, in the Musée des Tissus, Lyons, a tapestry that doubtless served as a mural decoration and may have been reproduced several times, unless the very similar piece in the Louvre is a fragment of the one in Lyons.

These fish inevitably call to mind the frescoes in the rich villas of Pompeii, or the mosaics unearthed in North Africa; they show the same keen powers of observation (fifteen different species can be distinguished) and the same treatment of shadows. Technically, this work is a good illustration of weaving methods of the Greco-Roman

period: the modelling is rendered by mixing (beating) the colours, a process invented by the Syrians, which consists in mingling different coloured weft picks in order to produce carefully graded shading giving a three-dimensional effect; the technique of hatching, which tapestry weavers of the medieval West would take up again, also helps to heighten the impression of relief and life.

Likewise more than true to nature, the *Wild Boar in Flight* of the Abegg Foundation exhibits the same characteristics and must be attributed to this first phase of Coptic production, as well as the so astonishingly expressive *Head of a Woman* in the Detroit Institute of Art. The curls and hair style as a whole, the somewhat heavy nose, the mouth, all recall Roman art and above all Roman mosaics.

WILD BOAR IN FLIGHT
3½″ × 10⅝″
Woollen weft and linen warp
Tapestry
4th century A.D.

42

HEAD OF A WOMAN
6¾" × 4¾"
Tapestry of polychrome wool
2nd–4th century

BACCHIC PROCESSION
Linen and wool
Tapestry, using the flying shuttle
Late 5th century

Egypt at this time reflects in its works the political sub-jection of the country as an imperial province and is only just beginning to find means of giving artistic expression to its own personality. For the time being, themes based on Greek mythology find their place in the iconographical repertory; the most popular are extracts from the legends of Aphrodite and Dionysus. These images, products of another cultural context, are little by little appropriated by Egyptian artists who discover Osiris behind Dionysus and recognize Isis in the features of Aphrodite. The hunting scenes in the marshes, which decorated ancient Egyptian mastaba and hypogea are updated, and from then on little cherubs or *putti* frolic in the midst of the aquatic fauna and flora.

43

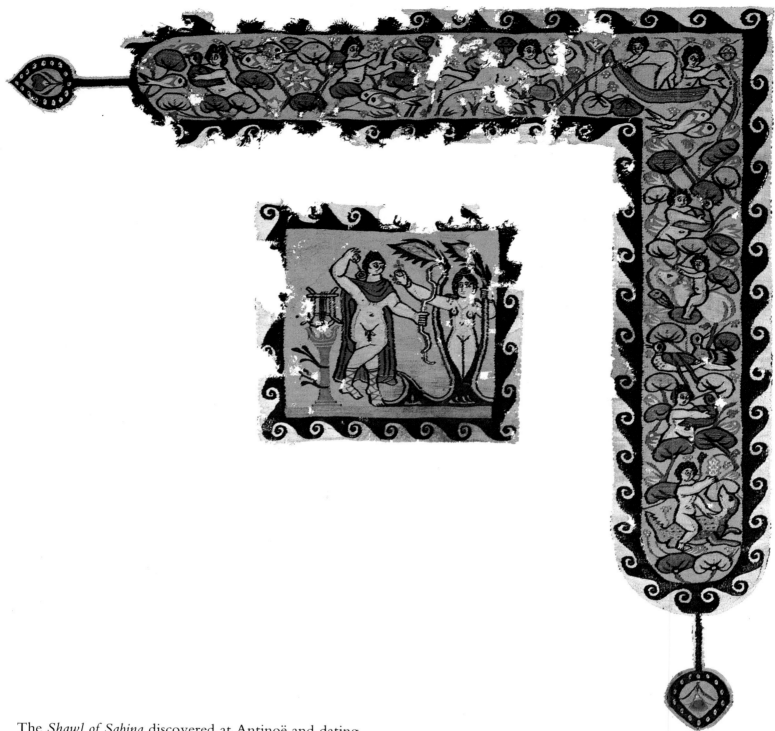

The *Shawl of Sabina* discovered at Antinoë and dating from the sixth century is a characteristic example of these scenes from the Nile. Curiously enough, whereas the general treatment differs considerably from that of the old frescoes and reliefs, the very peculiar lopsidedness of the young swimmers recalls the Ptolemaic bas-reliefs: the same distortion, the same bizarre position of the navel. On closer examination, this piece becomes even more interesting, since it is clearly a combination of various influences and at the same time a synthesis giving birth to original Coptic art. Another part of the shawl even introduces a new feature in the shape of a Christian element: a small representation of Daphne changing herself into a laurel tree in order to escape Apollo very subtly harmonizes Pharaonic, Greek and Christian themes. To protect herself from the darts of the god, the nymph waves under the eyes of her pursuer a small red cross; her gesture, which in this case is a means of averting danger, recalls very clearly the manner in which the gods of ancient Egypt presented to the lips of the Pharaoh the "ankh" cross, held to be the harbinger of eternal life.

FABRIC KNOWN AS THE "SHAWL OF SABINA"
55″ × 43¼″
Woollen tapestry on plain weave ground
Detail with flying shuttle
Antinoë, Egypt
6th century

The "cross of life," an essential hieroglyphic element appearing on monuments everywhere, is one of the rare Pharaonic symbols to have been handed on to Coptic weavers, who gave it a Christian significance quite naturally suggested by its form. The allusion to eternal life is strengthened by the transformation of Daphne into a laurel tree, a metamorphosis evoking the idea of another life, the life that the soul, also transformed, will know after death.

Conceived in the imagination of the Greeks, the personages are treated in a style recalling their origin: nude bodies, curled tresses, Greek capes and sandals. Here and there, it can be seen that details are brought out by means of the "flying shuttle," the second weft shuttle used by the weaver to indicate the folds of a garment or the features of a face, which was employed with growing frequency and became widespread particularly after the Arab conquest. A piece discovered by Albert Gayet at Antinoë, which must have adorned a tunic, evinces this addiction to the flying shuttle technique. On examination, it is easy to see that it might be compared with the method known as

LINEN FRAGMENT WITH ANKH CROSS
11¾" × 8¾"
Tapestry with coloured wools
Found in a tomb at Akhmim, Upper Egypt
4th-5th century

45

ANNUNCIATION AND VISITATION
10″ × 9″
Linen medallion embroidered
with coloured silk
Decorated part of a tunic
7th-8th century

outline painting used on Greek vases; the choice of scenes from Greek mythology (Hercules chasing a nymph, Narcissus gazing at himself in the fountain) strengthens this impression.

After the Council of Chalcedon, which in 451 consummated the break with the rest of Christendom by the condemnation of the Monophysite theses, Egypt experienced a sharp nationalist revival translated at the artistic level by growing reserve with regard to Greek standards. Concurrently with the proclamation of their religious independence, the Copts expressed their concerns in their art: themes of pagan origin were more and more often enriched with Christian significance at the same time that images of the Virgin and Child and the first representations of the saints, inspired by the great figures of St Pachomius, St Macarius and St Anthony, appeared on woven fabrics. Meaning became more important than the Hellenistic desire for realism, and simple conventionalized language was preferred to concrete details, as can be seen in the triangular faces of the figures, largely taken up by almost square bulging eyes. Similarly, bodies became deformed and natural proportions were no longer respected; craftsmen no longer sought to create the illusion of a body by the use of shading but obtained their effects by contrasting simple masses of colour.

In the sixth century, the introduction of sericulture in the Byzantine Empire was an important landmark in the history of textile art in the Mediterranean basin. Until then, raw silk had been imported from China via Persia, where the Persians stocked it and made it into cloths with which they flooded the market, and which had given Coptic weavers the inspiration for a number of their works. From then on, however, the Byzantines had their own mulberry plantations in Greece and were able to establish workshops for weaving silk on their own territories; the Alexandria gynaeceum specialized in making silk materials with a red ground.

MEDALLION WITH FOUR PUTTI ON RED GROUND
Diameter 3⅛″
Linen and wool
Tapestry, details with flying shuttle
7th century

SMALL SQUARE WITH RUNNING LION
FRAMED BY BUST MEDALLIONS
8″ × 7½″
Linen and wool
Tapestry; some parts with flying shuttle
7th century

HORSEMAN WITH HOUND IN A MEDALLION
Diameter 7⅞″
Tapestry of linen and wool
9th century

◁ TAPESTRY WITH MYTHOLOGICAL SCENES:
HERCULES PURSUING A NYMPH;
NARCISSUS GAZING AT HIMSELF IN THE FOUNTAIN
Decorated fragment of a tunic
Dyed wool on tapestry ground
All details done with flying shuttle
Antinoë, Egypt
4th–6th century

As regards traditional Coptic production, the flying shuttle continued in favour, but in the seventh century a new type of more complicated tapestry was developed. This was the "bouclé" fabric made by a process of oriental, more precisely Chaldean, origin known to have been used in Egypt from the time of the eleventh dynasty (about 2000 B.C.). To produce these cloths, which looked like our terry towels, the weaver made little loops rolling his weft pick at regular intervals round small rods, which he subsequently withdrew. The Louvre has a fine example of a bouclé fabric illustrating the story of Jonah swallowed by the whale. In the time of the Pharaohs, these pieces were used as blankets, but the Copts made them more often into cushion covers or, as would seem to have been the case here, simple wall hangings.

The seventh century was also for Egypt the century of the Moslem conquest and a new confrontation with another culture. The Moslems took over the Alexandria gynaeceum and made it into the first *tirâz* or State workshop on Egyptian soil. Next, they reorganized the structure of the official textile industry, which they moved to their new capital, Cairo, and several places on the delta, in particular, Tinnis. Coptic workmen employed in these *tirâz* were obliged to observe the constraints of Islamic religion in artistic matters. Thus, in conformity with the criticism in the *hadiths* (traditions) of silk garments as a useless luxury, official production was turned over to the manufacture of linen in which the use of silk was confined to the provision of a simple border or decorative fringe. The constraints eased with time, and these silk yokes tended to invade the rest of the fabric.

The greatest innovation to which Islamic tradition obliged workers in the State workshops to conform was undoubtedly the prohibition of the reproduction of the human figure, a prescription reinforced by the iconoclastic crisis in Byzantium, which the Moslems did not fail to turn to account among the Christian populations in their territories. Coptic fabrics of the time were therefore more often than before adorned with purely decorative motifs including frequent successful borrowings from the vocabulary of Moslem themes, particularly under the Tulunids (868–905). Coptic tapestries were covered with geometric designs, arabesques or eight-lobed rosettes set in regular octagons, designs the weavers could have seen on contemporary monuments such as the Mosque of Ibn Tulun in Cairo, founder of the dynasty named after him.

The administrative difficulties placed in the way of Christians wishing to build new places of worship benefited the sumptuary arts, to which all their efforts had to be transferred. In private workshops, Coptic craftsmen continued to weave for their own community. The

SQUARE WITH GEOMETRIC DESIGNS
8¼″ × 8″
Tapestry of linen and wool
Designs drawn with flying shuttle
7th century

49

decorations on their wool and linen or all wool tapestries remained at first largely faithful to the *clavi* and *orbiculi* motifs, evincing the continued use of the Coptic tunic alongside Arab dress. The abundance of religious subjects likewise witnesses to the cultural resistance of the Christian populations, even if Moslem influence made itself increasingly felt in respect of style. For although the figures, saints or prophets, recur, they have become barely identifiable owing to the extremely geometrical shape given to their bodies. Here and there, however, it is possible to recognize them in silhouettes draped in long robes with organ pipe folds, or groups of dancers with disproportionate limbs. The weavers used the flying shuttle technique with ever greater skill to adorn the surface of the figures with a layer of very tight padding, as on the fabric with the dancers, and created original twill effects using the double flying shuttle.

Little by little, influenced in particular by the use of silk fabrics, the ornamental style evolved. Breaking with the tradition of a decoration solely of original tapestry, themes became repetitive and were inserted in circles or diamond-shaped squares. The former decoration with vertical bands was replaced by horizontal fringes more suited to the display of Kufic inscriptions, which began to make their appearance, although slightly deformed, on Coptic fabrics. The court workshops in the Fayum, in Upper Egypt, specialized in this *tirâz* production, which for a while perpetuated Coptic textile traditions as they became progressively transformed.

From the twelfth century onwards, Egypt itself produced the cotton cloth it had formerly imported from India or other eastern countries. Times change: with the twelfth century, the last examples of original Coptic art disappeared.

FABRIC WITH DANCERS
10¼″ × 10¼″
Tapestry of linen and wool, with flying shuttle
Panopolis (Akhmim), Upper Egypt
12th century

50

MOSLEM FABRICS

TOMB VEIL (DETAIL)
Silk lampas
Turkey
18th century

Moslem civilization has sometimes been called a "textile civilization" (Maurice Lombard, *Les textiles dans le monde musulman*), and indeed the extraordinary expansion of textile production under Islamic rule is reflected still in the etymology of such words as muslin (from Mosul in Iraq), damask (from Damascus in Syria) or taffeta (from the Turco-Persian *taftah*, meaning woven), as well as in the treasuries of Western churches with their wealth of precious eastern fabrics, and in the amazement of Marco Polo. This success was undoubtedly due in large part to the unifying influence of the Arab conquest, which entailed the confrontation of the various techniques employed in regions with a long-standing textile tradition, such as Egypt, Iran and Syria, and contributed to technical progress through the exchanges that followed from the displacement of populations within the Islamic dominions. Furthermore, the rapid growth of the towns and the pomp of princely courts led to increased consumption, for which technical improvements had to provide.

The fibres most frequently used in Moslem countries were—by order of importance—linen, cotton, wool and silk. Other materials were employed in the manufacture of coarse or especially luxurious cloths: camel's hair or goat's wool for felts; hemp, palm fibre or woven hair for the production of precious fabrics in Fatimite Egypt, or work in marine silk extracted from the byssus of molluscs (the *prima marina*) for the manufacture of clothes whose colour changed with the light.

The fibres were first subjected to mordanting by an alkali or alum, prior to the dyeing process proper. In the East as in the West, the business of dyeing, whether before or after weaving, was virtually a Jewish monopoly. The colouring materials came from different provinces of the Empire. Spain, which was the first producer of kermes, also supplied woad for blue dyes and saffron for the yellows. But the demand was so great that foreign products had to be imported as well: wars from the Yemen and curcuma from India for yellow, and indigo and lake, likewise from India. The utilization of these numerous dyes was regulated by special legislation. Certain processes deemed unsuitable for quality products were prohibited; the use of henna instead of madder for red dyes was regarded as fraudulent because the colour faded in the sun.

Weavers of the Moslem period took over and improved the tools as well as the techniques of their predecessors, such as the low-warp loom, used very early in Egypt and Greece, or the draw loom, found in excavations in Syria dating from the third century A.D. They also discovered the treadle loom, invented in China, which served them better than the draw loom for the manufacture of cloths with complicated designs reproduced from cartoons; these figured pieces, which were at first samites, were progressively replaced and finally, at the beginning of the fourteenth century, altogether supplanted by lampas.

The innovations were rapidly adopted in the main textile centres but only later spread to the rural areas where the old private and cottage industries and the old instruments survived for a long time.

Consequent on the extension of Islamic culture in both time and space, textile production varied with the different epochs, local traditions and possibilities corresponding to each region (for example, the massive gold resources of the Sudan as a general rule favoured the use of gold brocade, whereas provinces rich in silver mines, such as Persia or Spain, preferred to brocade their cloths with silver thread).

After the reign of the first four Caliphs and the elimination of the Omayyad dynasty (660–750), under the Abbasid dynasty (750–1258) the production of silk was reorganized and the industry established in a special district of the new capital, Baghdad. As well as silk and the famous white cloth known as merv, the craftsmen made magnificent richly adorned gold brocade for the uniforms of an army that was, however, unable to halt the progressive disintegration of the central power and the advent of local dynasties in the ninth and tenth centuries.

"TIRÂZ"
10½" × 24¾"
Linen decorated with silk tapestry bands
Egypt
11th century

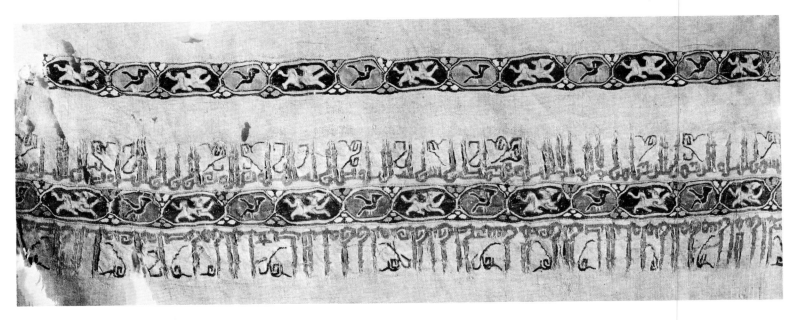

In Egypt, a Turkish officer, Ibn Tulun, seceded in 868 A.D. The Tulunid dynasty, which remained in power until 905, was famous for its wood carvings, and the cloths of the period reflected the vogue for this art: their sharply contrasted polychrome created an impression of hollowness evoking the idea of relief; the style was vigorous, and the decorative themes (plaits, cable stitch, spirals, birds or animals) were treated with a certain roughness accentuated by the choice of the material, for the most part wool. From this time on, Coptic weavers practised their traditional craft in the *tirâz*, under strict State control. There they produced in particular the fabrics also called *tirâz*, decorated with bands of wool and later silk introduced in the linen cloth using tapestry technique. In time, these bands came to cover an ever larger part of the fabric and often bore inscriptions dedicating them to the glory of the sovereign, who reserved them for his own use, or for making ceremonial robes *(khil'a)* to be offered as royal gifts. According to the fourteenth century historian, Ibn Khaldun,

this custom was inherited from the kings of Persia who, long before Islam, adorned the hems of their garments with royal portraits and various designs; as the Islamic princes belonged to a civilization that prohibited the representation of the human figure and exalted the use of writing, they quite naturally replaced these decorations by inscriptions.

The Egyptian workshops at Tinnis and neighbouring centres had the great privilege of making *kiswa*, the precious veils covering the Ka'aba at Mecca, which were regularly renewed. Black under the Abbasids, the *kiswa* was woven in white under the Fatimites (969–1171). This dynasty originatd in North Africa where it had its first capital, Kairouan, which it subsequently moved to Cairo, from where it controlled a vast empire stretching from Syria to Morocco. Under it, the production of artistic fabrics enjoyed a new boom, and designers on cloth inaugurated a delicate style resembling that of miniaturists. From the mid-eleventh century onwards, however,

the textile industry declined, and the Egyptian market was little by little taken over by Western cloths. It was not till the time of the Mamelukes (1250–1517) that a new type of silks appeared in the Nile valley; these were brocades inspired by Chinese products of the Mongol period, which were made first of all in eastern Asia for the court at Cairo, then copied locally by Egyptian weavers.

Syria, brought for a while under the domination of the Egyptian Fatimite dynasty, was the first cotton producing country of the Moslem world. In the workshops at Damascus, Tyre, Antioch and Tripoli it produced silk cloths brocaded on cotton. The techniques used were the same as in the Byzantine era, and the same decorations were reproduced, including Christian religious themes on pieces made for pilgrim buyers. In the eleventh and twelfth centuries, in the Frankish colonies in Syria, the workshops concentrated on this kind of fabric designed in the Western taste, and heavy gold and silver, diapered or brocaded silk materials were exported to the West where they were made up into vestments for priests and liturgical ornaments.

In 712 the Moslems conquered Spain, where an Omayyad prince, survivor from the massacre of his family, founded his own dynasty, which quickly threw off the authority of the central power and set itself up as an independent caliphate with its capital at Cordova. It was presumably the Arab conquerors who introduced sericulture to Spain, which soon specialized in the production of both raw and manufactured silk. Exported to European markets, Spanish cloths are mentioned from the ninth century onwards in pontifical inventories; the librarian Anastasius even uses the term *spaniscum* to designate silk cloth. In Almeria and Malaga, Murcia and Seville, Spanish fabrics soon began to compete with oriental products. Towards the middle of the twelfth century, under the rule of the Almohads, who came from North Africa, the decorative design was related to that of Egyptian and Syrian fabrics, in which geometrical forms and stylized inscriptions were mingled on brilliantly coloured, mainly red and gold, pieces. Among the themes probably transmitted by Coptic weavers to their Spanish colleagues in Moorish Spain, the eight-pointed star enjoyed particular favour.

These geometrical compositions, evoking contemporary jewellery, remained predominant despite the appearance in the late eleventh or early twelfth century of animal figures inserted in typically oriental circular compositions. The royal tombs of the period, such as those discovered at Las Huelgas near Burgos, brought to light pieces that are the more interesting because they can be accurately dated. This is the case, in particular, with the fragments of garments taken from the tomb of the Infante Don Felipe (died 1274) at Villalcazar de Sirga (Palencia); the magnificent gold *taqueté* reproduced here is a part of this. These fabrics were no doubt made at Granada where the Nasride dynasty (1235–1492) did its utmost to defend the last Moslem bastion holding out against the Christian reconquest. There, in the heart of the kingdom of Granada, the Alhambra style was created: on these cloths the decorations were arranged, usually against a red background, in parallel bands adorned with gold filigree feat-

uring scrolls inscribed with mottos and spangled with brightly coloured, red, yellow, blue and gold star-shaped polygons. In the fifteenth century, the decorative vocabularly was enriched with Gothic motifs, lancet arches and armorial bearings.

The Reconquest, completed in 1492 with the fall of the Nasride dynasty, was not the death blow to this typically Islamic textile art. Moslem craftsmen remained in Spain at least until the sixteenth century, and the *mudéjar* fabrics they made were a prolongation of the preceding period. At the same time, the Hispano-Moorish decorative vocabulary reappears, systematized and very pronounced, on North African fabrics.

In Sicily as in Spain, the Arabs introduced sericulture after their conquest of this former Byzantine province in 827. Under the rule of the Egyptian Fatimites, the production of silk materials knew a fresh period of expansion, favoured still further by the Norman conquest in 1062. Without making drastic changes in the existing institutions, Roger II continued to employ Moslem weavers, but called as well on the services of Greek specialists and reorganized the former *tirâz* of the Saracen emirs

SHROUD OF ST JOSSE
20½″ × 37″/9½″ × 24½″
Silk
Samite woven on a draw loom
Khurasan, Iran
Mid-10th century

SILK WITH PAIRED FIGURES SITTING FACE TO FACE
13⅜″ × 11¾″
Found near Rayy, Iran
11th-12th century

at Palermo famous for the production of embroidered braid and silk and gold cloths for the court. The decorations evoked at first the favourite themes of Byzantine and Moslem fabrics: medallions adorned with geometric motifs, herringbone pattern bands enhanced by rosettes or peopled by birds and dragons. In 1266, the transfer of the capital from Palermo to Naples brought this production to an end, and an art more clearly marked by Western culture succeeded it.

In the eastern part of the Empire, the dismantling of Abbasid power made way as early as the tenth century for the constitution of small, more or less independent Iranian States in which nationalist spirit created conditions favour-

able for the revival of former Sassanian textile traditions. It was in this century, under the rule of the Samanides (847–1004) established in the Khurasan region, that the *Shroud of St Josse* was made, the famous piece which was brought from the East on the occasion of the First Crusade. This figured samite woven entirely of silk on a draw loom contains many features borrowed from Sassanian art: the face to face arrangement of the elephants, the small tie hung round the neck of the cock and the camels recalling the kind of game reserved for royal hunts. Other elements, however, evidence its already Islamic character: the arrangement of strictly separate compartments within a rectangular frame, the inscription in Arab characters, the

55

independent treatment of each part considered as a wholly separate decorative element, the bright colours and the density of the patterns are clear indications of this evolution. As well as its aesthetic value, the *Shroud of St Josse* is therefore particularly interesting as a transition work, drawing at one and the same time on the local artistic heritage and a new artistic sensibility. The piece is also most instructive from the historical standpoint in that it is significant in its own way of the place occupied by the Turks within the Empire at that time. The Kufic inscription reading "Glory and Prosperity to quâ'id Abû Mansûr Bukhtakin—May God give him long life!" is indeed a real *tirâz* formula reserved normally for the sovereign. Its appearance here, bracketed with the name of a simple general, has a provocative air, an impression confirmed by evidence dating from a little later indicating that this Bukhtakin was executed for having fomented trouble at Khurasan.

In the end, however, the ambitions of the Turkish populations were realized and the Seljuks established their rule over Iran (1037-1194) and Asia Minor (1077–1307), where they patronized the development of a brilliant civilization harmoniously combining Turkish and Moslem elements. The cloths of this period owed much to previous productions but gave an ever larger place to arabesques and palmette patterns; the decorations became loaded with detail, the style was freer. At the same time, weavers adopted new and more elaborate techniques, such as the double cloth or lampas.

The Mongol invasions in the thirteenth century had a favourable influence on relations between China and Iran. Moslem weavers left to practise their art in the Far East and Chinese workers settled in Islamic countries. As a result, a mixed textile art came into being in which the familiar figures of the Chinese repertory and typical Islamic adornments appear side by side.

LAMPAS OF LAMÉ SILK
39" × 14"
Iran
14th century

56

YOUNG PRINCE IN A GARDEN
41¼″ × 26¾″
Silk brocade on satin ground
Iran
Late 16th century

It was not until the beginning of the sixteenth century that a national power came into being again in Iran with the advent of the Safavids (1502–1736). Under the two great sovereigns Tahmasp I (1524–1576) and Abbas I the Great (1587–1629) the artistic life of the country rose to such heights that Persian fashions even spread to Western courts. The fabrics in particular were incomparably luxurious and refined. Many were illustrated with historiated scenes, a rare phenomenon in Islam but more feasible in Iran than elsewhere since Shiism adopted a relatively conciliatory attitude in the question of images. The figures represented, always idealized (for even in Shiite countries no one was expected to reproduce the works of the Creator too precisely), were members of the princely entourage, lords or servants, loving couples, drinkers, whose stereotyped image was repeated on borders and bands

LAILA VISITING MAJNUN IN HIS DESERT RETREAT
27½″ × 11″
Silk lampas and satin serge, signed by Ghiyath
Yezd, Iran
Second half of the 16th century

"POLISH" BELT (FRAGMENT)
Gold brocaded silk lampas
Iran or Poland
18th century

DIVAN CARPET WITH FLORAL DESIGNS
48½″ × 26½″
Figured silk velvet
Turkey
Second half of the 17th century

TOMB VEIL
58¾″ × 27¼″
Silk lampas
Turkey
18th century

superimposed on backgrounds covered with plants, flowers, birds and butterflies recalling the omnipresent gardens of Arab and Persian poetry.

The subjects were sometimes taken directly from legends or literary works, as in the case of the fabric signed by the artist Ghiyath, illustrating the meeting of Laila and the poet Majnun related by the twelfth century writer Nizami. Several museums have a copy of this lampas—a typical production of Yezd, one of the chief textile centres of the period, together with Ispahan and Kashan—and it is impossible to say for certain whether these are dispersed fragments of a single cloth or series manufactures of a popular model. The weavers who executed these delicate designs worked from miniature cartoons and commanded a broad range of highly perfected techniques: brocaded double cloth, velvet of several piles. These products were so famous abroad that they sometimes led to the creation of independent industries. Towards the middle of the eighteenth century, for example, specialized factories in Poland began to make belts of a kind originally manufactured in Iran which were in great demand among Polish aristocrats. The copies were so close to the original that it is sometimes difficult to tell whether these "Polish belts" were made in Iran or Poland.

The influence of the Safavid workshops can likewise be seen in the first silks produced in Ottoman Turkey, which had become since the fifteenth century the leading Moslem power.

However, in the textile centres at Bursa, Damascus, Scutari and Hereke, where velvets were made, the weavers were not long in creating their own style differing from Safavid productions by the absence of any human figures (Turkey professed Sunnite obedience) which were replaced by geometric or floral designs. The two great sources of inspiration for textile art were the Koran and the Earthly Paradise. Quotations from the book went to decorate standards and veils for tombs on which they appeared set in medallions or written out in lines arranged herringbonewise. The gardens of the Earthly Paradise were evoked on fabrics, as on the beautiful wall tiles, by bunches of tulips, carnations and hyacinths, on which Italian weavers drew freely in the eighteenth century, at the same time that Ottoman artists were strongly influenced by Baroque and Rococo.

Whereas silk weaving was a strictly regulated imperial art calling for highly specialized qualifications, embroidery was practised by women of all classes who used it for the decoration of bags, turbans and cloths.

This art found particularly favourable scope for expansion in North Africa where, under Turkish rule, the famous "Algiers embroideries" were deeply marked by Ottoman influence.

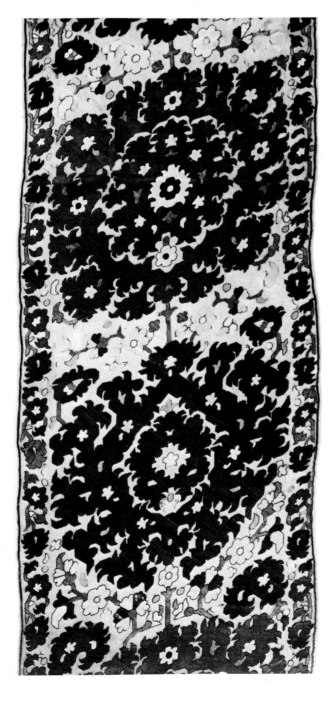

SO-CALLED ALGIERS EMBROIDERY (FRAGMENT)
Coarse linen and silk
18th century

ITALIAN AND FRENCH FABRICS

BROADCLOTH WITH VIOLET SATIN GROUND
PATTERNED WITH STARS AND ANGELS
17¼" × 13¾"
Lucca, Italy
14th century

In the thirteenth century Italian fabrics tended to supplant those of Islam. At the same time that Coptic production ceased, political instability in the eastern Mediterranean due to the Mongol invasions weakened the position of the workshops in Asia Minor, Persia and Syria. The Italians on the other hand benefited from favourable circumstances encouraging them to manufacture themselves more and more of the products which they had previously been content to distribute. In a general context of prosperity, at a time when the taste for luxuries was fostered by the influx of wonderful objects brought home from the East by the crusaders, the beginnings of the cotton and silk industries in the Italian peninsula and mass immigration of Sicilian workmen following the bloody episode of the Sicilian Vespers (by which the House of Aragon became masters of Sicily) gave a decisive stimulus to the textile sector.

It all began at Lucca, where the first Sicilians hostile to the House of Aragon migrated. Their experience and know-how merged there with those of equally highly qualified Jewish weavers from the south of Italy who had come to the town only shortly before them. Lucca benefited as well from a plentiful supply of capital and a commercial organization that enabled it first of all to supplement the supply of raw silk obtained from silk-worm breeders in Calabria, Sicily, Tuscany and Lombardy by imports from countries bordering on the Caspian Sea, and ensured it afterwards the necessary markets for the disposal of its finished products. Purveyor to the Church and princely houses, Lucca specialized early in very costly cloths. For ecclesiastical customers, the weavers made fabrics with religious designs in which they reintroduced the human figure abandoned since the time of the Copts and Byzantine silk-makers. Other towns at this time followed the same trend; Florentine fabrics illustrated scenes from the New Testament, and these are found again on embroidered orphreys from Siena. But while the unitary language of tapestry or embroidery was suited to religious iconography, the repetitive nature of production by the use of the flying shuttle was prejudicial to dramatic intensity and deprived the representation of a religious mystery of its suggestive power; very soon, Lucca weavers returned to profane subjects.

Sicilian craftsmen had already to some extent freed themselves from the restrictive heritage of the Orient by breaking the circular bounds set by the compartments that traditionally framed the confronted beasts to one side and the other of the tree of life. After this disappearance of the frame or *rota*, the dissemination of Chinese culture and above all of Chinese fabrics in the Mediterranean countries through the intermediary of the Mongol invaders speeded up the process of decompartmentalization and confirmed the renewed vitality and movement enlivening textile compositions. Asian influence also made its appearance in designs: eagles became dragon-like; the robes of the figures ended in curled and undulating ribbons inspired by the conventionalized representation of clouds by the Chinese. Less systematic symmetry, the expansion of secondary motifs, axes of action indicated by an animal bounding out of its frame, characterized the new productions.

LIONS DRINKING AND CONFRONTED EAGLES AMONG GEOMETRIC
AND FLORAL DESIGNS
23¼″ × 13¾″
Lampas, double cloth ground
Venice
14th–15th century

CHRIST RISING FROM THE DEAD
15¾″ × 9″
Gold brocade on satin ground
Italy
Late 15th century

The importance of Chinese influence was highlighted at
Lucca, as throughout all Italy, by the adoption of predominantly warp pattern lampas, which benefited technically from the appearance of the draw loom at the end of the
thirteenth century. Concurrently, the development of the
filatorium, the mill for reeling, winding and twisting silk,
made it possible to produce increased quantities and finer
qualities of yarn. In the new fabrics, crossings were multiplied and from then on almost invisible to the naked eye;
weavers were thus able to exploit contrasts in the weave
between the background and the motifs of the double
cloth lampas. Lucca produced a very special kind of brocaded silk, the diapered fabric, decorated in most cases
with confronted birds alternating with pairs of beasts, and
in between the animals large flowerets after the model of
the Sassanian Hom. The exaggerated length of the figures
reflected the predominance of the warp element.

EAGLE ATTACKING AN ANIMAL IN ITS ENCLOSURE
Silk brocade, with linen thread
covered with a membrane of gilt silver
Italy
14th century

LUCCA DIAPER
51½″ × 10½″
Green damask silk
14th century

In 1314 Lucca was ravaged by civil war and many of its craftsmen sought refuge in other towns. Some went to Venice where the Grand Council authorized the creation of a Lucca silk district near the Rialto. Their arrival coincided with the first development of silk weaving in the city of the Doges. Everything combined to favour the expansion of this processing industry. The Venetian explorers, among whom Marco Polo was the most famous, culled information about silk products and techniques in Syria, Persia and China; the Venetian colonies, which since the eleventh century had supplied raw silk as tribute, and finally the loss of Syria at the end of the thirteenth century, left a gap which allowed Venice to establish itself. After a first phase of production marked by very strong oriental influence owing to the close relations of the city with Constantinople, from the middle of the fourteenth century onwards, in Venice as in the rest of Italy, greater freedom

"Cut Velvet"
24" × 23½"
Italy
15th century

began to prevail in the matter of decoration. After the foundation, in 1347, of the guild of velvet makers, in the fifteenth century the industry became specialized. Introduced from the East, more precisely from Persia, velvet was worn by important personages as a symbol of dignity and power. As such, it appeared in the pictures of artists of the period, who sometimes supplied the master weavers with cartoons representing pomegranates, thistles or pine cones ending in wavy stems or opening out in diamond or almond-shaped compartments. The surface of the fabric was laminated so as to suggest different relations between the motif and the background; velvets in two, three or four depths of pile alternated with cut, tooled, figured or uncut velvets and with "antique" or "wrought-iron" velvets apparently of Venetian origin.

"Tooled Velvet"
17"¾ × 8"
Genoa
18th century

LAMPAS DECORATED WITH ARMORIAL BEARINGS, VASES AND GROTESQUES (FRAGMENT)
Silk
Italy
16th century

In the sixteenth century Italy came again under oriental influence, imitating Turkish velvets and copying the designs of Persian silks. The ardent enthusiasm of the Renaissance for antiquity was expressed in the textile area by the transposition of architectural elements, masks or vases. Combined with very stylized floral compositions intermingled with cornucopia, these same vases are found on very fine *jardinière* velvets sculpted at Genoa at the end of the century. In the seventeenth and eighteenth centuries,

factory was transferred to Tours, where Italian workers likewise contributed their technical know-how, and the industry progressed steadily under the reign of Francis I. "A family industry developed and it is estimated that, in the mid-sixteenth century, silk making gave a livelihood to forty thousand persons in this region; eight thousand looms were worked by a hundred master weavers established as master manufacturers, who handed down their offices and privileges from father to son" (Jo Guéde).

SILK WITH RED GROUND AND WOVEN DECORATION IN WHITE, PINK AND GREEN
First half of the 18th century

under the influence of Baroque art, the designs became more complicated and churches were embellished with luxurious, exuberantly decorated red and gold cloths. Distributed throughout Europe, and above all in Spain where they gave the textile industry a new outlook more in keeping with Italian taste, these fabrics served for a while as a model for French weavers who, however, freed themselves little by little and developed a style of their own, which soon eclipsed the productions of Italian workshops.

In France the practice of weaving had existed also since Neolithic times and was widespread in Gaul. After a long period during which textile activities were confined to the countryside and monasteries, feudal lords and kings employed weavers in gynaecea or workshops.

The twelfth and thirteenth centuries, on the other hand, saw the concentration of the industry in confraternities and guilds, whose statutes, previously transmitted orally, were compiled in the *Book of Crafts* by Etienne Boileau, provost of Paris merchants from 1261 to 1268.

During this period tapestry became an independent activity, but the *Book of Crafts* shows clearly that, from the twelfth century, silk weaving was known and practised in France in the textile centres of Reims, Poitiers and Troyes, and other materials were worked up at St Denis, Beauvais, Chartres and Arras. This activity in particular was given a fresh lease of life in Lyons in the fourteenth century with the arrival of weavers driven out of Lucca by the Florentines, and in 1450 Charles VII granted Lyons the monopoly of the silk trade for the entire kingdom. In 1466 Louis XII decided to found a royal manufactory at Lyons, but in view of the reservations of the Lyons Consulate the

In 1536, the Lyons Consulate agreed to the establishment of the manufactory, with its own statutes.

With the return of the Court of France to Paris, the industry in Touraine entered on its decline, but in Lyons, with the adoption of the big draw loom (1605), activity expanded and the city became a focal point for fabrics made in the Orient, Italy, Sicily and Spain, and in the seventeenth and eighteenth centuries Lyons was the recognized capital of the silk weaving industry.

A purely French style, however, only came into being with the centralizing policy of Mazarin, who in 1664 appointed Le Brun to manage the Crown Furniture Factory, and Colbert, who drew up uniform regulations for all the factories of the kingdom.

A very floral style became current in silk materials under the influence of Monnoyer and Dutilleu, and in the same period tapestry became more exotic following on the voyages of royal envoys to China, Siam and Turkey.

During the Regency, the reigns of Louis XV and XVI, the Consulate and the Empire, French silks developed a series of very striking creations including the productions of Charles Dutilleu, Joubert de l'Huberderie and above all Philippe de Lasalle, who was ennobled by Louis XVI.

The Malmaison hangings were made after designs by Jean-François Bony, who also designed the coronation robes of the Empress Josephine (1804).

After the adoption of the Jacquard loom, at the beginning of the nineteenth century, mechanization opened a period during which silks had to wait for nearly a century before they benefited once again from the collaboration of artists interested in the language of textiles.

SILK WITH REPEAT PATTERNS OF COILING DRAGONS
(ENLARGED DETAIL)
Woven silk with warp decoration
China
17th-18th century

According to an old Chinese myth, the Milky Way separates the worker, the masculine principle, from the weaver, his feminine counterpart. The latter was especially honoured for her silks, and her feast was celebrated in the spring, when the mulberry leaves were gathered.

According to another legend, the first person to cultivate the bombyx was the wife of the mythical emperor Huang-ti, in the third millennium B.C. Every year in the month of April the Empress, venerated as the goddess of silk, received offerings of mulberry leaves.

The number and antiquity of these stories witness to the importance the Chinese have from the first given to everything relating to silk. Indeed, the history of silk begins almost simultaneously with the history of China, and the two have often been closely linked. The first tangible evidence of the existence of sericulture was the discovery, in 1926, on a Neolithic site in south Shan-si, of an artificially cut bombyx cocoon. As regards the practice of weaving, indirect evidence of this is afforded by traces of silk fabrics encrusted on the sides of bronze vases dating from the end of the Shang period (1766– 1122 B.C.).

Classified in two categories according to quality, silk became very soon omnipresent in Chinese life. As well as clothes, it served to make quite a number of objects in everyday use: cords for musical instruments, fishing nets, etc. Considered to be specially valuable, it was given to civil servants as pay or a reward for outstanding services. It was above all the main Chinese export to the West, and a particularly important one owing to the fact that for a long time only the Chinese knew how to manufacture it: hence their monopoly of the production of raw silk.

A long period of prosperity opened for the trade in Chinese silks when the Han dynasty (206 B.C.–220 A.D.) began to develop the silk industry and organize the trade with the West, which had till then been intermittent. The second century A.D. was the golden age of the Silk Route linking the Syrian coast to Changan, the new Chinese capital, and the reputation of Chinese silk products became so great that Western peoples acquired the habit of calling the Chinese by the name "Seres" or silk (seric) people.

There was, however, reciprocity in these exchanges. While Syrian weavers, for example, were clearly influenced by Chinese silks, the impact of Mediterranean cloths on Asiatic production is also undeniable. Some pieces from the Han period prove, by their vine leaf and grape bunch designs, that oriental weavers knew and appreciated the principles of Greek art. Sassanian fabrics were likewise so faithfully imitated in China that it is sometimes difficult to tell the copies from their models.

Remains of silks dating from the Han period have been discovered in very widely separated places, evincing their extraordinary dissemination. They have been found in Syria, Mongolia and Korea, but the most interesting pieces were those unearthed by Sir Aurel Stein at the beginning of this century in the course of his excavations on the site of the ancient Lou-Lan in Chinese Turkestan. The technical quality of these silks, preserved in great numbers in tombs at what was formerly an important stage on the Silk Route, is very different from all other contemporary products, and they were already made for the most part by processes that continued in use until the eighteenth century. The simplest are monochrome tissues; these were

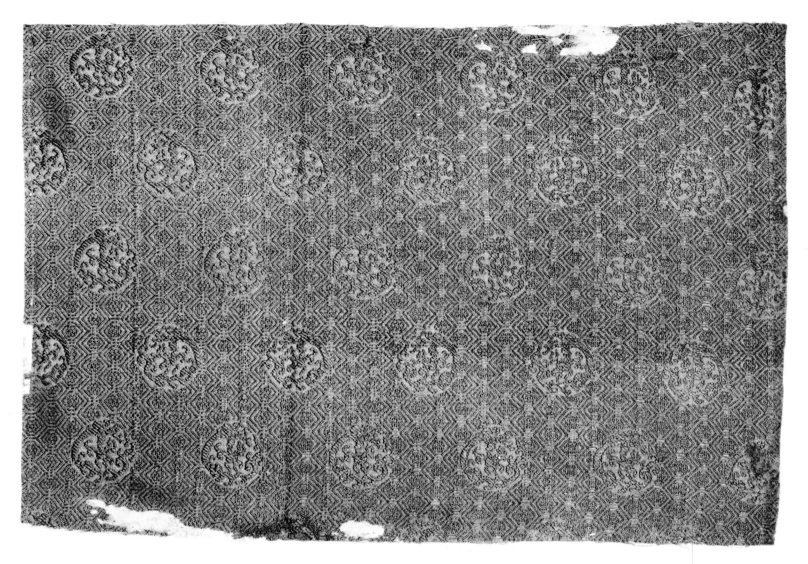

SILK WITH REPEAT PATTERNS OF COILING DRAGONS
7¼″ × 10½″
Woven silk with warp decoration
China
17th- 18th century

generally dyed after weaving and are especially striking on account of the fineness of the yarn, which gives them their great density. The polychrome weaves, manufactured by techniques that must have been known well before the time of the Han dynasty, are even more striking. Their designs, peopled with different kinds of birds and beasts moving among trees, are arranged in somewhat formal compositions bordered with foliated scrolls variously inspired by floral forms or spiralling clouds. These decorative elements, which recall those of contemporary lacquer work, are chosen from the time of the warping of the thread, implying detailed programming of the decoration since the weft serves only as a filling component, its influence on the design being the more reduced in so far as it is usually invisible, disappearing under the warp. The weft yarn, in view of its limited role, is therefore single and monochrome; on the other hand, there can be as many as four differently coloured warp threads, each motif being obtained by means of a float of the warp corresponding to the desired colour. The weavers were able to manufacture such complex fabrics because they had a perfect tool for the purpose, the reed loom, which seems to have remained in use over a long period.

In the fifth or at the beginning of the sixth century, the first reversible twill-weaves were made, for which draw looms must have been used. Their manufacture became generalized under the T'ang dynasty (618–907), which inaugurated a period of great development of the textile arts.

T'ang weavers made brocades or *kin* enriched by silk threads sheathed in gold, and improved printing techniques in order to brighten their fabrics with motifs emulating the forms and colours of contemporary ceramics. Three methods were used concurrently: *kyokechi* dyeing, in which the fabric was pressed between two wooden boards engraved with the design and impregnated with dye; a kind of batik, called *rokechi*; and, finally, a process consisting in the arrangement of undyed patches by squeezing the fabric tightly with little cords so as to isolate the fibres held fast together in this way when the cloth was dipped in the dye.

To conclude the description of this development of the textile arts during the T'ang period, mention must also be made of the fine silk tapestries, fragments of which have been recovered from the "Caves of the Thousand Buddhas" at Tun-huang, an outpost in north-western China, and some examples of which can be seen in the Shōsōin and the Taima-dera at Nara in Japan. These pieces were produced by a technique previously unknown in China and thought to have been introduced in the eleventh century via Iran by the Uighur Turks at that time settled on the western frontier of the country. What is not clear is whether the fabrics of this kind dating from the T'ang period can be regarded as Chinese, or whether they should still be taken to be the work of Uighur "teachers," a hypothesis supported by the discovery of very similar fragments in the ruins of ancient Uighur settlements. Whatever their origin, these tapestries deserve detailed study because they were very quickly going to enjoy great success in China and give rise to a new Chinese silk industry, even if the exact date of its appearance is not known. These contemporary products of the T'ang period already served the purposes that were to be those of future silk products: they were used chiefly for garments, had their place in interior decoration and may have provided covers for

PANEL WITH MANDARIN DUCKS AMID
LOTUS PLANTS AND LANDSCAPE
23″ × 15¼″
K'o-ssu (silk tapestry)
China
15th–16th century

PANEL WITH BIRDS ON TREES
IN BLOSSOM (FRAGMENT)
K'o-ssu (silk tapestry)
China
K'ang-hsi period (1654–1722)

literary and artistic documents. From the technical standpoint, they evinced the application of the old Western method of pounding colours and also the method of *gon* ("framed") tapestry, which consisted in edging the design with yarn of a different colour.

Support for the thesis of those who refuse to regard these T'ang period tapestries as genuinely Chinese works is found in the fact that the Chinese name for this kind of fabric, *k'o-ssu*, only appears in the next period, under the Sung dynasty (960–1280 A.D.). It is spelt in different ways according to whether it signifies crossed threads, weft thread or weft colours. These pieces are always Western

inspired, drawing on styles known in the West since the time of the Copts but progressively developing their own characteristics based on essential features such as:
- the use above all and even exclusively of silk for both warp and weft, which entails at once a degree of fineness beyond any comparison with Western products;
- the absence of any link between two differently coloured picks which, by leaving the vents apparent, give a peculiar impression of relief reflected, moreover, in the contemporary meaning given to the word *k'o-ssu*, since the character used for it today means in fact "engraved" or "cut silk";

PANEL WITH BIRDS AND FLOWERS
35″ × 25½″
Tsuzure, Japanese equivalent of the *k'o-ssu*
19th century

— frequent touches of paint on the woven tissue, so many indeed that in some works these tapestries are classed as paintings.

The *k'o-ssu* productions attributed to the Northern Sung dynasty (860–1126) reflect the influence of pottery, decorated like the latter with motifs showing birds fluttering round among flowers, but from the time of the Southern Sung dynasty (1127–1280) tapestry makers set themselves to reproduce the works of the great calligraphers and masters of painting who were captivated by floral and landscape subjects. Like pictures, these woven copies were signed and have handed down to posterity the names of

famous artists such as Chou K'o-ju, Chen Tseu-fan, Wu Hiu and Won K'i.

At the beginning of the thirteenth century, following the Mongol invasion, the Sung were succeeded by the Yüan dynasty (1279–1368). The trade routes were reopened and while Marco Polo visited China, Chinese weavers and fabrics again found their way to Western courts. The chief remains of Chinese silks of this period are those found in Egyptian tombs and in the treasuries of Christian churches.

The designs for these Asian fabrics were inspired by the output of Western workshops. In the sixteenth century

ALTAR CLOTH WITH DRAGON AND PHOENIXES
35½″ × 34″
K'o-ssu (silk tapestry)
China
About 1600

Lucca and Venice launched a new style permeated with oriental influence and this artistic confrontation led in the thirteenth and fourteenth centuries to the adoption of the lampas technique to the detriment of the samites. In China the lampas met perfectly the preference of weavers for warp decoration, stressing the vertical lie of the weave. It is interesting in this connection to recall that Chinese characters are written and read also from top to bottom in compositions that are clearly predominantly vertical. In the West the cultural context was different, and although artists let themselves be attracted by these lampas, it was not long before the predominant role in decoration was restored to the weft.

Under the Ming dynasty (1368–1644), Chinese silk exports came to a large extent under the control of Portuguese, Spanish and Dutch traders who flooded the European market with them. Japan was also a valuable market, a preserve of the Dutch and Portuguese who established special factories at Macao to manufacture damask and embroidered silks to sell to Manila and Japan; to attract buyers, these materials, although manufactured by Chinese workers, were woven with pseudo-European motifs treated to suit Japanese taste.

At the same time, works that were totally Chinese in character were still made to meet domestic demand in China. The town of Soochow, in particular, was during this period the chief centre supplying the Imperial Court. The rapidly growing prosperity of the upper classes in the late fourteenth and early fifteenth centuries gave a new stimulus to the decorative arts in general, and textiles in particular. Ming weavers indulged in every kind of luxury and fantasy, mingling weaving and embroidery, tripling the number of gold ends to give their creations greater contrast and brilliance. *K'o-ssu* became larger and more detailed, gold brocades multiplied, the elements of textile iconography became fixed in the forms they were to retain–apart from stylistic variations–until the twentieth century. These elements reflect a highly symbolical conception of art, in which each of them evokes a spiritual value: the prunus, purity; the duck, happiness and conjugal love. The Emperor alone had the right to wear robes adorned with the twelve symbolic emblems representing the universe in its entirety, a universe having at its centre the Dragon, that is to say China, enthroned over all.

In the late sixteenth century, from 1580 to 1590, ornamental hangings and velvet cushions began to be used in

EMPEROR'S DRAGON ROBE WITH THE TWELVE SYMBOLS
Height 60″
K'o-ssu (silk tapestry)
China
Mid-19th century

FLOWERED VELVET PANEL ENHANCED WITH GOLD THREAD
(FRAGMENT)
China, found in a Buddhist temple
17th century

Buddhist temples. It is not known from whom the Chinese learnt the technique for these productions, which was to enable them to "sculpt" some of their most delicate works.

Under the Ch'ing dynasty (1644–1911), the trend was more than ever towards concentration on the production of fabrics for export.

Despite protectionist measures adopted by the countries concerned, the volume of exports continued to rise, leading in the eighteenth century to the development of new and faster methods of production: additions in paint became more numerous and sometimes even the main lines of the design were painted in gouache. At the end of the nineteenth century, chemical dyes introduced from Europe came to be used more and more often in the place of natural colouring materials.

The prime importance given to work in silk should not be a reason to overlook less valuable textiles. Hemp appears to have been used in all periods for coarse fabrics, but the dates for the introduction of cotton and wool are uncertain. Sir Aurel Stein discovered fragments of pieces made with both these fibres in Chinese Turkestan, but if the written texts are to be believed, cotton only came into general use towards the end of the Sung period and wool under the Yüan dynasty.

CHASUBLE DECORATED WITH FLOWER DESIGNS
41¾″ × 24½″
Painting and printing on satin
China, export fabric
18th century

GUANYIN BODHISATTVA
Height 59½″
Silk lampas enhanced with gold thread
China, early 19th century

Silk tissues have always been the usual support for embroidery, which must have had its beginnings in China more or less contemporaneously with weaving, dating back presumably as far as the second millennium B.C., even if the oldest archaeological evidence for it, found in Central Asia or at Noin Ula in northern Mongolia–fragments of silk decorated with chain stitch, with differently coloured threads–dates only from the first millennium.

Among the oldest embroideries there are also several pieces dating from the second century B.C. which were discovered in the Baikal region and some T'ang period works now in the Shōsōin at Nara, Japan. It was under the last T'ang emperors that satin stitch seems to have supplanted chain stitch, concurrently with the spread of the practice of marking contours with gold and silver thread.

Under the Sung dynasty, embroidery, like tapestry, entered the orbit of painting, and the workers of the Embroidery Office founded by Emperor Hui-tsung (1082–1135) set themselves to reproduce the works of famous painters. The pieces of this period were very famous and were in turn often copied in later periods, particularly under the Ming and Ch'ing emperors.

After a period of expansion during which new processes proliferated amid an unprecedented wealth of decorative formulae, the end of the eighteenth century saw the inauguration of a more severe style with the adoption of the stitch known as the Peking knot, an authentic speciality of Chinese embroiderers; the threads are often gold and sometimes even peacock's feathers.

Chinese embroiderers became so famous that Europeans, delighted to be able to employ such highly skilled labour so cheaply, did not hesitate to send fabrics to the Far East solely to have them embroidered there. The widest variety of objects serve as a pretext for these needlework fantasies. Garments, temple banners, purses, spectacle cases, slippers are covered with flowers, birds, landscapes or scenes from everyday life. The choice of any given theme corresponds often to the expression of a wish, or serves to indicate the rank and function of the owner of the object.

PANEL WITH HAN XIANGZI, ONE OF THE EIGHT IMMORTALS, PLAYING THE FLUTE
36¼″ × 9″
Satin embroidered with coloured silk
China
About 1850

JAPANESE FABRICS

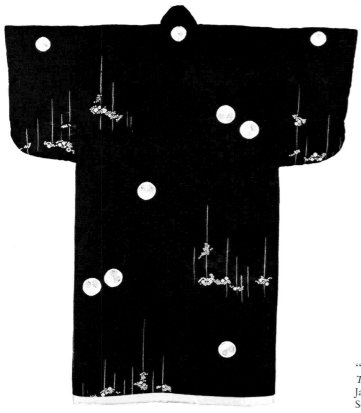

"KOSODE" WORN BY TOKUGAWA IYEYASU
Tsujigahana (dyed and painted fabric)
Japan
Second half of the 16th century

The beginnings of textile art in Japan were deeply marked by Chinese influence.

It was from China itself, through the intermediary of Korean weavers who migrated to Japan at the beginning of the Christian era, that the Japanese learnt first of all the technique of weaving hemp and linen, and a little later the secrets of silk-worm breeding.

In the sixth century, following the introduction of Buddhism to Japan, trade with China increased. Contact with this powerful neighbour with a rich, centuries-old textile tradition, completed the apprenticeship of the Japanese and led to the expansion of their production which was stimulated besides by the desire to decorate their newly built temples. The Japanese taught themselves the Chinese methods of tie-dyeing *(kōkechi)*, of resist-dyeing *(rōkechi)* or printing *(kyōkechi)*. At that time, however, they did not even try to exploit all the possible applications of these methods because they used them for the most part in the manufacture of fabrics for the people, who were not as a rule hard to please.

For the aristocracy, pieces embellished with embroidery seemed more appropriate, and the embroiderers of the Nara period (710–794) tried their hand at chain stitch and knot stitch, also imported from China, while at the same time improving their own *sashinui* methods of tambour-frame embroidery.

The Japanese made Chinese methods so much their own that it is difficult to distinguish their products from the models that inspired them. This similarity is particularly striking in the pieces of different origin that were collected by Emperor Shōmu Tennō in the eighth century and given by his widow to the Shōsōin at Nara, where they can still be seen.

The general expansion of production gave fabrics a new value: the provinces paid their taxes in cloths made of the silk and hemp distributed to them, and the various fabrics came to be related to the rank of their owner. This expansion led the authorities quite naturally to organize the constantly growing production of textiles: regulations were promulgated in 710, and a Weavers' Office was attached to the Court.

In 794, when the seat of government was transferred to the new capital, Heion-kyō (present-day Kyoto), the imperial weavers followed their patrons. There were no more innovations in weaving techniques, but printing methods were improved, and colours, increasingly numerous, were poetically named after plants or birds as an aid in distinguishing and classifying them.

The struggles of pressure groups led to the breakdown of the government, and Court customs, particularly in respect of dress, became more commonplace. At the end of the twelfth century, this trend was accentuated with the accession of the Samurai, who attached special importance to moral values and advocated an austere way of life from which textiles were among the first to suffer. Several centuries were to pass before there was a revival of the sector, favoured by the resumption of cultural exchanges with India and China during the Momoyama period (1573–1600). Tradition has it, moreover, that it was from Chinese craftsmen who settled in Osaka at the end of the sixteenth century that Japanese weavers learnt to use the draw loom, which was soon to replace the older reed loom for the manufacture of figured materials. As the largest weaving mills were established in the main importing centres, Osaka, Hakata or Yamagushi, the Japanese were always in contact with foreign techniques. The vogue for

DETAIL OF A NŌH ROBE
Overall length of the robe 63¾″
Kara-ori (gold brocaded silk)
Japan
17th century

THE GODDESS GATTEN HOLDING
THE MOON DISC IN HER HAND
Embroidery on brocaded fabric interwoven with
gold thread, with lampas frame
Japan
16th century

Ming brocades and embroideries became so widespread that to meet the demand, Japanese weavers reproduced the Chinese fabrics, adapting them at the same time to their own taste. In the Nishijin district of Kyoto, capital of the silk industry, they made *surihaku* fabrics with patches of gold or silver leaf stuck to the tissue and *kara-ori* (literally "Chinese weave") figured fabrics like embroidery, using the Chinese method as their name indicates.

Chinese fabrics were not the only ones appreciated by the Japanese; European fabrics likewise enjoyed some success, as is evidenced by the revival of interest in striped materials previously regarded as too easy to make to be highly esteemed. Japan borrowed from the West not only new decorative forms and motifs but also techniques previously unknown there, such as velvet making (late sixteenth–early seventeenth centuries). Sometimes elements of varied origin were combined to produce an original synthesis, as in the case of *tsuzure* based on Chinese *k'o-ssu*, and Western tapestries brought to Japan by Portuguese navigators.

At the end of the sixteenth century, the development of cotton growing had revolutionary effects in Japan. Ordinary cloths were from then on woven of cotton rather than hemp, and the *tsuzure* followed the same trend using cotton warp with silk weft, an innovation that made them stronger than Chinese tapestries. Despite the impact of foreign textile traditions, there was a parallel development of typically Japanese products featuring a proliferation of imaginative fantasy and a wealth of luxury embracing every kind of combination of techniques. These included *tsujigahana*, combining painting on fabric and dyeing; *kirishame*, using both appliqué and patchwork; and *nuihaku*, supplementing the gold or silver patches of the *surihaku* with additional embroidery.

NŌH COSTUME
Nuihaku (gold or silver) overlays and embroidered additions; *katami gawari* (the two halves with different designs)
Japan
17th century (early Tokugawa period)

The rules of composition were also very varied. The *katami-gawari*, literally "different half-bodies," consisted in contrasting the two halves of the same garment either by cutting them from different fabrics, or by changing the colours and motifs from one half to the other; the *katasuso* confined decoration to the shoulders and hems, and the *chirachimoyo* were adorned with dispersed designs leaving large plain spaces between them.

At the beginning of the Tokugawa period (1603–1867), the court at Kyoto was particularly taken with the type of decoration known as "Palace style." This was a very strange and somewhat affected style in which fragmented motifs were reproduced and suggestion played a large part: for example, half a wheel was represented to evoke the luxurious carriages of the nobles, or a simple white square to call to mind the sheets of paper on which courtiers composed their poems.

The iconographic textile repertory comprised originally the same main components as that of Chinese fabrics, but there again Japanese weavers little by little created their own vocabulary: each family kept an album of fabric designs and handed it down from mother to daughter. In their growing desire to imitate painting, designers gave pride of place to figurative motifs: flowers, trees, birds or natural scenes, linking up with poetry and song. Whereas previously stylized designs and economy of colours had been the rule, eighteenth century weavers sought effects similar to those of painting and had recourse to realism and polychrome. Dyeing processes were chosen rather than embroidery, which was only used to highlight or complete decorative elements. Artists preferred in particular a new method of resist-dyeing, *yuzen zome*, employing rice paste. The shading off made possible by this method made tissues look like a real picture, the more so since in order to accentuate the relation to painting and also to simplify their task, fabric designers often took a single big design for the whole surface of a piece, rather than cover the fabric with repeat patterns. Progressively, the symbolic value of design disappeared before the purely decorative function.

The authorities, the theatre and religion were the principal outlets for the manufacturers of luxury fabrics.

Besides the Emperor, members of the Court had to be supplied with due respect for the rules of dress, a deep science in Japan, where specific fabrics are prescribed for the various kinds of kimono, *kosode* (short-sleeved kimono), *obi* (simple cords developed into broad draped belts) or *furoshiki* (squares of cloth to be offered as princely gifts).

Dress has also an important place in the Nōh, the specifically Japanese form of theatre, which reached full maturity in the fourteenth century, and in which each role has a corresponding decor designed to create the appropriate impression. Extensively used to propagate Buddhist ideas, Nōh costumes combine profane and religious elements. The religious ritual calls besides for banners, temple ornaments and liturgical vestments woven with the donors' armorial bearings, the *mons*.

To complete this account of the wealth and refinement of Japanese fabrics and evoke their international fame, it may be recalled in conclusion that these fabrics certainly contributed to the craze for Japanese curios that overran the West in the nineteenth century, a craze that was not without its impact on an art movement as important as that of the Impressionists.

Marmot Beneath the Moon
Silk thread embroidery on satin ground
Japan
18th century (?)

INDIAN FABRICS

PRINTED COTTON FABRIC (DETAIL)
Gujarat, India

Archaeological textile remains on the Indian subcontinent are unfortunately few owing to the humidity spread by the monsoon. This is the more regrettable since specialists on the subject concur in thinking that India had a role of the first importance in textile art and that many techniques had their origin in that part of the world. This thesis is supported by the evidence of the most ancient piece of cloth to have come down to us, a fragment of cotton found at Mohenjo-Daro in the valley of the Indus and dating from about 1750 B.C., which reveals the existence already at that time of sure knowledge of the use of dyeing (particularly of mordant dyeing). This is the more remarkable since cotton is a less easy material on which to fix colours, requiring for the purpose specially delicate prior treatment.

This earliest piece is also already significant of two essential features of Indian textile art: primacy of cotton and wealth of dyeing techniques. That India might be the first of all countries for cotton had already been suspected by Herodotus who, in the fifth century B.C., observed that a "wool-bearing tree" grew in that country which yielded a product (cotton) much finer than Greek wool. As for dyeing, it seems that Indian craftsmen were indeed the first to develop fully all forms of dyeing. Very early, they knew how to prevent the colour from spreading too far over the fibres by previous treatment of the fabric and by adding gum arabic to the dye to thicken it. They learnt also how to make the best use of madder, oak gall and indigo. Only curcuma yellow (curcumin) was applied direct to cloth since, apart from indigo used in baths for dyeing in the piece, other dyes such as madder were applied on top of a mordant, the nature of the latter determining the colour

finally obtained. In this way, madder gave, according to the mordant used, reds, various shades of pink (aluminium), lilacs or blacks (iron).

The fame of Indian dyers spread quickly throughout the world, and when in the first century A.D. the Romans reopened the canal linking the Nile and the Red Sea, dyed cotton and silk fabrics manufactured in India were soon a substantial part of exports from the Orient to the West. It was perhaps at this time that the Egyptians were in their turn able, from their examination of these cloths, to discover the use of mordants.

Except for the Mohenjo-Daro fragment, the oldest Indian sources of information concerning textiles afford only indirect evidence. These are the Ajanta frescoes, painted between the fifth and seventh centuries A.D., in which the persons wear pieces of cloth obviously decorated by means of *ikat*, *batik* and *plangi* techniques.

The cotton fabrics discovered in Egypt, at Fostat near Cairo, at the end of the nineteenth century and recognized to be Indian by R. Pfister in 1938, include many batiks and prints. They were produced between the thirteenth and fifteenth centuries in the Gujarat factories, which were particularly skilled in dyeing and printing. Specialization on a regional basis was indeed characteristic of textile manufactures in India from very early times; it was already noted in the *Arthasastra*, an administrative publication containing regulations for the textile industry dating from the third century B.C. Gujarat was very soon famous for the production of printed fabrics. Those manufactured for customers in the Near East, such as the cloths discovered at Fostat, changed little in the course of the centuries. They were traditional models dominated by large geometric

motifs: stripes, zigzags, spirals or circles, alternating from time to time with figures of animals and flowers. These more or less standard models have remained in production down to the present day to meet conservative demand. Concurrently, however, other formulae have been adopted in the course of the years, and this novel type has little by little evolved, at least as regards the general output for the local market. Changes began to appear in the middle of the sixteenth century as the Mogul régime approached its apogee: the geometrical motifs became smaller and increased in number until they formed a regular pattern of small figures, generally flowers.

The western regions were justly famous not only for prints but also for *ikat* fabrics. As early as the eleventh century, the town of Patan in Gujarat was renowned for its *patola* silks. In the eighteenth century this term was finally applied exclusively to the most remarkable of these fabrics: the double *ikats*. These gems of patience and skill–they left the weaver no margin for error: he had to combine exactly the reserves saved on the warp threads with those he obtained from the weft yarn–were the pride of the Gujarat workshops in their heyday. They were produced in about twenty or thirty models representing different combinations of geometric, floral or figurative motifs distributed as a rule over the whole surface of the fabric. Most of the *patola* were used for making saris, but smaller pieces were also woven for divers uses. All, however, were in a class apart, surrounded with a sacred aura doubtless on account of the care required for their manufacture and their relative rarity. Supposed to be beneficial, the *patola* were worn by married or pregnant women; they were also used for robing liturgical images. Exported in large quantities, they gave rise in South-East Asia to local industries employing the same techniques and the same decorative themes: elephants, tigers, the eight-pointed star. This is fortunate since in India itself even the *patola* have almost disappeared, and the few families in Patan who keep up the tradition only make articles that have diverged widely from the original products: the designs are modern, the silks imported and the colours made with chemical dyes.

Unlike Gujarat in the north-west, Bengal and North-East India are more famous for weaving than for dyeing. The excellent quality cotton grown in the region has ensured for cotton materials the first place among their textiles, the finest of which are the muslins. These are curiously decorated with transient dyes which disappear in time, an effect that is not due to any deficiency but is deliberately sought, apparently for religious motives.

SILK BORDER OF A SARI (FRAGMENT)
Baluchar region, Bengal
Mid-19th century

BORDER OF A CASHMERE SHAWL (FRAGMENT)
Goat's wool
Shawl decorated with the traditional *buta* motif
Late 18th century

PAINTED COTTON WALL HANGING
8½ ft. × 5 ft.
Painting over underdrawing on cotton
Golconda while under Dutch control, c. 1640
Madras–Pulicat school

The Coromandel Coast was also renowned from the thirteenth century for its cotton fabrics, described by Marco Polo as "the most beautiful and the finest in the world, and the most valuable." In the seventeenth century, dyed and painted tissues for the Mogul court were made in the workshops at Masulipatam. During the same period, certain fabrics described as products of the Golconda school show obvious Persian influence and are recognizable in particular by the brilliance of their red colouring. Others, attributed to the Madras-Pulicat school, are comparable with Lepakshi and Anegundi Hindu paintings, which have the same kind of segmented composition. European influence is clear in the choice of subjects for the designs.

Among Indian products, one of the most highly prized in the West is undoubtedly the cashmere shawl. The origins of this remarkable weave are obscure. It is thought by some that the technique was known as early as the eleventh century; others say that it was introduced to Kashmir towards the middle of the fifteenth century by weavers from Turkestan. The term "shawl," derived from the Persian *shal*, signified first of all a quality of fine woollen material rather than a particular article of wear. The fineness of the shawl is a mark of dignity and evidence of the considerable care taken in its manufacture. The raw material is for a start exceptional: goat's wool from Tibet or Central Asia and the wool of wild sheep from the Himalayas. The women spin the wool at home before the specialists dye it. The workers who design on the fabric, and are in most cases different from those who colour it, are the best paid of all the craftsmen who take part in the work. Their position is far preferable to that of the weavers, whose living conditions worsened still further after the British took over Kashmir in 1846 and to such an extent that some of them left for the Punjab where they created a similar industry only inferior in quality.

The technique is the same as for tapestry: the looms are extremely simple, horizontal and with a maximum of two frames. At the beginning of the nineteenth century, the decorations were so elaborate that the weaving was

CASHMERE SHAWL (DETAIL)
Silk warp, Kashmir wool weft, cotton, silk
Lyons (?)
1844

distributed among several looms, the different fragments being joined later to reunite the piece as a whole. As this method proved too tedious, already at the beginning of the same century needlework copies were made, using stem and satin stitch, so as to speed up the work and increase output, since from the time of the first exports of cashmere shawls to the West in the late eighteenth century the demand had not stopped growing. Little by little, the style of the shawls evolved. The decoration, originally confined to the ends, spread to cover ever wider bands brightened by floral compositions; these were at first treated realistically after the Persian manner, but were progressively conventionalized to culminate in the famous palm-leaf motif (first quarter of the nineteenth century). Between 1850 and 1860, exports to Europe doubled.

The Europeans had not awaited the fashion for cashmere to take an interest in Indian fabrics. In France, the vogue for *indiennes* (printed calicos or chintzes) developed with the creation of the East India Company (Compagnie des Indes Orientales) in 1664, and the first competitive factory had opened in Marseilles about 1648. These calicos

were used initially for furnishing and in a second stage entered the clothing sector. In the seventeenth century Madame de Sévigné was mad about them, and Molière's *Bourgeois Gentilhomme* strutted around in costumes tailored in oriental cloth. The calicos fulfilled an important economic function serving as an ideal medium of exchange in the three-way trade in which merchants bartered the fabrics for slaves, who were shipped to the colonies to be given in payment for sugar, cotton and tobacco. Protectionist laws against calicos passed by the French authorities in 1686 and the English in 1700 and 1720 were unable to stop this traffic. Factories producing imitation cashmere shawls were established in Europe, where the invention of the Jacquard loom made it possible to produce ever more complicated designs, which the Indian weavers did their best to emulate. But the Franco-Prussian war of 1870–1871 closed the French market to them at the same time that changing fashions relegated cashmere shawls to the bottom drawer.

The famine that afflicted the workers in India from 1877 to 1879 led to the closing of the Kashmir workshops.

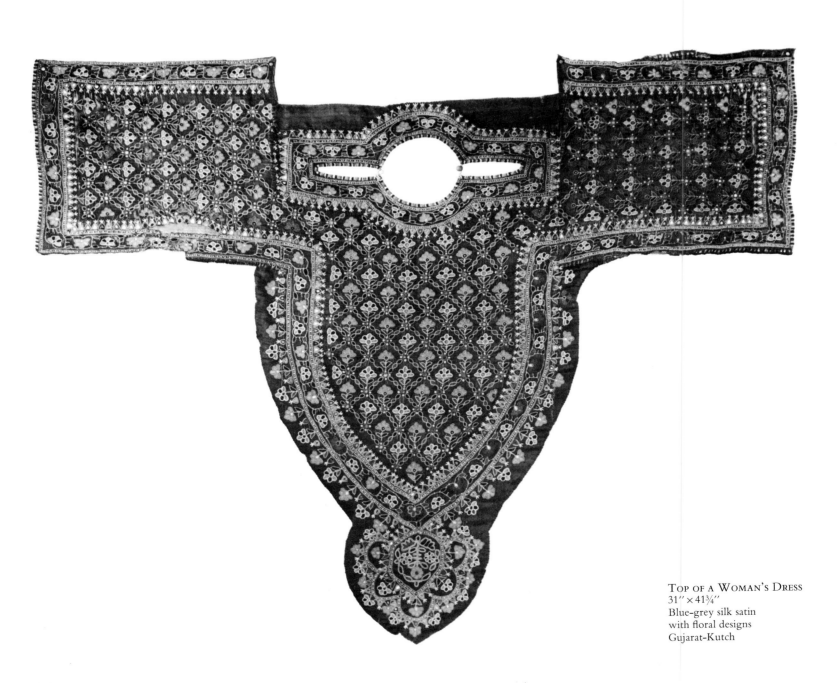

TOP OF A WOMAN'S DRESS
31″ × 41¾″
Blue-grey silk satin
with floral designs
Gujarat-Kutch

SOUTH-EAST ASIAN FABRICS

DETAIL OF A "LAU" (WOMAN'S GARMENT)
Decoration woven with extra warp
Eastern Sumba, Indonesia

It was a long time before researchers became interested in the fabrics of South-East Asia notwithstanding the incredible wealth of textile production in this region, particularly the island parts occupied by Indonesia, Malaysia and the Philippines. It was indeed not before the beginning of the nineteenth century that the first serious studies of Indonesian textiles were made. Owing to this long neglect, many points remain obscure and make it impossible to reconstruct a coherent history of the different techniques practised there. Some of these are, however, known throughout the world by the name given them in Indonesian-Malay: batik, *ikat* (to knot, to tie around), *plangi* (multicoloured), evincing their amazing development in this area.

One thing is certain: fabrics have for very long played a role of the first importance in the life of all the peoples of these regions, not only on account of their economic, but above all owing to their symbolic value. Fruit of the work of women, from the sowing of the cotton to the weaving of the fabric, textiles are essentially feminine, like the underworld, night or the moon. By virtue of their feminine nature, fabrics guarantee the fertility of future married couples and are often an integral feature of marriage rites: one of the culminating moments in a *Batak* (Borneo) marriage is when the newly married husband and wife are enfolded in a cloth held to ensure them posterity and harmony. Fabrics are likewise offered as gifts on other important occasions, such as births, circumcision, leave-taking for hunting or war, funerals.

Nowadays many cloths are manufactured industrially or imported and most Indonesian peoples no longer use their own production except on these ritual occasions.

Despite the gaps in our knowledge, it has been possible to establish approximatively some of the main stages in textile history in this area by taking account especially of foreign innovations and their influence on the native peoples.

The forbears of the present populations used for their everyday wear bark fabrics, which are no longer current outside certain regions where they have become the dress of the poor. The technique for the production of this fabric is very elementary: the bark of various species of locally grown trees is boiled and fermented and the mixture obtained is beaten to make a kind of sheet.

In all probability, the beginnings of weaving in these parts coincided with the introduction of the strap loom and the warp-pattern *ikat* by foreign immigrants from North Vietnam, known in Indonesia as representatives of the "Dong Son" culture (eighth–second centuries B.C.). The transition from working up bark to the exploitation of cotton was progressive, with an intermediary phase during which the weavers, here as elsewhere, tried out different vegetable fibres, such as agave.

The warp-pattern *ikat* has remained typical of isolated populations, little subject to progressive influences and with a way of life almost unchanged since megalithic times: the Bataks of North Sumatra, and the Ibans in Borneo. The work follows the seasons. Spinning and weaving are done during the dry season because cotton saturated with humidity would be too difficult to handle. On the other hand, the rainy season is no obstacle to the preparation of binding threads, getting the yarn ready for dyeing when the indigo plants, plentifully watered, are at their finest. After dyeing, the yarns are unbound and arranged

"SELENDANG" (SHAWL)
87" × 32¼"
Cotton *ikat*
Malaysia

for use according to the selected design; the background colour will be taken for the weft so as to heighten the effect of the more numerous warp threads. Weaving is a delicate operation; offerings are made to obtain the favour of the spirits because any mistake is fatal.

The most famous of the warp-pattern *ikats* are perhaps the *pua* made by the Ibans of Borneo. These fabrics are brought out for ceremonies connected with agriculture and war, formerly an essential part of the life of these head-hunters. After a victory, the women placed the remains of their enemies in these cloths, which they then carried in great state. For the fabric to be fully effective and afford all the protection necessary in a difficult period, the greatest precautions have to accompany its manufacture. The assembly of the warps with the mordants prior to dyeing, for example, is subject to the same taboos as the expectation of a birth. The designs decorating the fabrics, to be made later into skirts, jackets, ceremonial hangings or blankets, combine human or animal themes (crocodiles, frogs, etc.) and abstract figures; these motifs, of a very special kind, were formerly the property of the weaver and could be sold.

"PUA" (CEREMONIAL MANTLE)
76″ × 34″
Cotton, warp-pattern *ikat*
Sarawak, Borneo
Early 20th century

On the east coast of Sumba, the women weave very beautiful warp-pattern *ikats* for export, or to exchange with the peoples of the interior of the island who do not use this technique. The pieces called *lau* are worn by women, and the *hinggi* by men. The warp threads are wound continuously round the two uprights of a frame so that the worker can bind them easily. The two thicknesses of the hank are simultaneously bound tightly together so as to obtain symmetrical duplication of the motifs. The elements of the decoration, arranged by this means in pairs as in a mirror, are copied from the environment and include horses, scorpions, fishes, tortoises and anthropomorphic shapes, together with more peculiar figures such as trees of life hung in some cases with macabre trophies taken from the remains of conquered enemies, elements of Chinese origin like the Dragon, or typical European decorative themes.

Like the *plangi*, the weft-pattern *ikat* was introduced in the fourteenth–fifteenth centuries by Indian and Arab Moslem merchants trading in these seas. Contrary to the warp-pattern *ikat*, this technique has remained since that time a speciality of the Moslem coast peoples who live in

"LAU" (WOMAN'S GARMENT)
33½″ × 94½″
Decoration woven with extra warp
Eastern Sumba, Indonesia

DETAIL OF A "HINGGI"
(MAN'S GARMENT)
Cotton *ikat*
Decorated with the *tabala* motifs,
a tree or mast
with skulls and cockatoos

permanent contact with the outside world. That at least is true of the two main Indonesian centres for this production: Palembang in Sumatra, renowned for its silk *ikats*, and Bali, where the weavers use both silk and cotton. In the continental part of South-East Asia, weft-pattern *ikats* are, however, not unknown, and the agricultural communities of lower Thailand and Burma have their own output, originally produced to replace the Indian cloths woven to supply princely establishments.

The village of Tenganan Pageringsingan, south-eastern Bali, provides the only example in the region of the production of double *ikats*. In all probability, this difficult art was taught to the local weavers by Indian merchants who came to exchange the famous Patan *patola* for sandalwood and spices; evidence of these exchanges exists from the sixteenth century, but they may have begun as early as the fourteenth. Adopted and reproduced for their notable qualities, these double silk *ikats*, called *geringsing* in In-

SARONG OF SILK AND COTTON
35½" × 41⅜"
Weft-pattern *ikat*
Bali

donesia, were soon, as had already been the case in India, vested with special and sacred powers. Brought out on the occasion of village ceremonies, they appear also as parts of the costume of Javanese dancers, or hangings in the temples of Bali. Burnt and mixed with other ingredients, they even serve as medicaments.

The motifs for the decoration of these *geringsing* are to a large extent directly inspired by the Indian *patola*. Alongside various geometric and floral designs, both feature the eight-pointed flower or the friendly outlines of the elephant. Even more, however, than the choice and beauty of the decorative themes, the quality of the colours is the source of their value. This is not surprising, since the successive dyeing operations can take several years to complete. The slightest error makes the fabric unworthy of any religious or ceremonial function, reducing it to the rank of a mere article of sale. In order to simplify the production process and on account of the difficulty of preserving silk in humid surroundings, imitation double *ikats* are made in warp-pattern *ikat* and cotton.

The introduction of batik in the island of Java, doubtless connected with Indian influence, appears to have been relatively recent in so far as the first references to this technique date back no further than the sixteenth century. It should be noted that batik requires especially soft fabrics. For a long time, however, locally produced fabrics lacked the indispensable suppleness, so that in its Indonesian

DETAIL OF "KAIN PANJANG" (SKIRT MATERIAL)
Cotton batik
Central Java
Late 19th century

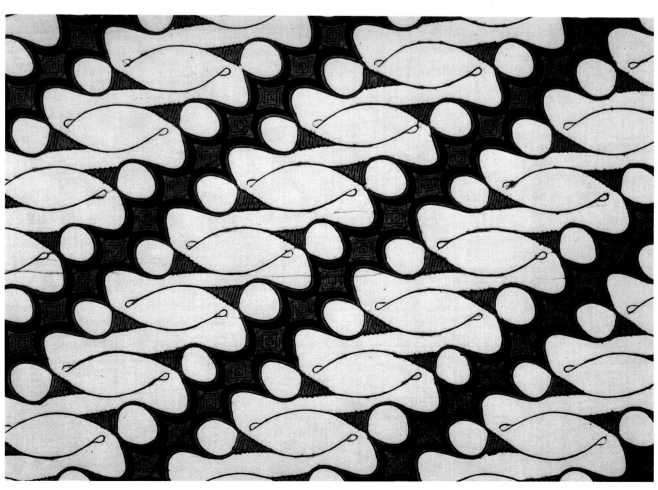

beginnings the method had to be applied to cotton fabrics imported first from India and then from Europe. As only the big commercial centres and princely courts could afford such costly supports, it was probably in these privileged circles that batik first made its appearance. The resist-dyeing methods using rice paste, which were already practised in western Java, may have served as a trial ground for this new technique destined for such a brilliant future. According to another hypothesis, not moreover incompatible with this, batik was first used as a substitute for the precious gold-covered fabrics from the centre of Java.

An important stage in the history of batik opened with the appearance and development of the *canting*, a reed or bamboo tube fitted with a small reservoir for wax, which was used by artists in a set of different sizes to work over the details as well as cover the surfaces to be filled in. At first this method, the *tulis* batik, was the only one used. (Several centuries ago the Javanese used the word *tulis* instead of batik; in modern Javanese *tulis* still means the kind of Javanese batik that is designed by hand with a wax pencil.) But the very long time required for this wholly manual execution of the design led to the adoption and concurrent use of another more rapid process. Since the middle of the nineteenth century, the invention of a copper seal, the *cap*, has enabled the worker to treat with wax twenty pieces a day instead of one piece in twenty or even forty days. At present, the *tulis* batik and the *cap* batik exist side by side and sometimes even together on the same fabric, but the considerable saving in time obtained with the *cap* and the need to produce more in order to withstand the invasion of European products and keep the tourist market supplied, all tell in favour of the *cap* batik. Just as paraffin has progressively taken the place of beeswax, so artificial colouring materials have replaced natural dyes. Today Javanese batik is the only Indonesian textile speciality manufactured on a semi-industrial scale, with the inevitable falling off in quality consequent on the break with the tradition of a cottage industry. Uniformity of production little by little becomes the rule where in former times many types of fabric were produced, and the secrets of their manufacture handed down and improved from generation to generation.

Fortunately, some contemporary artists, fascinated by the possibilities afforded by batik, have recently set themselves the task of restoring it to favour by seeking specifically modern uses for this traditional technique.

Foreign influences have been decisive factors in the history of Indonesian textiles, and they continue to modify local traditions. There is, indeed, a striking correlation between the symbolic potential of fabric and the age of its technique: warp-pattern *ikat*, known since megalithic times, has a stronger ritual power than weft-pattern *ikat*, introduced much later by Moslem merchants; batik, still more recent, no longer has the same sacred value, and to all appearances, current industrialization will not help to give it anything of the kind.

SARONG
30¼″ × 49½″
Batik
Java

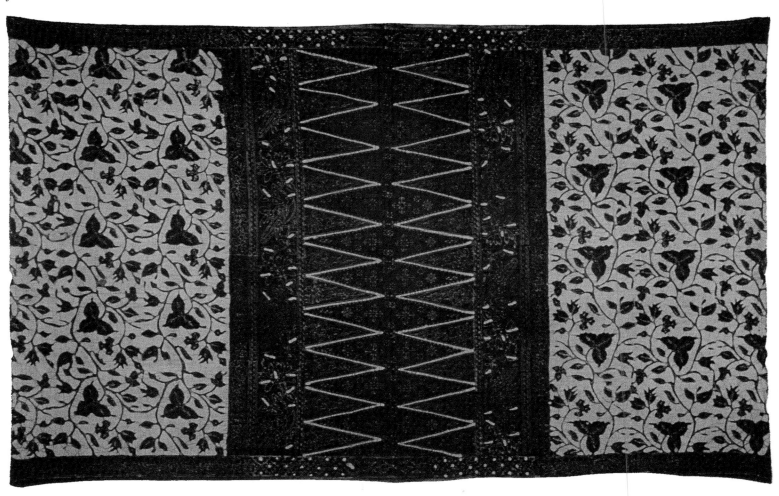

92

CENTRAL ASIAN FABRICS

FELT MATERIAL
33½″ × 69″
Afghanistan, Konar province

Central Asia has been from all time a transit zone and has in consequence experienced an almost uninterrupted succession of confrontations and invasions, the latest being the Soviet offensive in Afghanistan. In this part of the world at present divided between Iran, Afghanistan, the Soviet Union and Pakistan, Greek, Indian, Chinese, Turkish and finally Russian civilizations have come face to face and mingled. Since the prosperous days of the Silk Route and the first foundation of post towns along it, the peoples of very different origins who live on these territories have been divided between sedentary city dwellers and steppe-land nomads. Although this distinction is no longer pertinent owing to the general settling process, it is still valid to the extent that recently settled peoples keep many habits inherited from their former itinerant life. The Uzbeks established in north Afghanistan and the Tadzhiks, of Iranian origin installed in Soviet Turkistan and Afghanistan, are essentially city populations whereas the Turkomans, recently settled in the south of the Soviet Union (Turkmenistan) and Afghanistan, have a long-standing nomadic tradition. These two modes of life have their respective, different, textile productions.

With the wool from their sheep, the nomads make the structural and decorative elements of their tent, the yurt, protected from the wind and the rain by felt facings. The women use a horizontal loom and weave very long narrow bands which adorn the walls and serve to hang knot-stitch or *kilim* bags for their effects. The ground is covered with plain or decorated felt, and sometimes *kilims* when guests are received.

Craftsmen in the towns prefer to work in cotton or silk, with which they make magnificent *ikats* for many uses. Some weavers also practise a resist-dyeing technique applying wax to the printing block, or keep up the old *plangi* tradition. For their part, the women reproduce with their needles the designs specific to each region, and each town has its own type of *susani* (needlework), serving alike to make wall hangings, curtains, prayer rugs or shrouds. Since the beginning of the twentieth century, however, the quality of these pieces has become much poorer: synthetic dyes have replaced natural colouring materials, and in the Soviet Union embroidery is now done on sewing machines.

Textile handicrafts as a whole have suffered greatly from mass importation of Soviet fabrics. Printed materials copying the *ikat* designs are offered for sale, and local taste is changing at the same time that new economic directives are prescribed in Soviet territory where extensive cultivation of medium quality cotton has replaced the former quality production. In Afghanistan the last handicraft workers fight to uphold the tradition of work in silk, in particular at Herat, rival of the Iranian centres at Yezd and Ispahan and the emirate of Bukhara. The confrontation of civilizations, formerly a factor of cultural enrichment, seems today to have only a debasing influence.

SILK NECKERCHIEF DYED BY THE "PLANGI" TECHNIQUE
41¼" × 20½"
Akcha, Afghanistan, province of Jozjan

IKAT FROM TURKISTAN
42½" × 40½"
Silk
Bukhara, Soviet Uzbekistan
18th-19th century

94

AFRICAN FABRICS

BANDS OF DYED POLYCHROME COTTON
Bamako, Mali; Mandingo work

Little is known about the origins of weaving in Africa. In the absence of archaeological evidence (fragments or imprints of fabrics, remains of weavers' implements), hypotheses can only be based on the cross-checking and comparison of myths and oral traditions relating to weaving, contemporary African techniques and those known to have been employed in other parts of the world. By the use of this method, and after long observation in the field, Mrs Renée Boser-Sarivaxévanis (former keeper of the Department of African Arts and Fabrics, Ethnographical Museum, Basel) has been able to reach a number of conclusions, set forth in various authoritative works, which have laid the foundations for a history of African tissues.

In the third millennium B.C., the populations which occupied the then fertile lands of the Sahara must have already known the mechanical loom because the rock paintings left by them on the walls of Tassili portray persons whose clothes are obviously not cut from animal hides but well and truly woven. In all probability, these ancient Africans wove the vegetable fibres available to them on the horizontal loom, which appeared in hither Asia as early as 5000–4000 B.C., from where it was adopted by Egyptian craftsmen under the pharaohs. This loom was originally designed for the weaving of previously spun fibres, wool or linen in the Near East, linen only in Egypt where wool was only introduced at a relatively late date. In Africa these raw materials did not as yet exist, and the available vegetable fibres were not easy to spin, which seems to have limited the development of weaving during an initial period. It was not until the beginning of the Christian era that more rapid expansion of this activity took place. At about this time, a Syrian Semitic people

from the north-east, who had crossed the Sahara bringing with them a Syrian breed of sheep, settled among the Peuls in the western part of West Africa and taught them how to use a more elaborate horizontal treadle loom suitable for the weaving of wool. The Peuls, at the same time that they accustomed themselves to working with the new loom, began also to rear sheep for wool.

After an initial phase during which the Peul weavers, with their improved loom and a suitable fibre, were no doubt the only Africans to practise the art of weaving, the discovery of the possible use of cotton for the production of textiles was a new step forward. Cotton bushes grew wild in the region, and the Africans learnt from the Arabs how to turn them to good account; indeed, the oldest known mention of the local production of cotton fabrics is a reference in a book by the Arab writer El-Bekri, dated 1068. Apparently the weavers of wool from Upper Senegal soon began to work this new raw material, using at first the frames that had served previously for wool. It is not, however, always possible to adapt methods devised for wool to the weaving of cotton, and the development of a new loom derived from the previous one but suitable for cotton quickly became necessary. From then on, weaving techniques spread very rapidly, since the peoples taught by the Peuls learnt at one and the same time both to produce the easily spun fibre they had lacked hitherto and to operate the loom they needed to exploit it. Both loom and cotton industry were thus transmitted first to the Tukulors, the Wolofs and the different Mandé peoples of the Sudan, then, very soon, to the Bambaras and the Dogons; by the late thirteenth century they had reached Gambia and from there spread southwards.

APPLIQUÉ FROM DAHOMEY (DETAIL)
Cotton hanging with silk and muslin inlays
Abomey, Dahomey; Fon handicraft

PRINTED COTTON (DETAIL)
Ivory Coast; Sienuf handicraft

Although it had been supplanted by the cotton industry and fell off to some extent, the production of woollen fabrics went on in the Peul country, where the caste of weavers, the Maabubes, continued to use two types of looms: on the one hand, the old model reserved for wool, a light loom easily carried from place to place and therefore well suited to pastoral tribes; on the other, the more recent type, adapted for the weaving of cotton.

Alongside the diffusion of this Sudanese loom (so called from the area where it was used), another, much more archaic type made its appearance in southern Nigeria. This was a vertical woman's loom, of a very peculiar kind, whose equivalent, curiously enough, is only to be found in Palestine, Syria, Turkey and Greece in early times. This loom is thought to have reached Africa by the intermediary of the foreigners who, coming from the north-east in the tenth century and mingling with the native population, gave birth to the Yoruba people. It is possible that in the course of their wanderings these immigrants may have fallen in with Semitic tribes and learnt the use of this Near Eastern technique.

What is certain, anyhow, is that this loom was first adopted by the Yorubas who, having no wool-producing live-stock and knowing nothing as yet of linen or cotton, used it initially to weave local fibres which are still exploited today. They very soon transmitted this newly acquired skill to neighbouring peoples–Igalas, Igbiras, Igaras, Ibos, Edos, Nupes and Hausas–and Yoruba weavers who had settled in Dahomey and Togo trained new workmen there. A little later, the introduction of cotton into southern Nigeria gave a fresh impetus to the new art of weaving.

Besides the West African horizontal and vertical looms, there was also the East African pit treadle loom, introduced at a very early date in Abyssinia and along the Somali coast. The characteristics of this loom relate it very closely to the Indian loom (fairly massive structure, great width of the reed and very deep pit for the treadles and feet of the weaver), and it is not therefore impossible that this invention was discovered by the black weavers through the exchanges that took place between the Indian sub-continent and the East African coast.

The study of African textile techniques would be relatively simple if, starting from the three initial bases, Sudan, Niger and Ethiopia, the situation had remained static. In the course of the centuries, however, the different people exchanged their tools and skills and invented new models. Social-cultural factors also have to be taken into account; for example, religion had its impact on the history of clothing. Islam, which disapproved of nudity, favoured dress covering the entire body, such as long shirts or *boubous*, whereas in other regions, a small loincloth of beaten bark or even a simple slip were considered adequate. These vestimentary habits had obvious repercussions on the textile sector, increasing or reducing needs. The Masai and other East African stockbreeding peoples quite naturally clothed themselves in the skins of animals from their flocks, which created a context unfavourable in the main to the development of weaving and explains in part the superiority of West Africans in this respect. Unfortunately, although this sub-Saharan region is richer in textile traditions, it has a humid climate hardly favourable to the preservation of fabrics: indeed, with rare exceptions, the oldest examples to have survived date no further back than the nineteenth century.

African fabrics comprise a relatively limited number of weaves, confined to variations on the principle of the cloth; the most frequent means of producing the decorations, which are sometimes very elaborate, are the use of tapestry weave and above all shuttle weave and brocade.

The use of tapestry is limited but worthy of note on account of a curiosity: the existence of tapestries made entirely of cotton. This is easily explained by the fact that wool was worked before the appearance of cotton. The Peuls had become accustomed to decorating their traditional woollen fabric–the *kasa*, which they made up into blankets and coats–by inserting geometric motifs in tapestry in the weave. When they discovered the new material, cotton, they naturally began to produce, using the same principles, tapestries in cotton as well as wool.

Easier and therefore faster to work than tapestry, brocade and shuttle weave decorative techniques were perhaps also introduced in Africa by Semites, but their astonishing diffusion would appear to have been due to the Portuguese, who discovered the advantages of these techniques in the weaving and dyeing workshops they had set up in the Cape Verde Islands where they employed the slaves they captured on the continent. Indeed, many of the brocade and shuttle weave motifs use the same geometric designs as the Portuguese school fabrics clearly marked by Hispano-Moorish influence.

Very special decorative effects can be obtained by putting together woven bands with different motifs completing or contrasting with each other. These fabrics, also produced in West Africa in a zone reaching from the south of the Sahara and the Atlantic coast in the West to the Lake Chad region in the East, have been studied by two great experts in African textile art, Venice and Alastair Lamb. The extremely narrow width (some are less than an inch wide, the average width being between 3½ and 10 inches) distinguishes them from the bands woven in other parts of the world such as the Balkans, the Near East or North-West India. The kind of material varies with the region and local resources: cotton among the Bambaras, sheep's or goat's wool or camelhair along the south-east border of the Sahara, elsewhere reeds, palms or raffia. Heirs to an ancient silk-working tradition in Niger, the Ewe and Ashanti have since the seventeenth century imported the raw material they formerly produced themselves and continue to employ silk for their most beautiful fabrics.

Tapestry, *ikat*, *plangi*, printing, embroidery, appliqué, all decorative techniques except batik are drawn on in Africa for the adornment of these woven bands and applied sometimes before, sometimes after, the bands are assembled. The sewing is done with over-edge stitch so that the joins are almost invisible. Once completed the

LOINCLOTH DECORATED BY THE "PLANGI" TECHNIQUE
(FRAGMENT)
Cotton
Made up of nine bands each 5 inches wide
Indigo dyeing
Mali
Late 19th century

whole piece is generally used as a garment, or sometimes as a furnishing fabric.

It may be wondered why the craftsmen weave narrow bands which they have afterwards to go to the trouble of sewing together, when they could have used techniques that would enable them just as well to manufacture the entire fabric in a single piece. Venice and Alastair Lamb offer three possible and perhaps complementary explanations. First of all, a practical reason: the bands are woven on a light and easily portable loom, an important consideration when it is remembered that many West African weavers are still itinerants. The second is an economic reason: it is suggested that financial problems make the weaver hesitate to embark straight away on the manufacture of a whole piece. Finally, account has to be taken of the tradition that makes it obligatory in many ceremonies to wear garments composed of these bands.

Another original process including sewing is employed in Dahomey (now Benin) where appliqué specialists, perpetuating an ancestral skill, continue to produce illustrated hangings of a kind formerly intended for use as tapestries or pictures in the palaces of tribal chiefs but today offered to the general public. Motifs cut out of brightly coloured fabric are affixed to a generally yellow or black background support; shaped to more or less stereotyped models, the iconographical elements are often the same from one hanging to another, but according to the way they are arranged, they represent either a battle or a hunting or fishing scene, or a typical scene from country life or court ceremonial.

It seems that hangings of this type were formerly manufactured specifically for the purposes of funerary ritual, in which each image had a symbolic value or constituted, in association with others, a kind of puzzle.

Yoruba Batik
70½″ × 77″
Industrial cotton fabric
Manufactured and purchased at Ibadan, Nigeria

MAN'S ROBE
71½" × 55"
Industrial cotton fabric, indigo dyeing,
crease-decorated by the *plangi* technique
Soninke handicraft

Dyeing techniques had a large place in the decoration of African fabrics. As a general rule cloths were dyed after weaving except in the case of *ikats*, which require prior treatment of the yarn. This, however, is one of the least common dyeing techniques. In Upper Volta (now Bourkina-Fasso) and Ivory Coast the Baules learnt this technique from the Dyulas, who migrated there from Mali in the eighteenth century. In Upper Volta, warp-pattern *ikats* are not produced regularly but only made to order; they are manufactured in large quantities in Ivory Coast, where they provide ceremonial wear for Baule chiefs and supply the tourist market. In Nigeria, where warp-pattern *ikats* are also manufactured, the Yorubas are the only purveyors of finished cloths. The foregoing, together with the weft-pattern *ikats* made by the Tamale Mossi in Ghana, more or less cover the entire production of *ikats*. Mention should, however, be made of the manufacture, today virtually at an end, of raffia *ikats* in Madagascar, which are disturbingly similar to Indonesian pieces previous to the tenth century and to the earliest Yemen *ikats*, featuring in common with these the same zigzag pattern decoration. This may perhaps be a vestige of Arab-Moslem influence in the north-east of the island dating from about the fourteenth century.

Confined to a somewhat narrow area, the manufacture of *ikats* in African territory, although of quite long standing, would appear to have been introduced by foreign craftsmen, probably Asians. This hypothesis is in any case much more plausible than that of its spontaneous appearance there.

The knowledge of indigo dyeing also reached Africa from Asia, more particularly from India. This technique, although its development was limited in North Africa, enjoyed on the other hand considerable success in the western part of the continent. It was probably introduced shortly after the appearance of cotton, the two being complementary. The Yorubas in south-west Nigeria may have obtained their knowledge of indigo from their Proto-Yoruba forbears, already mentioned in connection with the vertical loom. To eke out their stock, they employed concurrently raffia, thread or various pastes, most often tapioca; and to obtain the alkaline salts that had to be added to the indigo bath, they kneaded bread of damped

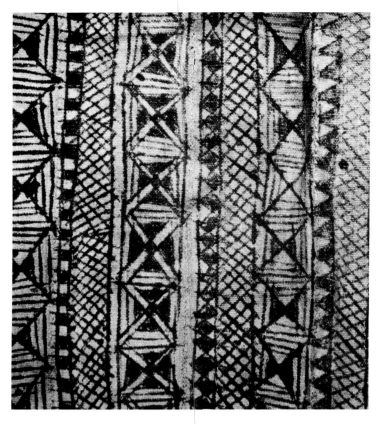

"EARTH DYED" LOINCLOTH (DETAIL)
Cotton
Mali (Sudan), circle of Bafulabe Kulugidi

"RAFFIA VELVET"
62¼" × 27¼"
Old fabric of soft vegetable fibre
embroidered over a large strip of plain raffia
Zaïre, Kuba handicraft

ashes, whose combustion, controlled by the Mother of Ashes with her ancestral know-how, produced a residue containing the alkali.

In Senegal, the Soninke were past-masters of the art of resist dyeing, and although it is not known in what period they acquired this knowledge, they had already mastered its secrets so well by the time of the conquest of their territory by the Almoravid Berbers in 1076, that when they afterwards spread throughout the African continent they became, with the Mandingo, the principal vehicle for the transmission of dyeing techniques to Gambia, Portuguese Guinea, Sierra Leone, Ivory Coast and even Yatenga and the Sudan. The Soninke themselves remained the greatest dyers of the region. As they did not weave, they worked in collaboration with the Maabube-Peuls, who supplied them with cloth to dye. They often used the method of creasing fabric, which enabled them to obtain very peculiar cloud form motifs; strangely enough, some of their processes created designs unlike anything outside Japan. It is not impossible, moreover, that there might have been an exchange in the sixteenth century when Portuguese ships provided a bridge between these two parts of the world.

In Mali, cloths are decorated by the method known as "earth dyeing" because the motifs are drawn by means of mud tinctures. First, the fabric is dyed in the piece, yellow or brick red. Next, two alternative processes are possible: the first consists in drawing the design directly with the mud, which when the cloth is washed leaves a "positive" print on the fabric; in the second, a resist substance is applied so as to protect the future design from the dyeing effect of the mud, with the result that after the mud and resist have been removed, the design appears as a "negative" on the dark background.

The dyed cloth is sometimes enriched with embroidered designs. These comprise many combinations of a few basic geometrical forms, which are used above all in the Islamic regions of West Africa. Legend has it, moreover, that it was among the people of the West that the seventeenth century Zairian legislator, Shamba Bolongongo, learned the arts of weaving and embroidery before he introduced them in his own country where very beautiful embroidered raffia fabrics, sometimes called "raffia velvet," are made even today. The piece in the Paul Tishman collection features traditional motifs, each of which has its name and its specific significance. This often happens in African countries, where each people has its own iconographical vocabulary handed down from generation to generation. Geometrical elements generally predominate, particularly in Islamic territory where religious prescriptions prohibit the representation of figures, and it is certainly because the Bambaras have remained pagans that they are among the rare West African peoples to produce fabrics decorated with animal and geometric figures.

Like the motifs, the organization of work is codified according to a general plan that can be summarized as follows. Women are taught spinning and dyeing, while weaving and embroidery are reserved for men; in communities where the women weave, they use a different instrument from their male colleagues. The men who weave are sometimes free, as is the case among the Bambaras and the Malinkes, and sometimes members of a caste.

The distribution of tasks is strictly regulated, as is well illustrated by the following example: the Peuls have their cloth made up by the weaving caste of the Maabube, but take it back for finishing before giving it next to the Soninke who, as stated above, do not know how to weave but excel in the art of dyeing.

The complexity of this organization is alone enough to show the importance of cloth in these communities and the almost magical powers often attributed to it. An essential element of social life, clothing is in many cases a status symbol, as for example the *gandoura*, still a sign of prestige in Cameroon, or the *ndop* band of cloth dyed blue with a white motif which, again in Cameroon among the Bamoums and the Bamilekes, indicates royal or noble rank.

Many stories are told in Africa concerning the invention of weaving. In the Dogon country, it is said that one of the descendants of the primordial human couple drew cotton threads between his teeth, crossing the warp threads by opening and shutting his jaws, and pushing the weft yarn with his forked tongue in an act closely connected with that of speech. "The loom brings together the whole of Dogon symbolism. It is oriented north-south, in the general direction of creation. It is situated in the sun, weaving being a work of light. It represents the home, where the weaver and the spinner unite. It is the symbol of the tomb of the eighth ancestor. Its four vertical supports are related to the four basic elements: earth, air, fire and water" (Molly Formel, in *Textile/Art Driadi*, No. 14).

LARGE CLOTH WITH GEOMETRIC AND ZOOMORPHIC DESIGNS
7'2" × 18'4"
Benin

MYTHS AND RITUALS

The course followed by textile art in the different centres raises certain issues about the fundamental role of textiles in these civilizations. Apart from its daily use for purposes of protection and adornment, one can easily see that it came to serve a still more essential purpose in these communities, as a living link between their members, as a medium of exchange with other communities, and as a link with the divinities.

In some civilizations, textiles acted in reality as an omnipresent social link. Such is the case with both the pre-Columbian and the present-day Indians of South America. Their fabrics, which are never inscribed but on the contrary were a matter of oral or visual knowledge handed down like a set of codes directly connected with the operation of weaving, are present at all stages of life. As stated by J.V. Murra: "According to Morua, the participants in the funeral procession wore a special garment. They took the clothes of the deceased to the places where he had lived. His widow and other relatives went and washed the clothes at a particular place on the river bank or the irrigation canal." The same author points out that the Incas carried out the sacrifice of textiles by fire: "The economic basis of such offerings and sacrifices calls for further information. The graves of the place were situated near the fields and flocks, and many of the textiles sacrificed were the fruit of the labour provided by the community in these domains."

Having its place in the labours and doings of everyday life, the textile kept very close to the human being: it was at once his double and his metaphor. In speaking of the fabric as a living being, Sophie Desrosiers illustrates her meaning with reference to four-edged fabrics: "All the technical, practical and economic reasons seem inadequate to explain the permanence of the straight garment... The fabric designs were almost like body paintings. The garment would become a body-garment or skin-garment." Hence the ban on cutting textiles.

As we have noted, Indonesia is another region of the world whose textile tradition connected with mythology is very much alive. One of the most interesting examples from this area is the *pua*, an *ikat* piece made by the Ibans who live in the north-western part of the island of Borneo. The fabric intervenes to hide the primordial episodes of creation, to delimit the ritual spaces of initiation, to represent what transmits life. Here again it is connected with the body, with its coming into the world and its going out of it, with its changes of status.

To quote Rémy Prin on the subject of fabrics, in the light of the course followed by the centres of textile art: "The fabric is the place of friction of men's memory, of their imagination and knowledge, if not of a certain science. And so to question with patience and rigour the memory and living space of men may possibly lead us, from one resewn shred to another, to discover how much of the body and mind can be read into these fibre objects."

THE PRIMACY
OF TAPESTRY
IN THE WEST

THE BAYEUX EMBROIDERY
England, late 11th century
(Abbey of St Augustine, Canterbury?)
Linen and wool
William the Conqueror and the Normans
Going into Battle (detail)
Overall size: 19 in. high, over 230 ft. in length

TAPESTRY AND EMBROIDERY

ABRAHAM AND THE ARCHANGEL ST MICHAEL
Quedlinburg, Lower Saxony, mid-12th century
Tapestry
St Michael Slaying the Dragon (detail)
Overall size: 3½ ft. × 33½ ft.

All over the world textile art arose in centres which worked out techniques of their own, and the productions of each have their specific features. For many people, however, textile art is synonymous with one particular technique: tapestry.

The main reason for this privileged position is that, of all the media of textile expression utilized in America, on the shores of the Mediterranean, and in the Middle and Far East, tapestry, together with embroidery, is the technique which best lends itself to the working out of complex designs: it is the one, in other words, whose connections with painting seem most evident. And in the West, since the Renaissance, painting has asserted itself as the major visual art, so that tapestry, being closely connected with it, has to some extent come to share this privileged position.

Over the centuries, however, the question of the relations between a miniature, a painting and a drawing, and today a photograph, has always been an ambiguous one. These relations have varied. They have not followed a linear evolution such as would justify us in regarding medieval tapestries as an independent textile art with respect to those of the eighteenth and nineteenth centuries, which would then be seen as the most striking examples of tapestry's subordination to painting.

This over-simple view was apparently given currency by Jean Lurçat and the commentators on his work, intent as they were on presenting Lurçat's approach as a revolutionary return to the original autonomy of tapestry. The fact is that the relations of tapestry with painting have at all times been complex and ambiguous, and this ambiguity

has been heightened in the postwar period in which works woven from pictures by dead or living painters have arisen alongside works by painters who have designed their own cartoons, works by painters who have woven their own cartoons, and works by creators who have woven their own tapestries without starting from a pictorial design.

One cannot share the viewpoint expressed in the editorial of the 1973 tapestry number of the *Revue de l'Art*: "Is it not time to face the issue and ask whether tapestry is not essentially a minor art, or at least an art of reproduction and accompaniment which, with a varying time-lag, follows the evolution of the major arts, and of painting in particular?" This view is belied by the fact that each of the periods dealt with here has produced tapestries which number among the major achievements of Western art. Nor can we agree with the contemporary painter and tapestry designer Mario Prassinos when he states categorically that "whenever tapestry joins up with living art, it is in one way or another the textile application of that art." Many examples exist to show that certain artists have made designs expressly intended for tapestry weaving which in no way answer to the styles or trends of the applied arts. Tapestry weaving has been and remains a self-sufficing medium of expression, and its close relations with the other visual arts, even when it sometimes imitates them, must not be allowed to obscure the fact that it has its own specific features, as clearly marked as those of drawing or engraving.

Moreover, while the different textile techniques that we have referred to, including tapestry, were enlisted in the service of daily life and sometimes put to ceremonial purposes (weaving or adornment of garments, making of nomad dwellings, making of sacred or sacrificial fabrics, etc.), tapestry in the West was soon confined to domestic and ecclesiastical uses, covering the walls of castles, princely dwellings and religious edifices, and serving as partitions between the pillars of churches.

Pierre Verlet has emphasized the close connection in the Middle Ages between the tapestry and the wall; he has pointed out that the evolution of Gothic architecture promoted secular tapestry over religious tapestry because the available wall space in churches was reduced as the number of stained-glass windows increased. As for the examples of tapestries of different heights and widths within the same hanging, this may be explained by their being intended for some specific place in a castle. The inventories drawn up after the death in 1380 of Charles V of France show, in

accessorily a diplomatic arm of some trenchancy, tapestries were also and above all, together with goldsmith's work, a means of asserting rank and wealth, and consequently a means of making the prince's power felt and seen."

This explains why the inventories of Philip the Bold, Jean de Berry and Philip the Good included many more tapestries than were necessary for current use. Francis Salet records the fact that Philip the Good, about 1440, built a storehouse "to lay up his said tapestry and keep it safe from fire."

Their value as furnishings was evidenced again in the 1950s when tapestry weaving was revived by the Association of Painters of Tapestry Cartoons. According to them, tapestries were the best means of warming the cement walls of contemporary architecture. Le Corbusier developed this idea for his "town homes." "Modern man,"

THE BAYEUX EMBROIDERY
England, late 11th century
(Abbey of St Augustine, Canterbury?)
△ The Normans Crossing the Channel to Pevensey, Sussex
▷ William the Conqueror and the Normans Going into Battle

particular, that the *Story of Judas Maccabaeus and Antiochus* was woven to the size of the great wall in the gallery of the Château de Beauté-sur-Marne. But this does not seem to have been a general rule. We know that the great merchants of the Middle Ages did not only order tapestries to be woven for a particular place, but also kept in stock a supply of pieces of different sizes, the larger ones for main halls, the medium-sized for chambers, the smaller for use as door curtains. It must be remembered, too, that kings and princes were often on the move and liked to take with them the furnishings they had chosen, which represented a considerable investment, so that tapestries were often taken down, rolled or folded up in chests, and then rehung on hooks. They therefore had to be of a size answering to the average position that might be met with in different residences. Finally, there seems to have been no hesitation about cutting down tapestries that were too big. Their value as personal furnishings was on a par with their social value. Francis Salet writes: "As a reserve of capital and motor of economic activity, as a reserve of presents and

he wrote, "is a nomad. Our nomad moves because his family has grown or on the contrary because his children have got married. Tapestry gives him the chance of acquiring a 'mural'; that is, a painting of large size, with an architectural potential. He unrolls his tapestry and spreads it over the wall, touching the floor. Is he moving out? He rolls up his 'mural,' puts it under his arm, down the stairs he goes, and he unrolls it again in his new home."

Because of the prestige attaching to tapestry in the West, it seems necessary and fitting to devote a whole chapter to this unique form of expression which, for centuries, tended to overshadow the other forms of Western textile art. But by the very fact of this privileged position, it is advisable to emphasize the specific features of this art and distinguish it from embroidery, with which it is sometimes confused.

In its widest sense the term tapestry is synonymous with art fabric. More strictly defined, it may be described as an indivisible work (i.e. not divisible into patterns), executed manually with yarn whose extension is limited to that of the coloured design (Nicole Vialet, *Principes d'analyse scientifique. Tapisserie, méthode et vocabulaire*, 1971).

There are two great varieties of tapestry: loom-woven tapestry and needlework tapestry. The former is a fabric made by weaving weft threads alternatively over and under the warps. The weft thread, generally of wool, more rarely of silk, silver or gold, completely covers the warps consisting of raw wool, cotton or hemp. Needlework tapestry is distinguished from woven by the fact that it is executed by needlework on a taut canvas, made up of crisscrossing weft and warp threads regularly spaced; it is similar to it, on the other hand, in that the support is again completely covered over.

In practice the contrast between these two techniques may be more or less marked. Thus the shuttle carrying the weft thread during weaving is sometimes manipulated like a needle (flying thread procedure), to allow a faster and

strip of coarse linen, worked in four colours of wool divided into eight tones (brick red, full-bodied yellow, buff yellow, light and dark green, and three shades of blue), in two kinds of needlework.

The circumstances in which it was made remain obscure. Some authorities think it was conceived and executed by Queen Matilda, wife of William the Conqueror. Others believe it was made in Canterbury by the monks of the abbey of St Augustine. It seems safe to say that the *Bayeux Embroidery* is not the work of a single artist, and that it was probably based on a preliminary design. True, no trace of any such design can be detected on the linen. But having noticed that the scenes or ensembles within a scene correspond to a length of from two to three feet, which is the length of a sheepskin, Simone Bertrand, who for many years was the keeper of the work, has suggested that the preliminary design may have been drawn on skins

finer making of certain parts of the design. Furthermore, some pieces of needlework tapestry are executed on a plain-weave fabric, with no interval between the threads, or even on a canvas fastened to a fabric.

Embroidery, on the contrary, is done on a soft material which, since it is not entirely covered, itself forms an active part of the composition.

An example of this confusion is the "Bayeux Tapestry," mistakenly so called since the nineteenth century. Actually it is an embroidery, one of the finest that has come down to us, and also the one that raises some of the most enigmatic questions. It was made in England in the latter half of the eleventh century (probably between 1067 and 1082) for Odo, Bishop of Bayeux and half-brother of William the Conqueror. It tells the story of the events leading up to the Norman Conquest and illustrates the Battle of Hastings itself (14 October 1066), in which William, Duke of Normandy, defeated Harold, King of England.

The scope of the story and the variety of the subjects contrasts with the sobriety of the means employed: a long

before being transferred to the linen. This monumental work, with 79 scenes accompanied by Latin inscriptions, includes some 1255 figures: men and women, horses, dogs, ships, castles, churches. It is bordered with friezes in which animals of all kinds and small stylized figures face each other on either side of the cross. Though it is executed with no notion of perspective, the idea of movement is remarkably well conveyed by the position of the overlapping figures, turned in every direction, and by the many arrows and spears which, in the battle scenes, set the rhythm of the composition.

While the *Bayeux Embroidery* has remained famous because of its antiquity and scope, and because it heralds the figured tapestry, it is in fact only one among many examples of the art of embroidery in the West. From the eleventh to the fourteenth century, this art form was almost exclusively devoted to religious use, to the ornamentation of liturgical vestments (copes, pluvials, chasubles, dalmatics, etc.) and altar cloths. England excelled in this needlework to such an extent that medieval embroidery in the

West was dominated by what was known as *opus anglicanum* (English work). It was in demand all over Europe, thanks to the popes, bishops and rulers who purchased it or contrived to have it presented to them. According to Louis de Farcy (as Odile Brel-Bordaz reminds us), "The English occupation of France, together with the sojourn of the popes in Avignon, contributed greatly to making it known in France."

The stitchery used is of two kinds: flat stitches for the gold threads and split stitches for the silk threads. This needlework was executed in the London workshops which, in the reigns of Edward I, II and III, ensured the English supremacy, before competition from Italy, Spain and Flanders led to the adoption of quicker methods and a simplified style, and before the French wars and domestic unrest caused a decline in English work in the late fourteenth century.

One of the best known and most finished examples of *opus anglicanum* is the *Tree of Jesse* of the fourteenth century. Measuring 58½ × 13¾ inches, it illustrates a Biblical theme which links up the ancestors of Christ: Jesse, King David, King Solomon and the Virgin, showing them together with the infant Jesus and Christ on the Cross between the Virgin and St John the Evangelist. Its almost unfaded colours, and its admirable display of foliage, geometric designs and fantastic animal figures, make it a bright and attractive work, of flawless technical mastery. In its perfection, despite its small size, it can vie with fourteenth-century tapestries and stands in the same stylistic relation to stained glass and miniatures.

Outside England, according to Nadine Gasc, each country worked out a specific style of embroidery: Germany with its *opus coloniense* technique (samite embroideries), Spain with its death's-head motifs, and France with its metal-work in relief.

In France embroiderers–including both men and women–were registered as an autonomous trade guild in Etienne Boileau's *Livre des Métiers* (Book of Crafts), of the mid-thirteenth century, together with several more specialized guilds: the "pattern cutters and scratchers," also the "church-vestment makers and Saracen alms-purse makers."

Between the fourteenth and the twentieth century, embroidery designed as interior furnishings has a history akin

THE CREATION TAPESTRY
Gerona, Catalonia, late 11th–early 12th century
Embroidery
12 ft. × 15½ ft.

to that of tapestry. Certain themes are common to both, and both obtained designs from the same painters, Raphael and Derain for example. Likewise, needlework tapestry sometimes served to adapt prints made on the same theme as those inspired by loom-made pestries: for example, the famous piece known as *The Reward of Virtue, the Dangers of Pleasure* (Musée Jacquemart-André, Paris), after Hans Holbein, embroidered about 1540–1550 in a provincial French workshop.

But while embroidery and needlework tapestry gave rise to some remarkable masterpieces, they did not by any means enjoy the success of loom-made tapestry, which from the fourteenth century on became the most widespread form of textile art in the West.

For its execution, two types of loom had appeared in Europe during the Middle Ages: the upright or high-warp loom, and the horizontal or low-warp loom. (The latter term only appears in the seventeenth century; for convenience, it will be used here without taking account of that date.) The same result can be obtained with either frame, and this fact, as Julien Coffinet points out in *Métamorphoses de la tapisserie*, has done something to obscure the impact which the use of different frames has had on the history of tapestry weaving.

Descending from the traditional weaver's loom, the low-warp loom obviously appeared in the West before its rival. But it did not immediately influence the development of tapestry. It is in a French text of 1303, recording an agreement between the low-warp weavers and another "manner of weavers who are called high-warp workmen" that the expression high warp *(haute lisse)* appears for the first time. The low-warp weavers formed a powerful guild which this new "manner of weavers" seemed all too likely to compete with: they therefore wished to subject them to the same rules. The agreement of 1303 records their victory. The two trades were united and ten "high-warp workmen," designated by name, pledged "both themselves and all the men of their trade" to adopt the "ordinance" of the low-warp weavers (that is, the regulations of December 1290 and July 1277).

Historians of tapestry have been puzzled by this union. For the low-warp weavers made "shaggy carpets," the stitches being knotted, then cut; they did not make fine tapestries. Furthermore, several documents attest that they worked "with the treadle," not with the high-warp loom. Why then should they have feared being supplanted by this new "manner of weavers"? Geneviève Souchal has shown that the similarity "in the materials employed, in the warping and above all in the nature of the works executed" (single panels forming a unit) amply justified the fears of the low-warp weavers.

It is in any case a significant point that the adherence of the high-warp weavers to the statutes of the low-warp guild exerted no influence on the working methods of either. The latter kept to their low-warp looms (as we know from the Tournai Ordinance of 9 December 1410 on "low-warp tapestry styled treadle work").

And, what may seem more surprising, the "high-warp workers" continued to operate on an upright loom. It has been repeatedly pointed out that the periphrasis used in the text of 1303 (a "manner of weavers") expressed the perplexity felt at the rise of a new industry; and new means vulnerable. If the high-warp weavers saw fit to persevere in their technique, it was obviously because they had decisive reasons for doing so.

THE TREE OF JESSE
14th century
Embroidery ("opus anglicanum")
58½" × 13¾"

According to Julien Coffinet, there were at the time at least two reasons for relinquishing the low-warp loom: it was impossible to produce with it pieces of any great size (nothing exceeding ten feet); and, because the warps were not divided into independent groups, the low-warp loom was unadaptable to the simultaneous and independent work of several heddlers. But the major objection against low warp at that time is that it did not permit the heddler to stand back from his work. For it must be remembered that tapestry is executed from the *back*, so that with a low-warp loom the cloth faces downwards; therefore no direct control of the design is possible. With high warp, on the contrary, the weaver can follow the progress of his work by getting up from his seat and going round to examine it from the front. This option, appreciable at all periods, was

particularly necessary in the fourteenth century, because the designs were imprecise, if not non-existent. "Low warp ruled out improvisation; high warp, on the contrary, enabled weavers to make discriminating use of the freedom granted them" (Julien Coffinet).

It was not until the first half of the fifteenth century that, "by a back-lash from high warp," the low-warp loom received the impulse which permitted it to be developed. Here the painters' workshops, in particular those of Arras and Tournai, played a decisive role by providing weavers with full-size working models, perfectly finished, which they could place on the warp threads and copy directly. At that point high warp could boast of no particular advantage. This aesthetic transformation probably accounts for two technical modifications that now occurred: the

110

lengthening of the beams and the division of the warps into independent groups.

But this evolution did not proceed by clear-cut stages. High-warp weavers may well have employed the low warp–placing the model behind the warp threads–for the weaving of fine pieces, akin to painting, or for certain details. Conversely, some particularly skilful low-warp weavers doubtless ventured as early as the fourteenth century to produce small tapestries based on the aesthetic of painting. But, for large-scale work at least, it was not until the seventeenth century that high warp could vie with low warp. High warp did not of course disappear for two centuries; it is found in the sixteenth century, notably in Paris and Fontainebleau. But it was still unsuited to the exact copying of designs, for the techniques of transposition were unsatisfactory. The simplest technique consisted in tracing out squares on the cartoon and on the warp threads, and marking each stitch on them with a compass. For large pieces, this system of guide marks resulted in significant distortions. Another technique was to draw the design on assembled sheets of paper: in this case, if the room was well lighted, the lines of the drawing showed through, and with chalk or pen the weaver could trace them on the warp threads.

The introduction in the seventeenth century of the technique of transferring the design to the warp threads with tracing paper marks a decisive stage in closing the gap between high and low warp–though the latter retained (and retains today) the advantage of being less costly because more rapid.

Unexpectedly, then, the "back-lash" of high-warp weaving was not accompanied by any challenge to the pictorial conception of tapestry; and it was not until the late nineteenth century, as we shall see, that the question of the relations between tapestry and painting was raised with all its implications.

From the evolution outlined above, it would be a mistake to conclude that the history of tapestry may be summed up in two conflicting conceptions of the weaver's art, one specific, the other pictorial, each having prevailed alternately. The truth is that a double current has always existed, and it has tended, according to the place, the workshop, and indeed even the weaver, to make one conception prevail (more or less consciously) over the other. A further point is that, in itself, the artistic context has not always systematically conditioned the choice of the loom. For reasons that may be either incidental (availability of one type of frame or one category of weavers) or structural (the corporate spirit of the high and low warp weavers, in particular), the two different looms have sometimes been used for identical purposes.

However, if we take an overall view of the history of tapestry, it may be said that, when Pope Leo X ordered from the Brussels workshops the *Acts of the Apostles* designed by Raphael, that step was an essential factor in orienting tapestry towards a "subjection to the rules and procedures of painting" (Francis Salet). Thereafter, from the early sixteenth century on, the techniques employed necessarily evolved on the lines best suited to a faithful interpretation of the designs supplied by painters.

THE ORIGINS OF TAPESTRY

Not much is known about the origins of tapestry. As Jules Guiffrey wrote at the end of the nineteenth century: "The earliest written evidence that we have about the history of tapestry only dates from the first years of the fourteenth century. But at that time tapestry was already a flourishing art... The period prior to this blossoming has remained till now shrouded in darkness."

In the early Middle Ages, as we have seen, tapestry was being practised in different parts of the world–by the South American Indians, by the Coptic and Byzantine weavers. While any connection between the Old and the New World is obviously to be ruled out, we do know that after the three crusades of the twelfth century, which were purely religious in spirit, those of the thirteenth century and the Fourth Crusade in particular (1202–1204) were prompted in part by commercial and political motives. The sack of Constantinople (1204) yielded a large booty of fine fabrics, and there may well have been some tapestries among them. It is also possible that some weavers may have accompanied the crusaders or, conversely, that eastern craftsmen may have migrated to Western Europe.

One essential work is significant in this respect: the *Tapestry of St Gereon* (now divided between the Musée Historique des Tissus, Lyons, the Victoria and Albert Museum, London, and the Germanisches Nationalmuseum, Nuremberg). It was discovered in the church of St Gereon in Cologne by Canon Bock, who published a detailed description of it in 1862: "In the textile before us, the outer diameter of these circular medallions measures 23½ inches. The ground, setting off these circles and the other figures and ornaments, is coloured in two shades of brown and blue, which form a small triangular design with alternating colours, like a chessboard pattern... The medallion on a bluish brown ground represents a scene of natural history in tones of yellowish white. The mythological winged griffin is attacking another monster, a horned animal with cloven hoofs. We do not say that these animals have a symbolic meaning. We only note in passing that the monster known as a griffin, half bird, half quadruped, was represented in the earliest times; originating in the East, it figures in the earliest traditions of India and Persia."

And Canon Bock concludes: "After a careful comparison with oriental fabrics, we have reached the conviction that our fabric originated not in the West but in the East, the true home of weaving in silk and wool."

A few years later Alfred Darcel, administrator of the Gobelins manufactory in Paris, expressed a different view

(*Gazette des Beaux-Arts*, 1877): "We should be inclined to think that it was made nearer to us, but under the influence of some Eastern fabric." And indeed the *Tapestry of St Gereon* is now thought to have been woven in Cologne in the late eleventh century; but it is clear that, by its theme and the arrangement of its motifs, this tapestry establishes a close connection between Byzantine and Romanesque art. Some other pieces from Halberstadt Cathedral, treating both religious themes *(Christ and the Apostles, Abraham and the Archangel St Michael)* and a secular one *(Charlemagne and the Philosophers)*, provide a further link in the history of tapestry, before the monumental pieces of the fourteenth century. The weaving of the first two is attributed to Abbess Agnes of the Quedlinburg convent, between 1150 and 1175. These two are compared by Julien Coffinet to the figures in the painted ceiling (c. 1160) in the church of St Martin at Zillis (Grisons, Switzerland); he connects the third with "a hanging from Quedlinburg Cathedral, the *Marriage of Mercury and Philosophy*, dating to about 1200 and woven by a technique of thick wool." This technique of knotted tufts of wool was borrowed from the East by medieval European weavers; such work is referred to in early inventories as "shaggy carpets from overseas."

It has been pointed out by Madeleine Jarry that the tapestry of *Charlemagne and the Philosophers* "may be compared to a miniature of the ninth century, such as the *Bible of St Calixtus* in San Paolo fuori le Mura in Rome."

Another tapestry (Oslo), from a hanging of the *Twelve Months*, may have been woven in Norway in the first half of the thirteenth century. By its technique and its highly stylized figures, set off by sharp outlines, it is related to the *Bayeux Embroidery*.

The period from the late eleventh to the mid-fourteenth century is marked, then, by two salient facts. First, the scarcity of extant tapestries, despite the many mentions of fabrics in records of the period; but owing to the looseness of the terms employed, it is difficult to know whether these fabrics were actually tapestries. Secondly, their close connection with religious communities, a connection soon to be broken by a growing secularization which became characteristic of post-medieval tapestries in the West.

TAPESTRY OF ST GEREON (FRAGMENT)
Cologne, late 11th century
Tapestry
Size of fragment: 28¾″ × 28¾″

THE TWELVE MONTHS, DETAIL OF APRIL
Norway, first half of the 13th century
Tapestry
Overall size: 4 ft. × 6½ ft.

THE ANGERS APOCALYPSE
Paris, c. 1380
Tapestry
◁ The Third Reader
▷ The Great Whore

THE GREAT CENTRES OF TAPESTRY

PARIS

The earliest information we have about the textile industry in Paris goes back to the close of the reign of St Louis (1226–1270). Etienne Boileau, then Provost of Paris, in his *Livre des Métiers*, refers to weavers of swaddling-clothes, quilters, silk spinners, alms-purse makers and so on, as well as to "weavers of Saracen carpets and weavers of our own carpets." The so-called Saracen carpets were "shaggy" carpets similar to Turkey carpets. According to Jules Guiffrey, the secrets of their manufacture were revealed to the Christians by the infidels, known by the generic name of Saracens. "Our own carpets," meaning native French work, designated on the contrary "the kind of work which was done in our regions before the introduction of the Saracen technique and which continued to be made along with the others... because they cost less to make and answered different needs." This indigenous work, according to Geneviève Souchal, consisted of household fabrics "serving to cover walls, beds, seats and tables." They were made of wool or a mixture of wool and linen, or even of wool and hemp, loosely woven and no doubt of a downy texture, sometimes decorated with regular designs, "but only such designs as could be executed with a shuttle thrown from one end of the loom to the other."

In 1303 the so-called Saracen weavers were joined by a new "manner of weavers." Their production, though comparable in some respects to that of their elders, was distinguished from it by some fundamental features: it consisted of tapestries that were not shaggy, with complex designs, executed on a high-warp loom from a rough model. The uses to which they were put were not, however, a decisive criterion of differentiation.

As pointed out by Geneviève Souchal in her masterly study of Parisian tapestry, "The people of the Middle Ages seem to have distinguished their work much less by the purpose it served than by the quality of the materials employed, their implementation, and the dimensions of the finished product, and they must have walked on high-warp tapestries as readily as they hung up shaggy carpets on the wall."

According to the same scholar, the appearance in Paris of this new form of expression may well have been connected with the decline of the Arras cloth trade, hitherto famous throughout Europe. Some powerful Parisian cloth merchants—"figuring among the subjects most highly taxed, by far, in the different tax rolls drawn up under Philip the Fair," and maintaining close relations with the northern towns, Arras in particular—are thought to have given asylum to cloth workers from Artois driven out by the disturbances of 1285. "At the prompting of these great merchants the new manufacture was presumably acclimatized (or possibly even invented) on the banks of the Seine." We shall have occasion to return to this point, for the decline of the Arras cloth trade was no doubt also at the origin of the development of high-warp weaving in the capital of Artois.

No tapestry from the Paris workshops of the first half of the fourteenth century is known to exist. Archive documents do, however, prove the existence of a limited production of such work, featuring geometric designs and heraldic emblems for the most part. From the latter half of

THE ANGERS
APOCALYPSE
Paris, c. 1380
◁ Christ with Sword
▷ The Fourth Trumpet

the fourteenth century we have several fragments of a hanging with the arms of Beaufort-Comminges (Camphill Museum, Glasgow, and Metropolitan Museum, New York). It may be taken as representative of the work being done at that period, and reveals an imperfectly mastered technique. Some details are reversed, and anomalies differing from one fragment to another are to be found in the arrangement of animals and the representation of armorial bearings.

The first figured tapestries make their appearance, it would seem, between 1360 and 1380. In the inventory of Charles V of France (1364–1380), drawn up in the closing years of his reign, figure innumerable "shaggy carpets" and heraldic tapestries, together with thirty-three "carpets with pictures," each including several pieces. At the French court the Dukes of Anjou, Berry and Orléans owned a large number of hangings, and among them were some "storied tapestries." More than to anyone else, however, the rise of figured tapestry seems to have been due to Philip the Bold, who in 1384 inherited the counties of Flanders and Artois. After the purchase in 1383 of a *Battle of the Thirty*, his account books testify to something like a passion for this kind of work.

The largest and unquestionably the finest hanging of the fourteenth century to have survived is the *Apocalypse*, preserved in the Tapestry Museum at Angers. It is also one of the few Gothic hangings about which we are well informed. The accounts of Louis I, Duke of Anjou (1339–1384), refer on 7 April 1377 to a payment of 1,000 francs to Nicolas Bataille for "two tapestry cloths

with the story of the Apocalypse which he made for the Duke." In January 1378 an advance of 50 francs was paid to Hennequin of Bruges, "painter to our lord the King," for "the pictures and patterns made by him for the said tapestry with the story of the Apocalypse." Finally, on 16 June 1379, Nicolas Bataille received an advance of 300 francs for three "tapestries with the story of the Apocalypse" which he engaged to finish "by Christmas" of that same year. Further, an Apocalypse manuscript figuring in 1373 in the inventory of Charles V's books in the palace of the Louvre is listed as missing in the verification of 1380, for "the king has given it to the Duke of Anjou for the making of his fine tapestry." So we know who commissioned the hanging, who executed the designs, who wove it, and when. There remain, however, several controversial points.

The one which in the past few years has been most discussed may be eliminated outright. Recent studies have shown that, contrary to what has been written and repeated for over a century, the *Apocalypse* was not woven by Nicolas Bataille. He was not a weaver in the strict sense (though sometimes designated as "weaver and varlet to the duke" in the records), but a "tapestry merchant"; he was a "promoter" (to use the expression of Jean Lestocquoy) who acted as middleman between the court, his chief client, and the high-warp workshops. Many documents vouch for the extent of his business: "six carpets of Arras work" (1373), for example, and, among others, a carpet for Bertrand de Claiquin (1396). With a few exceptions, these hangings were all intended for Philip the Bold,

Duke of Burgundy, and to a less extent for the Duke of Orléans. In 1397 we find Nicolas Bataille associated with another merchant, Jacques Dourdin, engaging to supply the king with a sumptuous chamber of tapestries "with imagery woven with fine gold Arras thread": this was the *Jousts of St Denis*, commemorating the admission of the Duke of Orléans, brother of Charles VI, and his cousin Duke Louis II of Anjou to the Order of Knighthood in 1389.

If the activity of this great merchant has not always been well discerned by art historians, the reason is, apparently, that one particular payment was long overlooked: the payment of 20 June 1379, attesting the remittance to Nicolas Bataille of a sum of 20 francs, for him to distribute "for their wine" (i.e. by way of a gratuity) "to the servants of Robin Poinçon who worked on the tapestry of his Lordship." This entry is crucial, for it gives us the name of the master weaver under whose orders the Apocalypse hanging was made: he was Robin Poinçon, more commonly known today as Robert Poisson. Very little is known about this man, apart from the fact that he lived in Paris and that "he seems to have had some connections with northern France, like so many other artists and high-warp weavers" (Jean Lestocquoy). In 1367 we come across a Jehan Pisson (but does he really belong to the same family?) charged with conveying some Arras tapestries from Lille to Paris. A whole family of the name of Poisson is known to have been established at Arras in the early fifteenth century. Does this mean that the Angers *Apocalypse* was woven at Arras?

There is no evidence to settle the question definitely. According to Jean Lestocquoy, it might well have been woven, in part at least, at Arras, for the tapestry industry was more prosperous there than in Paris. But this argument is not decisive. The fact is that at this period we have very little information about the respective importance of these two centres. Yet Lestocquoy's view is borne out by the work of Mme Stucky, who has pointed out a great many similarities, notably in the foliage and the "crab-leg" motifs, between the Angers *Apocalypse* and the hanging of *St Piatus and St Eleutherius*, which is known to be Arras work.

There can be practically no doubt, on the other hand, that a second *Apocalypse* hanging–of which no vestige now survives–was indeed woven at Arras. The accounts of Philip the Bold for the year 1386 record a payment of 1,176 livres to Jehan Cosset, a competitor of Nicolas Bataille at Arras, for "the said cloth of the Apocalypse which Robert Pisson is commissioned to make." It is clear from this entry that Robert Poisson undertook to produce a second set of *Apocalypse* hangings, this time for the Duke of Burgundy. That this set was made at Arras is attested by an entry of 1387 referring to "six large high-warp tapestries of Arras weave with the story of the Apocalypse." According to Donald King, four pieces out of six were finally delivered; divided in two, for reasons of convenience, in 1403, they appear to have passed successively to Philip the Good, Charles V and Philip II, being recorded for the last time in 1731, when two of them perished in the fire that ravaged the royal palace in Brussels.

THE ANGERS APOCALYPSE
Paris, c. 1380
△ St Michael Slaying the Dragon
▷ Death on a Pale Horse

Another point has been much debated by scholars for decades: the number and division of scenes within the *Apocalypse* hanging. Intent as they were on a division into *seven* pieces (seven being the recurring number used in St John's writings to symbolize perfection), even the best scholars were long misled. They argued that this hanging must originally have included seven readers (perhaps the seven bishops of the Churches of Asia) and ninety-eight small pictures (seven times fourteen), divided into seven pieces each with fourteen scenes (two rows of seven each). But this reconstruction was by no means self-evident. After all, twenty-eight pictures had disappeared and the alternation of blue and red grounds had to be respected. So it was assumed, for want of anything better, that the second and third pieces of the set must have included, in all, only fourteen pictures, thus bringing the number of scenes in the whole set to eighty-four (seven times twelve).

This hypothesis has recently been questioned by Donald King. The "seventh" piece (now lost) bequeathed in 1490 to Angers Cathedral by Anne of France–and corresponding to the piece which in 1416 figured in the inventory of the Duke of Berry–had, Donald King surmises, never formed part of the Duke of Anjou's hanging (which was given to Angers Cathedral after the death of King René). This "seventh" piece more probably belonged to a third *Apocalypse* set commissioned by the Duke of Berry after those of his two brothers and left unfinished. The Angers *Apocalypse*, Donald King concludes, consisted of only *six* pieces, the second and third forming but a single one.

While the "pictures and patterns" of Hennequin of Bruges have not come down to us we do possess several manuscripts from which this artist apparently took inspiration. Much interest was formerly directed to French MS 403 in the Bibliothèque Nationale, Paris, for it was known that Charles V of France had lent it to the Duke of Anjou "for the making of his fine tapestry." But it was shown by Leopold Delisle, in the early twentieth century, that this manuscript was doubtless not the only one with which the king's painter was acquainted. It would seem that he was also inspired by the manuscript in the Seminary of Namur, Latin MS 14410 in the Bibliothèque Nationale, and MSS 432 and 38 in the Cambrai and Metz libraries. Nevertheless, Hennequin of Bruges may be said to have created an original work. To convince oneself of this, one need only compare some of these miniatures with the corresponding scenes in the hanging. As Geneviève Souchal has aptly put it, "the rather stiff figures in the manuscripts have been turned into figures pulsing with life, with varied expressions, wrapped in cloaks with abundant and elaborate drapery... the small book illustrations are seen to be transposed into a mural scale with an economy of means which imparts to St John's prophecies a monumental simplicity enhanced by racy accents." Examining the hanging, Julien Coffinet has noted that outlines are rare and that the drawing of forms is generally indicated by the simple juxtaposition of tones. From this he infers that "the weavers received models from Hennequin of Bruges which were not only drawn, but on which the lighter and darker values were clearly indicated, with perhaps at the top some indications for the tones." But it seems difficult to agree with Fabienne Joubert that the re-use of certain figures–especially in the last three pieces–was the result of a "fairly extensive reworking" of Hennequin's models by "a discriminating cartoon-designer" who considered them inadequate. These re-uses (the readers and St John's shelter, for example) were undoubtedly deliberate on the part of the painter of the small sketch-designs. Moreover it was not current practice at that time to make full-size cartoons. At least it was not institutionalized: there was then no intermediary between the painter and the weavers, and while the latter certainly enjoyed great freedom in the transcription of models, they were not free to "correct" the composition of the "pattern maker" as they might see fit.

Discrepancies between the earlier and later pieces of the *Apocalypse* set testify nevertheless to the creative latitude left to the weavers. The grounds, uniform to begin with, are adorned with motifs from scene 30 on: for the most part, a scattering of flowers, sometimes in sheaves, and also, and above all, some foliage scrolls similar to vignettes. In several pictures the foliage scroll is developed within a motif alluding to the scene of which it forms the background. Thus in the *Adoration of the Image of the Beast*, some birds recall the shape of the doves which come and restore life to the two prostrate witnesses. Stylized in a bird-of-prey attitude, other winged creatures go to emphasize the abomination of men worshipping the statue of the monster arisen from the sea.

These background elements are undoubtedly the work of the weavers. For what reason could Hennequin of Bruges have had to provide for plain backgrounds to begin with, and figured ones afterwards? All the less reason since it would have been so easy for him to modify his design in the course of the work. One may presume, on the contrary, that for reasons both decorative (to break the monotony of the scenes, a monotony amplified by the division of the woven panels) and practical (to strengthen the weave of the cloth and diversify the weavers' work) Robert Poisson took it upon himself to fill the broad red and blue surfaces. One may further assume that for each picture the weavers proceeded empirically, as shown by the cusps inscribed in the decreasing lozenges which pattern the background of *St Michael Slaying the Dragon*.

Though on the whole the style of the *Apocalypse* hanging remains homogeneous, some further differences–obviously arising from the work of the weavers–can be seen between the earlier and later pieces. As Fabienne Joubert has rightly pointed out, the monumental figures at the beginning–clad in solid draperies hollowed out with squarer recesses, with rugged features framed by thick wavy locks of hair–stand in contrast to other figures treated with more elaborate detail. These latter have "more complex and sinuous draperies [and] more refined faces framed by tight and nervous curls of hair." It has been observed by René Planchenault that in certain pictures of the earlier pieces the figures huddled on the left side leave "a pointless void" on the right, while other figures in "a composition too lax at the start" are cramped on the right

119

THE PRESENTATION IN THE TEMPLE
Paris, last quarter of the 14th century
Tapestry
5 ft. × 9½ ft.

side. These differences can in reality be easily accounted for. We must remember, first, that the hanging may have been woven partly in Arras and partly in Paris. And several groups of weavers, each group working on a different loom, were probably mobilized at the same time; according to Julien Coffinet, three looms at least must have been used to complete the weaving of six pieces in the space of seven years. No doubt too, in order to press ahead, several groups of weavers worked in shifts on the same loom. This, as René Planchenault writes, "would explain why in one and the same scene we find some figures of admirable quality beside others of less skilful workmanship."

Very few tapestries survive whose style can be compared with that of the Angers *Apocalypse*. One of them is the *Presentation in the Temple* (Musées Royaux d'Art et d'Histoire, Brussels). The serene expression of the figures, the sculpturesque design of the draperies, the clouds edged with double festoons, the stylized vine branches patterning the background, also the colouring and the grain of the weave, all testify to a close kinship with the *Apocalypse*. Too high to be an altar frontal, as formerly supposed, this piece was probably made up, like the *Apocalypse*, of two superimposed rows, as evidenced at the bottom of the panel by part of an angel's wing and the top of a small building. Once attributed to the Paris workshops, this tapestry is now thought to be Arras work. Some resemblances have been pointed out between the female figures in the *Presentation* and the Virgin in the Duke of Berry's *Psalter* by André Beauneveu. Here one seems to be "in the presence of one of those productions of around 1380 in which flowered the so-called Franco-Flemish style of those northern painters who, in the time of Charles V and Charles VI, came in numbers to seek their fortune from French patrons" (Geneviève Souchal).

The hanging of the *Nine Heroes* (several panels exhibited at the Cloisters, New York, a branch of the Metropolitan Museum) also has many features in common with the *Apocalypse*. With less refinement perhaps, we find here again a similarity in the drawing of the figures, the architectural setting, and the butterflies and foliage scrolls adorning the background. The colours in both moreover–the grey of the stonework, the red tones which with time have turned pink, and above all the deep blue–answer each other to a remarkable degree. Generally attributed to the Paris workshops on the strength of these analogies, the panels in the Cloisters may however, according to Geneviève Souchal, have been woven at Arras. The stark and sometimes awkward design of the *Nine Heroes* cannot in any case be the work of Hennequin of Bruges. Nor, contrary to what was once thought, can the maker of the designs have been the painter and sculptor André Beauneveu, who was employed at the court of Jean, Duc de Berry (who presumably commissioned the hanging), and whose great skill was vaunted in 1393 by Froissart. For Millard Meiss, the *Nine Heroes* reflects rather the style of the painters of Charles V who in the late fourteenth century were working in north-eastern France and Flanders.

While we have very little information about the activity and production of the Paris workshops in the late fourteenth century, we do know that a considerable trade in tapestries was carried on in Paris. Apart from Nicolas Bataille, whose activity was particularly prolific, two other merchants participated in the rise of this industry in the royal capital: Jacques Dourdin and Pierre de Beaumetz.

Jacques Dourdin, who died in 1407, carried on his business at least as much in Arras, of which he was a native, as in Paris where he lived. Between 1386 and 1397 he delivered some twenty tapestries to the Duke of Burgundy;

but the King of France, Queen Isabeau de Bavière and the Duke of Orléans also numbered among his customers. Tapestry was not his only source of income: he occupied himself in 1399 with "heritages" (i.e. real estate) and was also a wine merchant.

Pierre de Beaumetz, who died in 1418, was chiefly in the service of the Duke of Burgundy, whom from 1383 he supplied with hangings on heroic and religious themes, together with more modest works such as cushions "with a green field intermingled with white ewes under a gold-coloured hawthorn." It is not always known where these works were made, but they appear to come as much from Paris as from Arras. In 1388 he formed a partnership with Jean Cosset, a rich merchant of Arras, the two men engaging to supply the Duke of Berry with "Shepherds and Shepherdesses." Their partnership seems to have lasted until 1396. Presumably Pierre de Beaumetz was also in charge of a high-warp workshop, for in 1399 mention is made of his "varlets" and in 1412 he is recorded for the last time as a "high-warp workman."

Nicolas Bataille died in 1408, preceded on 22 October 1407 by Jacques Dourdin and followed by Pierre de Beaumetz, who apparently ceased his activities in 1412 and died in 1418. With the passing of these three leading merchants, the Parisian tapestry industry fell into a decline: according to Jean Lestocquoy, "there is no need to call in the English occupation of 1420." Other, more numerous scholars would attribute the disappearance of the Paris workshops to the social and political disturbances that afflicted the capital at the beginning of the fifteenth century: the plague epidemic of 1418 and civil war followed by the English occupation in 1420. But this explanation seems inadequate, inasmuch as other luxury crafts, goldsmithery for example, continued for many years yet to offer a livelihood to a large number of artisans.

Actually, the presence in the tax rolls of at least two weavers in 1421 and of three, including a woman, in 1423, shows that such work continued in Paris for some years more. According to R.A. Weigert, "the Paris workshops seem to have resumed their activity, even if only on a limited scale, after 1450." Further, this author states that, "though neither particularly numerous, nor particularly flourishing, tapestry workshops continued to operate in Paris during the first half of the sixteenth century." Thus two Parisian weavers, Jean Pinel and Claude Bredas, are said to have supplied "a set of over twenty pieces... on the occasion of the marriage of Renée of France and the Duke of Ferrara in 1528." Francis I is thought to have commissioned a hanging woven in gold and silk from the Parisians Nicolas and Pasquel de Montagne, while in 1552 one of their competitors executed for the Archbishop of Sens, Louis de Bourbon, six pieces of a *Life of Jesus Christ* destined for the abbey of Saint-Denis. Other weavers also seem to have been at work in Paris around the middle of the sixteenth century: Antoine de Larry, Gérard Laurent (whose descendants occupied an important position in the workshops of the Louvre and the Gobelins), Guillaume Torcheux (or Tricheux), and Pierre Blasse.

THE NINE HEROES
Paris, 14th century
Tapestry
Julius Caesar (detail)
Overall size: 10 ft. × 11½ ft.

ARRAS

The industry of high-warp weaving appeared at Arras, as in Paris, in the early fourteenth century. Which centre preceded the other hardly matters, though it was once an issue passionately debated among historians of tapestry. One thing is known for certain: tapestries were being woven at Arras in 1313. This is formally attested by a receipt of that year signed by Isabiaus Caurrée "for five cloths in high warp."

The history of Arras tapestry seems to be closely connected with the decline of the cloth industry in that region. As has been shown by Henri Laurent (*La draperie des Pays-Bas en France et dans les pays méditerranéens*, 1935) and E.J. Reynolds ("Merchants of Arras and the Overland Trade with Genoa, Twelfth Century" in *Revue belge de philologie et d'histoire*, 1930, Vol. IX), "up to 1200, at every stage of the overland trade route from Flanders to the shores of the Mediterranean, it was the merchants and products of Arras that opened the way to others." During the thirteenth century, however, this pre-eminence was lost. The cloth trade developed in other northern towns, and Brabant gradually prevailed over Artois. Indeed, by the end of the century Arras was hardly producing anything more than serges of ordinary quality.

A reconversion was necessary. The cloth industry left behind both raw materials and highly qualified labour which the Arras "financiers"–bankers keen on putting their capital to work in all branches of economic activity–naturally hoped to reinvest in a more lucrative production. The cultural and artistic ferment then being experienced by the town, added to the economic slump, favoured the rise of a luxury industry. Described as "the best wrought that can be found on this side of the Alps," the tapestries woven "with fine Arras thread" very soon acquired an international renown. From London to Constantinople, Arras was synonymous with the weaving industry, and the name of the town passed into several European languages as a generic term for tapestry–arras in English, *arazzo* in Italian, for example.

Philip the Bold–heir to the counties of Flanders and Artois on the death of his father-in-law Louis de Mâle–and later John the Fearless (1371–1419) and Philip the Good (1396–1467) contributed to a large extent to the prosperity of the Arras tapestry works. Their orders, together with those of other rulers and lords of that day, kept the looms busy.

As in the case of Paris, we have little information about the life and production of the Arras workshops in the fourteenth and fifteenth centuries. The *Register of Burgesses* lists over a hundred "high-warpers" at Arras in 1423. As Jean Lestocquoy has pointed out, this list only includes the more well-to-do persons and leaves out the workmen. A large number of weavers, no doubt several thousand, must have been employed at Arras in the early fifteenth century. The princely accounts mention only a few of them by name, and "it is evident that we must distinguish between the tapestry employers or merchants and the actual weavers, even though this term has a very broad meaning in the documents" (Jean Lestocquoy). Among the names recurring most frequently are Vincent Boursette and his son-in-law Huart Walois, Michel Bernart, André de Monchy, Pierre Le Conte, Guillaume au Vaissel, Jean Cosset

THE STORY OF SS. PIATUS
AND ELEUTHERIUS
Arras, 1402
Tapestry
◁ St Piatus Preaching at Tournai
▷ St Piatus Baptising Irenaeus
   and his Wife and Son

and Jean Walois (son of Huart?). All of them came of well-to-do patrician families established in the Arras region for several generations, the same families no doubt which two centuries before had contributed to the rise of the cloth industry. To varying degrees, all of them also occupied positions in the town administration and combined the tapestry trade with one or more further activities. The case of Huart Walois is not untypical. Eight times a municipal magistrate between 1372 and 1409, mayor of the famous brotherhood of Notre-Dame des Ardents and *"nostelain de saies"* (cloth merchant) in 1375, he was put in charge of the town artillery in 1388 and made "treasurer" in 1399; he was "wine steward" in 1395, and in 1403 the Duchess of Burgundy employed him as her trusted agent to redeem some bonds in the amount of 500 livres. The example of Jean Cosset is no less revealing. Five times a municipal magistrate, a publican and cloth merchant, he was also *valet de chambre* and confidential agent to the Duke of Burgundy. He conveyed the Duke's tapestries and plate from Arras to Dijon and carried secret messages for him, "riding his horses to death from Dijon to Paris and Boulogne."

These powerful merchants did no weaving themselves. They farmed out the work and, when necessary, advanced the money needed to buy raw materials and pay the weavers. It is safe to say that they did not always wait for a particular order to come their way; the demand was steady enough for them to run no great risk in building up stocks. "The more or less hazardous initiative of the great

contractors" (to use the words of Francis Salet) would go far to explain the extent and above all the pace of such an output. How could so many tapestries have been turned out year after year if the merchants had had to wait every time, before setting the looms to work, for the prince's goodwill, the choice of the subject, the design and perhaps final approval? It may be taken for granted that these great merchants were also in close touch with the workshops which specialized in making tapestry designs, those of such artists as Bauduin de Bailleul, Jacques Daret, Robert de Monchaux or Jacques Pillet.

The commercial network animated by these Arras "capitalists" extended well beyond the frontiers of Artois. It was they who set in train the development of tapestry in other northern towns (Tournai, Lille, Oudenarde). So it is understandable that designs made in one place might be executed in another many miles away, and that the manufacture of a hanging might occupy several workshops located in different towns.

While a large number of tapestry hangings are listed in princely inventories, only a few scattered pieces have come down to us. Of these, the oldest Arras tapestry and also the best known is the *Story of SS. Piatus and Eleutherius*. In fourteen scenes divided into four fragments, it illustrates the legend of the two patron saints of Tournai, who lived in the third and sixth century respectively. The first six scenes refer to St Piatus. Having been sent out to evangelize Gaul, he went to Tournai, in modern Belgium, where he persuaded the people to destroy their idols and build a church on the ruins of the pagan temple; in the last scene he baptises Irenaeus and his wife and their sons, as the wondering crowd looks on. Three other scenes once completed the cycle. A chronicler described them in the seventeenth century: they represented the beheading of Piatus and his disciples, the carrying of the saint's body to Seclin, near Lille, and the miracles occasioned there when it arrived. The story of St Eleutherius occupies eight further pictures. First he goes to Rome with his followers to receive investiture from the Pope. On his return to Gaul, Blanda, daughter of the governor of Tournai, tries to seduce him. Failing in this, she runs away and dies soon afterwards. Eleutherius brings her back to life. Converted as a result of this prodigy, Blanda has herself baptised. The governor and pagan population of Tournai try to force her to abjure her faith, but they are punished for their impiousness by a plague which ravages the town.

THE STORY OF THE DEEDS
OF JOURDAIN DE BLAYE
Arras (?), c. 1390–1400
Tapestry
The Visit of Fromont to Girart (detail)
Overall size: 10′9″ × 12′6″

An inscription which has how disappeared, but was copied in the seventeenth century by Canon Dufief, recorded the place (Arras), the year of execution and completion (1402), the weaver's name (Pierrot Feré) and that of the client who ordered it (Toussaint Prier).

Toussaint Prier, who died in 1437, was clergyman of the chapel of Count Louis de Mâle and chaplain to Philip the Bold, before becoming a canon of Tournai Cathedral. It was for his cathedral that he ordered the tapestry to be made. Did he go by way of one of those powerful merchants of whom we have spoken or did he apply directly to the specialized workshops in Arras? There is no evidence to settle this point. The distance between Tournai, where he lived, and Arras, where the work was done, suggests that Toussaint Prier may have employed the services of a middleman.

The researches of Adolphe Guesnon have shown that Pierrot Feré was a weaver who enjoyed a certain affluence. A "notable" of the town of Arras, his name figures in the records of burgher assemblies convoked by the municipal magistrates. He was a member of the Twenty, a tribunal annually re-elected which sat in judgment on infractions to the rules of the cloth trade and related crafts. At various times he was also a member of the "Quatre des Héritages," another municipal commission whose business was to share out undivided property and settle disputes at law concerning charges on real estate and joint ownership. His means and social status, however, are not to be compared with those of the great Arras merchants, for he was a weaver, not a broker. "It would be useless to look for his name among the purveyors inscribed in the Duke of Burgundy's accounts. It is not there, and for good reason. These names usually refer to the middlemen, the tapestry merchants or tapestry contractors, not to the craftsmen themselves, whose names are unrecorded" (Adolphe Guesnon).

Here then, most unusually, we have the name of at least two persons concerned in the making of the SS. Piatus and Eleutherius hanging. But we do not know who the painter was who supplied the designs. Some have assumed that there was none; had their been, his name would have been recorded in due place alongside the two others. In the view of Julien Coffinet, Pierrot Feré may have worked from an illuminated manuscript depicting the life of the two saints, himself preparing the full-size models.

In any case, one cannot help noticing that the work of the weavers is much more apparent in the Tournai hanging of SS. Piatus and Eleutherius than in the Angers Apocalypse. The outlines are more prominent and the drapery, falling more heavily, is emphasized by broad shadings in three tones similar to those used later for the modelling of furs. The skies composed of broad horizontal bands contrast with the clouds in festoons characteristic of earlier work, while the flowering plants and grass, more abundant than in the Apocalypse, are drawn from an oblique angle. As noted by R.A. d'Hulst, "For the first time an attempt is made to spread out the landscape and deepen it. Proportions, however, are not always respected. Most of the buildings represented are too small; deliberately, no doubt, for their purpose is not only to figure towns and monuments but also to isolate the different pictures from each other." And this view is borne out by the scene of Eleutherius' departure for Rome. Taking place in the open air, it is limited on the left by the church where the four Gentiles are being baptised, and marked off on the right by

THE ANNUNCIATION
Arras (?), early 15th century
Tapestry
11'4" × 9'6"

an architectonic frame. "The relationship with the art of Van Eyck, and the homely realism of the landscapes and accessories, bear witness to an artistic environment more Flemish than French" (R.A. Weigert).

The *Deeds of Jourdain de Blaye* (Museo Civico, Padua) is generally attributed to the Arras workshops on the strength of its analogies with the *Story of SS. Piatus and Eleutherius*. Also related to the latter is the *Annunciation* (Metropolitan Museum, New York). The gnarled tree-trunks, the round or fern-shaped leaves, the plant life mingling and overlapping on several planes, the sky made

up of contrasting horizontal touches, indicate a close connection between the two works. From the absence of outlines in the *Annunciation*, however, it may be inferred that the weavers disposed of a highly finished model, possibly an actual painting. In view of the analogies with the *Champmol Altarpiece* (Musée des Beaux-Arts, Dijon), painted between 1394 and 1399 by Melchior Broederlam for Philip the Bold, James J. Rorimer has attributed the designs for the *Annunciation* to this Flemish master. Broederlam certainly executed some tapestry designs; he is known to have drawn the "small patterns" representing "shep-

DESCENT FROM THE CROSS, ENTOMBMENT AND RESURRECTION
Arras (?), first quarter of the 15th century
Wool, silk, gold and silver thread
3'8" × 9'11"

herds and shepherdesses" for Margaret of Flanders. But scrutiny of the two pieces shows that he can hardly have been the maker of the designs in question. In the tapestry, the architecture is more developed and the effect of depth more marked than in the painted panel in Dijon. Further, as Geneviève Souchal points out, "the impetuous and twisted gesture of the tapestry angel does not reappear in the painting where a thicker-set Gabriel, with both wings erect, raises his hands to breast level to present his banderole. Nor does the Virgin in the painting, to express her surprise, have anything of the strange and mannered hand movement shown in the tapestry." It seems more reasonable to assume the existence of a common model. Alain Erlande-Brandenburg thinks the model might have been Italian in view of the "acanthus adorning the top of the arcade" and the patches of colour on the architecture

which evoke, according to him, "the Cosmati technique of polychrome marble inlays."

Some features in common with the above-mentioned hangings are also to be seen in two other tapestries on religious themes: the *Descent from the Cross, Entombment and Resurrection* (Victoria and Albert Museum, London) and the *Resurrection* (Musée de Cluny, Paris). Both are small-sized, finely woven pieces, probably intended to adorn an altar. The vegetation with rounded and indented forms, the skies made up of horizontal blue and white touches, again suggest Arras work. Outlines, non-existent in the Cluny piece, are used with a precise aesthetic purpose in the London tapestry–to emphasize, for example, the transparency of the shroud enveloping Christ's body–and not, it would seem, to make up for the shortcomings of an imprecise model.

THE RESURRECTION
Arras (?), early 15th century
Tapestry

THE OFFERING OF THE HEART
Arras (?), early 15th century
Tapestry

Another group of tapestries, representing amatory scenes, has also been attributed to the Arras workshops. Among the most significant of them are the *Offering of the Heart* (Musée de Cluny, Paris), five *Scenes from a Romance* (Musée des Arts Décoratifs, Paris), two versions of a *Lord and Lady with a Hawk* (sometimes also called *Le couple seigneurial*) and a *Lady with a Hawk* (Metropolitan Museum, New York). In each of these works reappear the leafage, tree-trunks and skies described above. With one exception (the *Offering of the Heart*), outlines are non-existent. Both versions of the *Lord and Lady with a Hawk* were certainly executed from the same design; but they are distinguished from each other by the quality of the weaving–much less careful in one of them–and by the reversing of the motif, due perhaps, according to Julien Coffinet, "to low-warp weaving: the size of the piece (8½ × 9½ ft.) would suggest that already by about 1420

there were low-warp looms transformed or enlarged. This possibility cannot be dismissed, but it is by no means forced upon us... Possibly the design was redrawn in reverse at a client's request... Possibly, too, the piece was woven in high warp on a loom lighted from behind, as for the long-wool carpet with the design placed behind the warp threads and followed directly by the weaver."

Comparison of the foregoing pieces with the *Lady with a Hawk*–also woven from the same design–reveals something of the way in which a model in existence for a decade or more could be adjusted to the taste of the day in order to satisfy a new generation of clients. Thus the high-collared dress and peaked coif fashionable in the 1420s and figuring in both versions of the *Lord and Lady with a Hawk* were replaced in the *Lady with a Hawk* by a décolleté and finery "with hairnet, fillets and flowing headgear" in vogue in the years 1435–1440.

127

THE DEVONSHIRE HUNTING TAPESTRIES
Arras (?), mid-15th century
Wool
The Boar and Bear Hunt
13½ ft. × 32½ ft.

The *Devonshire Hunting Tapestries* (Victoria and Albert Museum, London) also show common features with the "reference hanging" of *SS. Piatus and Eleutherius*. They consist of four pieces of unusual size (c. 13 × 33 ft.): the *Boar and Bear Hunt*, the *Otter and Swan Hunt*, *Falconry*, and the *Deer Hunt*. W.G. Thomson has suggested that these tapestries may have been woven for the marriage in 1445 of Margaret of Anjou (daughter of King René) and Henry VI of England, which would explain their presence in England. This view has been contested by G. Wingfield Digby and Wendy Hefford.

Hunting scenes were frequently represented at this period. Jean Walois in particular owned many fine designs on this theme. In 1413–1415 he supplied John the Fearless with a "high-warp tapestry with figures engaged in hunting"; in 1416 he supplied Duke John of Touraine and his wife Jacqueline of Bavaria with "a chamber wrought with a deer hunt and a boar hunt"; in 1428–1429 Philip the Good ordered from him "a chamber with a bear hunt"; finally, in 1434–1435, he received payment for "a chamber decorated with a bear hunt" offered by Philip the Good to his brother the Duke of Gelderland. So it is generally assumed that this well-known merchant, Jean Walois, played a leading part in the commissioning of the Devonshire tapestries.

These pieces, however, were long attributed to the Tournai workshops. Dora Heinz and Madeleine Jarry saw in them "one of the finest examples... of the early Tournai style still very much under the influence of Arras work." But this was to go "strangely beyond any permissible supposition" (Jean Lestocquoy), for no documents relating to the Tournai industry make any mention of hunting scenes, whereas the Arras records abound in references to them. Moreover the Tournai workshops were at the time undeveloped, and one cannot see any reason why Jean Walois, presumably the "promoter" of these hangings, should have applied to the Tournai weavers rather than those of Arras, who were at hand and better prepared to cope with so large a project. According to Marthe Crick-Kuntziger, the presence on the ground in the *Boar and Bear Hunt* of "kidney-shaped flints," common in the Arras region but unusual around Tournai, would warrant the assumption that both cartoons and tapestries were made at Arras.

Who supplied the cartoons, is difficult to say. All students agree that the *Devonshire Hunting Tapestries* show some striking analogies with the *Livre de la Chasse* of Gaston Phébus, dating to around 1370. But it has been pointed out that they are also related to certain miniatures in the *Très Riches Heures du duc de Berry*, illuminated about 1415 by the Limbourg brothers (one notes in particular the continuous tree frieze overlapped by castle towers and roofs), as well as to Melchior Broederlam's *Champmol Altarpiece* in Dijon (the figure of St Joseph, the stylized rocks, the trees and landscape recall certain parts of the *Otter and Swan Hunt*).

G. Wingfield Digby and Wendy Hefford have pointed out significant differences of colouring and weaving in the four Devonshire pieces. In their view the *Boar and Bear Hunt* (the earliest piece) and the *Deer Hunt* (the latest) are of inferior workmanship to the other two, and the *Otter and Swan Hunt* differs from *Falconry* by its more emphatic outlines and the use of crimson and wine-red tones. It is possible, as these scholars suggest, that the Devonshire tapestries actually belong to several successive sets of the same hanging. It may also be surmised, however, that they were simply woven in different workshops, or in the same workshop by different groups of weavers, for the weaving of these four pieces is known to have spanned some fifteen years, from 1430 to 1445. From the reversing of certain motifs in the *Boar and Bear Hunt*, Digby and Hefford have inferred that this piece may have been woven in low warp. But, as Julien Coffinet notes, these reversals are only to be found on the right side of the tapestry; better, then, to assume the existence of a design grouping "two series of separate hunts, one of which, for reasons of balance in the composition, must have been reversed."

When did the Arras workshops cease production? This question gave rise to some lively controversy in the late nineteenth century between two scholars of Arras,

Adolphe Guesnon and Eugène Van Drival. The former maintained that the tapestry industry there had begun declining in 1460 and that the siege of 1477 put an end to it. "For a time," wrote Guesnon, "Arras had no more cloth trade, no more serges, no more weavers; Louis XI had swept them away. This may be said to have been the *coup de grâce* for Arras manufacturing. It was extinct, so completely, that when reorganization began the king did not even attempt to revive it." For Guesnon, then, the Arras production had continued down to 1460. Jean Lestocquoy has shown that the latter's view, though inexact on some points, is probably close to the truth. The decline of Arras apparently began well before 1460, for in 1426 the municipal magistrates were already complaining about the departure of "serge and high-warp merchants and workmen" for "other towns like Valenciennes, Tournai, Bergues and others." And in 1449 it was the Tournai workshops, not those of Arras, that were engaged to weave one of the most sumptuous tapestries of the period, the *Story of St Gideon*. The siege of 1477 can hardly have been as fatal to the Arras industry as Guesnon supposed. After a lull of about two decades the Arras weavers appear to have resumed work under the abbacies of Jacques de Kerles (1497–1508) and Martin Asset (1508–1537), for a revival of art work is traceable to the abbey of Saint-Vaast in the early sixteenth century. Jean Lestocqoy categorically states that weaving was still being done at Arras in 1528.

The fact is that the decline of Arras seems to be connected with the rise of high-warp weaving in the Tournai region. Was it the prosperity of Tournai that caused the decline of the Arras industry, or was it the latter's decline that favoured the development of the Tournai workshops? There can as yet be no definite answer to these questions. It has been established that members of the same family, of the Sarrazin or the Molin families for example, were sometimes active concurrently in both towns; further research will no doubt bring to light more evidence of this kind. But the reasons for such emigration are unexplained. The fact that in 1423 the Tournai weavers obtained a "banner" consecrating the autonomy of their craft may have promoted this movement. Yet it would seem that there must have been "negative" reasons inciting the Arras weavers to emigrate well before 1477. Had competition become too strong or were the regulations of the profession too cramping? Was it a migration carried out in conjunction with the powerful merchants of the region intent on extending their business beyond the frontiers of Artois? Or was it the consequence of a decision handed down by the royal power? Historians of tapestry weaving may one day come to grips with these questions.

THE DEVONSHIRE HUNTING TAPESTRIES
Arras (?), mid-15th century
Wool
The Otter and Swan Hunt (detail)
Overall size: 14 ft. × 38 ft.

Tournai

Less than ten high-warp weavers seem to have been at work at Tournai during the latter half of the fourteenth century. In a standard work on the subject (*Les tapisseries de Tournai*, 1892), E.J. Soil de Moriane numbered five, about the same as in Paris and Arras, at the end of the thirteenth century. We have no precise information about the rise of the tapestry industry in the Tournai region. It therefore seems rash to state that "the history of Tournai tapestry reproduces that of Paris and Arras with a time-lag of thirty or fifty years" (Jean Lestocquoy). True, it is generally assumed that at both Tournai and Arras, with a by-effect in Paris, the high-warp workshops came into existence to counteract the decline of the cloth industry. But how to account for a time-lag of several decades? One cannot exclude the possibility that, after restoring the situation in Arras, some capitalists of that town–descendants perhaps of those originally responsible for the rise of Arras–may have undertaken to extend the field of their activities and promote the development of tapestry workshops where circumstances seemed favourable to it.

Two documents relating to the manufacture of "carpets" and "shaggy woollens" show that at Tournai, in the late fourteenth century, there existed a production comparable to what had been done in Paris for a century past by the "Saracen tapicers" or low-warp weavers. One may therefore wonder whether, like their Parisian confrères, the first Tournai high-warpers had to submit to the yoke of these low-warpers who were afraid of being supplanted by a new "manner of workmen." One might suppose so from an ordinance of 1397 concerning the "trade and wares of high-warp tapestry and shaggy woollens." Another document regulating the manufacture of "so-called high-warp cloths" shows that at Tournai in 1408, as in Paris in 1303, high-warp was still an unfamiliar technique. As Jean Lestocquoy has noted, these "cloths" were actually long strips measuring about thirty-eight Tournai ells in length by three quarters and a half wide (i.e. 82 by 2 feet)–dimensions in no way comparable to those of the figured tapestries woven in Paris and Arras at the same period. Things must have changed in the next fifteen years, for in 1423 the high-warp weavers separated from the makers of "shaggy woollens." Who were the latter, and since when and why were the high-warpers associated with them to form an independent guild with its own "banner," authorized to hold its own patronal festival?

All scholars are agreed in thinking that Philip the Good gave a decisive impulse to the Tournai workshops, when in 1449 he ordered one of the most sumptuous tapestries ever woven, the *Story of St Gideon* (now lost), intended to adorn the enclosure where the knights of the Order of the Golden Fleece met once a year. According to Jean Lestocquoy, the affair was negotiated on the duke's behalf by a man of Arras, Jean Aubry. The cartoons of the eight pieces each measured about 50 by 16 feet. They were entrusted to Bauduin de Bailleul, head of an Arras workshop which specialized in making designs of all sorts, for sculpture, goldsmith's work, stained glass, copper and so on. This workshop is famous, for it is the only one of the period of which any trace remains. But little or nothing is known

THE STORY OF
THE SWAN KNIGHT
Tournai, mid-15th century
Tapestry
The Knight Elias and his
Brothers Turned into
Swans (fragment)

about how it operated or what its relations were with the workshops employed to transcribe the small designs or models.

The eight pieces of this immense *St Gideon* set were woven by two "merchant workmen of tapestry" of Tournai: Robert Dary and Jehan de L'Ortye. It is surprising that a work of such scope was not executed at Arras, all the more so since the designs were made there and the middle-man negotiating the affair was a native of Arras. It may be that Dary and L'Ortye were chosen "simply because their workshops had some idle looms and... available labour" (Julien Coffinet). If this were so, no significant value could be attached to the commission. From the prestigious character of the hanging, however, it seems more likely that Dary and L'Ortye were chosen for their skill. While the *St Gideon* hanging seems to have brought the Tournai workshops "the recognition they had lacked" (R.A. Weigert), one must also remember that it was the fruit of close collaboration with Arras. The two towns seem to have had close connections in the 1440s. In 1446 Guillaume au Vaissel of Arras supplied Philip the Good with a tapestry intended to complete a chamber "worked with several figures and devices of children going to school" which "my lord has had taken and purchased from Jehenne Patequin... widow of the late Jehan Baubrée residing at Tournai." In 1449 the abbot of St Vaast at Arras applied to Guillaume au Vaissel for the making of a *Resurrection* from designs "on canvas coloured in tempera" supplied by the painter Jacques Daret, a former pupil of the Tournai master Robert Campin.

From 1450 on, one name dominates the history of Tournai tapestry weaving, that of Pasquier Grenier. Like the Cossets, Walois and Bernarts at Arras, Pasquier Grenier was a merchant, a broker in tapestries and wines, who in pursuit of his various concerns had branch-offices in several towns (at Bruges and Guise in particular). He also took part in the town administration at Tournai, occasionally acting as ambassador. Described in 1449 as *marcheteur* or merchant, Pasquier Grenier was not a weaver. Like his counterpart at Arras, Jean Walois, he nevertheless owned a large number of designs, which shortly before his death he bequeathed to his children, "to be divided among them equally." One of the first commissions given to Pasquier Grenier by the Duke of Burgundy was for the *Story of the Swan Knight* (remaining fragments in Wawel Castle, Cracow, and the Museum für angewandte Kunst, Vienna). Probably woven between 1454 and 1462, it was intended, together with a *Story of Esther and Ahasuerus*, for the "Cardinal of Arras," Bishop Jean de Jouffroy. Its execution is thought to have followed the performance of a poem by the same name, which took place at the famous *Vœu du Faisan* (Vow of the Pheasant) held at Lille in 1454. Most scholars agree in assigning the *Story of the Swan Knight* to Tournai. Marthe Crick-Kuntziger surmises that the designs may have been supplied by Robert Campin, the probable initiator "of that so homogeneous style, so curiously tinged with archaism," which we find in many hangings of this period; or if not Campin, then one of his pupils, Jacques Daret or perhaps Henri de Beaumetiel. Some inscriptions in the Tournai dialect would confirm this hypothesis. But Jean Lestocquoy thinks the designer may have been Bauduin de Bailleul (died 1464).

In 1459 Pasquier Grenier sold to Philip the Good a *Story of Alexander* heightened with silk and with gold and silver Cyprus thread; it comprised six wall hangings and several other small pieces, including a canopy, a dossal, a cover and several valances. Only two pieces are extant (Palazzo Doria, Rome), and it took many years before they could be identified with the purchase made by the Duke of Burgundy; the identification had been rejected, from the apparent lack of the gold thread mentioned in the deed of sale, but Marthe Crick-Kuntziger has shown that the gold is there all right, however tarnished. The subjects seem to have been taken from the *Livre des conquestes et faicts d'Alexandre le Grand* compiled by Jean Wauquelin for the Comte d'Estampes, a book much appreciated at the court of Burgundy, where flattering parallels were read into it, and also abroad, for in January of the same year, 1459, the Duke of Milan, Francesco Sforza, summoned to his court Guillaume, son of the late Jean, and Melchior, son of Pasquier "de Garneriis," both of Tournai in Picardy, "*causa portandi et ostendendi certum disegnum regis Alexandri et certas alias tapezarias.*"

THE STORY OF THE SWAN KNIGHT
Tournai, mid-15th century
Tapestry (fragment)

THE TROJAN WAR
Tournai, 1475–1490
Wool and silk
13½ ft. × 24 ft.

THE TROJAN WAR
Tapestry cartoon, perhaps by Henri de Vulcop
Later 15th century
Pen and ink, heightened
with watercolour and wash

132

The two *Alexander* hangings in the Palazzo Doria have been connected with several drawings (British Museum, London, and Historisches Museum, Berne), so closely related to the hangings in style, composition and clothing details that they are thought to be either preliminary drawings for them or contemporary copies of them. According to J.P. Asselberghs, a fragment of a drawing in the British Museum would prefigure the extreme left side of a tapestry in the Petit Palais, Paris (Dutuit Collection), "technically so close to the Tournai tapestries of the *Trojan War* that it presumably came from the same workshops." This piece and another, *Alexander Accepting the Submission of the Kings of Cappadocia, Cyprus and Phoenicia* (Burrell Collection, Glasgow), may both belong to a later version, adjusted to the taste of the day, of the hanging delivered to Philip the Good. Also attributed to Tournai is a hanging of the *Seven Sacraments* (several fragments in the Metropolitan Museum, New York, the Victoria and Albert Museum, London, and the Burrell Collection, Glasgow). This hanging originally comprised fourteen scenes set out in two superimposed rows: above, Old Testament prefigurations of the sacraments; below, the seven sacraments.

These *Seven Sacraments* fragments have been successively connected with a *Story of the Sacrament* purchased in Brussels in 1440 by Philip the Good for his son Charles (G.L. Hunter, 1925); with a donation made in 1475 by Pasquier Grenier and his wife to the church of St Quentin in Tournai (Paul Rolland, 1936); and with "another tapestry of the VII sacraments of Holy Church figured according to the Old Testament and the New [which] we have made at this place" (i.e. at Tournai), bequeathed in 1458 by Jean Chevrot, Bishop of Tournai, to the collegiate church at Poligny, his native town (L. Fourez, 1954). Fin-

ally, a Spanish art historian, F.J. Sánchez Cantón, has suggested that these fragments may be the remnants of "another large cloth of wool and silk which is of the seven sacraments" thus listed in 1503 in the inventory of Isabella the Catholic and purchased in 1871 by the painter Mariano Fortuny from the chapter of the Capilla Real in Granada. While it is impossible to give any definite answers, we may at least assume, with J.P. Asselberghs, that apart from the hanging purchased by the Duke of Burgundy for his son, these tapestries probably have a common origin. William Wells has connected this hanging with several orphreys (Historisches Museum, Berne) and with the *Altarpiece of the Seven Sacraments* (Antwerp) painted by Rogier van der Weyden for Jean Chevrot, Bishop of Tournai. Other scholars–Friedrich Winkler, Jakob Stammler and Micheline Sonkes–have pointed out analogies with several prints in the Ashmolean Museum, Oxford, and with two drawings in the Louvre by painters schooled in the tradition of Rogier van der Weyden.

The foregoing hangings have some points in common with the *Justice of Trajan and Herkinbald* (Historisches Museum, Berne). This tapestry was based on two pictures by Rogier van der Weyden painted at two different times for the Brussels Town Hall; the pictures were destroyed in 1695 in the bombardment of the town by the French under Maréchal Villeroi. The description of them given by Dubuisson-Aubenay in his *Itinerarium Belgicum* (1623–1627) shows that the copying was very approximate. The subject is a tribute to two just judges. On the left, the Emperor Trajan executes one of his soldiers who had killed the only son of a poor widow. The rest of the story relates to events long after Trajan's death: Pope Gregory the Great, kneeling at the altar of St Peter's, prays to God for the salvation of the pagan emperor; in another scene he

THE JUSTICE OF TRAJAN AND HERKINBALD
AFTER ROGIER VAN DER WEYDEN
Tournai, c. 1460
Gold and silk thread
15 ft. × 34½ ft.

contemplates the skull of Trajan, whose tongue, the instrument of just judgment, has been miraculously preserved. In the two other scenes, Herkinbald (i.e. Archambault, Count of Bourbon), on his death bed, slays his own nephew for raping a maid of honour; his bishop refuses to administer the last sacrament, but the Host is miraculously conveyed to his mouth.

This *Justice* hanging seems to have belonged to Georges de Saluces, Bishop of Lausanne from 1439 to 1461 (the year of his death); but it is not certain that it was made for him, inasmuch as his arms are sewn on, not woven. Anyhow the *Justice of Trajan and Herkinbald* cannot have been woven before 1455, when Rogier van der Weyden finished his picture of the *Justice of Archambault*. Though illustrating very different subjects, the *Swan Knight*, the *Seven Sacraments* and the *Justice of Trajan and Herkinbald* all have a composition of great clarity, contrasting with the almost inextricable disorder of several battle scenes, with their tangle of horses and knights in gorgeous armour: the *Story of the Mighty King Clovis*, the *Story of Caesar*, the *Story of Charlemagne*, the *Capture of Jerusalem*, the *Story of Hercules*.

One of the most spectacular of these involved hangings is the *Story of Caesar* (Historisches Museum, Berne). It is believed by R.L. Wyss to have been commissioned by Charles the Bold around 1465–1470, while Jakob Stammler and J.P. Asselberghs regard it as one of the tapestries confiscated by Charles after the beheading of King Louis of Luxembourg, Count of St Pol and High Constable of France, convicted of treason by Louis XI. In any case, it seems to be closely connected with a manuscript of about 1453, the *Privilèges de Gand et de Flandres*.

The *Story of the Mighty King Clovis* (Musée de l'Œuvre Notre-Dame, Reims) reflects the same aesthetic. Only two fragments of this hanging survive; it consisted originally of six pieces. The person of King Clovis here has been equated with King Charles VII of France, but this hypothesis is unproven.

Probably made for Philip the Good between 1465 and 1467, the *Capture of Jerusalem* (Notre-Dame de Nantilly, Saumur) also belongs to the cycle of great battle scenes. Inspired by the apocryphal legend of the *Acta Pilati* and the *Jewish Antiquities* of Flavius Josephus, it illustrates the battle between the besieging troops of Titus and the defenders of Jerusalem (in 70 A.D.).

The same involved composition recurs in the *Battle of Roncesvalles* (remnants in the Musée d'Histoire et d'Archéologie, Tournai, the Victoria and Albert Museum, London, Museo del Bargello, Florence, Musées Royaux d'Art et d'Histoire, Brussels, and private collections). These pieces have been connected by J.P. Asselberghs with part of a *Story of Charlemagne* (Musée des Beaux-Arts, Dijon). He has shown that both probably belonged to two versions of the same hanging: "greater vigour in the colouring" points to the more "original" character of the Florence and Brussels fragments, while the antecedence of the London and Tournai fragments is indicated by sharper relief, more delicate shades of colour, and the presence of a transparent cloth badge surmounting Roland's helmet.

Of all the warrior hangings attributed to Tournai, the most famous is the *Trojan War*. Not only is it the only Gothic hanging for which we have the designs; it is also one of those with the largest number of surviving pieces. Inspired by a long poem of the twelfth century by Benoît de Sainte-More, the *Romance of Troy*, this tapestry was very popular in the fifteenth century; at least four versions

of it are known to have been made in less than half a century, and there were probably more. According to J.P. Asselberghs, the original work may have been offered by the town of Bourges to Charles the Bold and Margaret of York in 1472. Nicole Reynaud thinks it was originally commissioned about 1465 by Charles VII, younger brother of Louis XI; after his death, the hanging–i.e. the remnants in the Victoria and Albert Museum, London–would have passed to the king, then to Charles VIII, who would have "removed the armorial bearings" and replaced them with "a sun in each piece." Contrary to the assumption of J.P. Asselberghs, Charles VIII then would not have been the initial purchaser of a hanging executed between 1489 and 1493. Anyhow at least two versions are thought to have been made between 1472 and 1484: one for Ferdinand of Naples, the other for Matthias Corvinus, King of Hungary (1458–1490). Another "istorye of Troyes" –perhaps the last of the series–was delivered to Henry VII of England in 1488.

Of these various hangings, there survive today four pieces at Zamora (Cathedral of Holy Saviour), one in London (Victoria and Albert Museum), one in Madrid (Collection of the Duke of Berwick and Alba), and further fragments, some of fair size, in New York, Boston, Montreal, Worcester, Glasgow and Paris. In his remarkable study of them, J.P. Asselberghs has shown that each set consisted of eleven tapestries, each 15¾ feet high by 31 feet in length. For the known hangings as a whole, this would

THE STORY OF JULIUS CAESAR
Tournai (?), c. 1465-1470
Silk thread
The Crossing of the Rubicon (left side)
Overall size: 14 ft. × 25 ft.

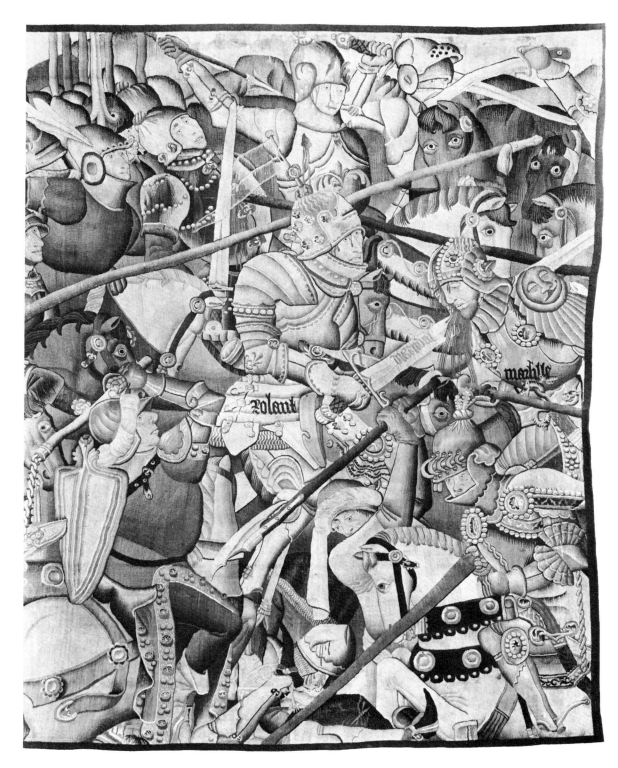

The Battle of Roncevalles (fragment)
Tournai, c. 1450–1475
Wool and silk

represent "the work of about ten weavers using three or four looms over a period of thirty years" (Julien Coffinet). So it is not surprising to find discrepancies in the pieces and fragments that survive. "While it is true that all the tapestries have the same texture (6 to 7 threads per centimetre), that the same colours with buff and red dominants are employed, that the figures wear the same clothes and have the same expressions..., some differences do exist: they are to be found within one and the same hanging as well as from one hanging to another" (J.P. Asselberghs). Thus the colours, the reds in particular, and the treatment of hatchings sometimes differ quite noticeably. Some of the tapestries, rather "stiffer" than others, betray a more laborious execution. The piece in the Victoria and Albert Museum

is "technically and stylistically the feeblest" (J.P. Asselberghs). These differences are understandable, given the size and number of the hangings. They are due to the diversity of the workshops concerned. No single workshop, however large, could have coped with the weaving over many decades of so many thousand square feet of tapestry. A more delicate point is deciding whether one or several centres attended to the work. At that time, according to Asselberghs and Coffinet, only Tournai "met the conditions necessary to undertake and successfully carry through a work of this scope." Jean Lestocquoy assumes on the contrary that several centres must have been involved, not only Tournai, but also Lille, Douai, Valenciennes and Saint-Omer. The *Trojan War* tapestries are of keen

135

THE BATTLE OF RONCEVALLES
Tournai, c. 1450-1475
Wool and silk
5'4" × 18'8"

interest to art historians because of the fact that eight designs for them have come down to us (Louvre): their survival is unique in the history of medieval tapestry. While several extant drawings (Berne and Lyons) relating to the *Story of Alexander* were probably used as tapestry designs, no trace of the actual tapestry remains.

These small drawings are executed in pen and brown ink, heightened with watercolour and touches of wash. Their provenance has been much discussed. In a study remarkable for its fine scholarship, Nicole Reynaud has demonstrated that the Louvre drawings were probably the work of one Henri de Vulcop, painter to the Queen of Anjou, wife of Charles VII, then of Charles of France, brother of Louis XI. "At the cost of some compositional artifices," Vulcop contrived to make of tapestry "a place like the panel or the book in which to set forth with coherence and continuity" some original solutions to the problems being raised at the same period by a Fouquet or a Master of King René. "The qualities peculiar to himself are best revealed in the artist's overall layout. In keeping with the principle of *horror vacui* which governed tapestries of the third quarter of the fifteenth century, his battles are not only massive and intricate mêlées, but are distinguished from other battle scenes in contemporary tapestry by their tumult and movement. In them one recognizes a true history painter, gifted not for epic grandeur like Fouquet, but for narration and action. And with a highly personal sense of decorative styling, he knows how to ease the impact of these masses of bodies and helmets by a subtly

calculated interplay of bristling lances and coiling oriflammes which with him play an essential part." The *Trojan War*, for Nicole Reynaud, marks "a forward leap" with respect to the hangings of the previous generation, such as the *Justice of Trajan and Herkinbald*, the *Story of Julius Caesar*, the *Story of St Peter* or the *Story of Jephtha*. "The seething life, the realism and deliberate variety of attitudes and expressions, strike a sharp contrast with the immobility of the composition, the stiff uprightness of the figures, and the stylized hieraticism of the great previous series."

So far as we can tell, the *Trojan War* tapestries kept closely to the preparatory designs. Some differences can of course be noted, but they "lie chiefly in the elaborate ornamentation of the fabrics, in the adding of cloaks and caparisons, of embellishments in the architecture and small flowers in the foreground, sometimes in the lengthening of the figures." Such differences do not affect the overall composition, "the fancifulness of armour and clothing, the attitudes and gestures, the very peculiar expressions." According to Julien Coffinet, it was by no means "the general custom" to keep so closely to the design, and the care taken with the Troy tapestries would be accounted for by the rank of the patrons, the importance of the painter and "a conscious effort at closer collaboration between painters and weavers." Here one may be "in the presence of the first deliberate attempt to replace the weavers' independence by subordination to the painters, an attempt presumably made with the assent of the weavers" (Julien Coffinet). This statement cannot be accepted without reserves: how indeed are we to appreciate the importance of the *Trojan War* when it is the only Gothic hanging whose designs have come down to us?

A *Passion* hanging (Musées Royaux d'Art et d'Histoire, Brussels) is also attributed to Tournai, though a Brussels origin is sometimes surmised. According to Marthe Crick-Kuntziger, the weaving of this piece would seem to connect it with the *Story of the Mighty King Clovis*, and its design would connect it with the *Story of St Peter* (Beauvais Cathedral). Presented to the cathedral in 1464 by Bishop Guillaume de Hellande, this last-named hanging made in Tournai has been related by Geneviève Souchal to a painted *Crucifixion of St Peter* on the left wing of an altarpiece in the Metropolitan Museum, New York, attributed by Charles Sterling to a "painter of the school of Picardy strongly influenced by Rogier van der Weyden"; also to a little known tapestry, the *Judgment of the House of Ahab* (Isabella Stewart Gardner Museum, Boston).

EPISODES FROM THE PASSION (FRAGMENT)
Tournai (?), c. 1475
Tapestry
Overall size: 14 ft. × 30 ft.

Another group of tapestries on country themes also seems to originate from the Tournai workshops. Among the best known are the *Grape Harvests* (Burrell Collection, Glasgow), the *Woodcutters* (Musée des Arts Décoratifs, Paris) and *Sheepshearing* (Musées Royaux d'Art et d'Histoire, Brussels). These pieces are characterized by "calm and simple workmanship, with no particular research" (Julien Coffinet), and so they have nothing in common with the showiness of the martial and religious scenes evoked above.

The fact is that, from all the tapestries referred to so far, and many others as well, it seems difficult to single out any well-defined "Tournai style" recognizable in both design and weaving. Yet some scholars have ventured to do so, putting the emphasis now on the composition, now on the procedures of transcription. According to Marthe Crick-Kuntziger, most of the hangings discussed here (*Story of the Swan Knight, Story of Alexander, The Seven Sacraments, Justice of Trajan and Herkinbald, Story of the Mighty King Clovis, Story of Charlemagne, Story of Hercules, The Passion, Story of St Peter*–but not apparently the *Trojan War* and the *Vengeance of Our Lord*) would seem to come from "a very homogeneous group of designers" working at Tournai around the middle of the fifteenth century. It is true that these hangings present some similarities of composition: a crowding together of richly clad figures over practically the whole surface of the tapestry, an all but total absence of sky and landscape, and plant life less schematic than in earlier works. But can this be said to amount to a style peculiar to Tournai? No monopoly was held by the painters' workshops located at Tournai; that of Robert Campin and his pupils is generally cited, but it was certainly not the only one. The workshop of Bauduin de Bailleul was still active at Arras, and it is reasonable to suppose, given the abundant output of the period, that other painters working in northern France and elsewhere (in Brussels perhaps) were also catering for princes and merchants.

From a study of the weaving, not the design, Guillaume Janneau has pointed out a procedure peculiar to the Tournai workshops. It consists in "heightening the intensity of a local tone by a bright reflection and a muted brown... The Tournai tapestry maker noticed that a highly saturated blue, even over an extended surface, is less blue than it becomes when aroused by a dark purple area of the right size. Then the eye no longer perceives the secondary tonality, which the blue reabsorbs in its irradiation. If the quality of the two colours is well proportioned, one goes to stimulate the other and heightens its splendour. Does the weaver need to brighten up a local red at one point? No longer is it enough for him to weaken the hanging: from another body of colours he takes a yellow which he 'lays in' at the right place. It is not a question here of adjusting a complementary tone to a dominant tone; the effect of these two would be to neutralize each other. Clashes of colour are what the weaver aims at, not fusions. Thus the complementary tonality of the blue is quite remote from this brown purple: it is yellow. What the weaver wants is not to reconstitute the state of achromatism, but on the contrary to separate the vibrations whose conflict excites the constituent colours." But, as Janneau admits, this technique would seem to have remained "experimental"; its practitioners had only "a rough idea of its resources." It was apparently combined with another technique, originating at Arras, which consisted in rendering modelling by a gradation of tones–"that is to say... by the reciprocal re-entry of the brights and browns employed as hatching."

There was more than one high-warp workshop at Tournai, and one may readily suppose that they did not all apply the same techniques. As already pointed out, the quality of the weaving (fineness and regularity of the stitch) and the choice and scheme of the colours may vary considerably from one hanging to another. The extent of these differences is such that one may wonder whether

THE WOODCUTTERS (FRAGMENT)
Tournai, c. 1450-1475
Silk thread
Overall size: 10½ ft. × 16¾ ft.

SHEEPSHEARING
Tournai (?), c. 1475
Silk thread
5'5" × 7'4"

certain tapestries from peripheral centres of less importance, like Lille, Bruges, Antwerp and Oudenarde, have not been wrongly attributed to Tournai. Can diversity have been peculiar to the Tournai workshops?

According to Julien Coffinet, these painters and tapestry makers were jointly intent on "breaking with tradition." While his analysis has the merit of emphasizing the evolution of the relations between painters and weavers, it is, again, by no means certain that it applies specifically to the Tournai tapestries. For lack of information about other centres, too much has probably been made of Tournai. Further research may help to put things in the right perspective.

We are no better informed about the reasons for the decline of the Tournai workshops. Weaving was still being done there at the beginning of the sixteenth century, a decade or so after the death of Pasquier Grenier, but it is difficult to say how much longer it continued, and above all to what extent. Dramatic events shook the town at the dawn of the Renaissance. In 1513 Tournai escaped from French domination and became an English possession. Sold back to François I in 1517 by Henry VIII, the town was captured in 1521 by the Emperor Charles V, who there promulgated his fierce edict against the Reforma-

tion. The persecutions that followed, combined with a terrible epidemic, had disastrous consequences for all the arts and crafts. It is not certain, however, that these events alone account for the decline of the Tournai tapestry industry. For in the second half of the fifteenth century the workshops seem to have benefited in turn from the rise of other tapestry centres, notably in the Scheldt basin at Lille, Oudenarde, Ghent, Enghien, Louvain, Malines, Saint-Trond, Herenthals, Antwerp, Bruges and Brussels. In 1454 Gierozzo de' Pigli, the Medici representative in Bruges, wrote to Florence that the most skilful tapestry weaver in the Low Countries, *"Il sommo dei maestri,"* was a man of Lille. In 1461 the weavers of Ghent informed the municipal magistrate that Louvain and Bruges were the most prosperous centres of the tapestry industry.

In view of these facts, one cannot help wondering whether, over the past century, the importance of Tournai may not have been overestimated. Further research might well reveal that the decline of the Arras workshops was not in fact followed, as so often assumed, by a "refocusing" of activity at Tournai, but by a splintering into various centres of production, carried out at the prompting of some of the great merchants and high magistrates of the towns concerned.

BRUSSELS

To Sophie Schneebalg-Perelman goes the credit for throwing light on the Brussels tapestry industry and clarifying its history, much neglected since the late nineteenth century. What happened was this. The standard work (*Histoire générale de la tapisserie*, Paris, 1878–1885) had been divided into three parts, Jules Guiffrey writing the volume on French tapestries, Eugène Müntz the one on Italian tapestries and Alexandre Pinchart the one on Flemish tapestries. Unfortunately Pinchart died before he had written an essential chapter of his volume, the one on Brussels. Guiffrey took over and wrote the chapter, basing himself not on Pinchart's notes but on the recent book of Alphonse Wauters (*Tapisseries bruxelloises*, Brussels, 1878), which had remained very incomplete.

In her thesis and a series of articles which break new ground, Sophie Schneebalg-Perelman has shown that weaving was practised in Brussels as early as the mid-fourteenth century, while hitherto its origins there had not been traced back beyond the late fifteenth century: "An irrefutable source, the accounts of the Dukes of Brabant, proves that from 1366 these princes were patronizing the Brussels workshops and provides us with the names of some fifteen tapestry makers of the fourteenth century." Their output was considerable, so much so that John of St Pol, Duke of Brabant, lent "several hangings" to his uncle John the Fearless for a diplomatic meeting held at Lille in 1415. Examination of the archives suggests, however, that these were "rather primitive," unhistoriated works, comparable in make and price to those of Arras at the same period.

An important document published in 1912 by J. Cuvelier (*Registre aux statuts, ordonnances et admissions du métier des tisserands de laine ou grand-métier de Bruxelles*) shows that for the period 1418–1446 "the total number of tapestry makers enrolled comes to nearly 500." Their mobility may be inferred from the fact, noted by Sophie Schneebalg-Perelman, that the names of some of them indicate that they originated from Picardy or Tournai. As at Arras and Tournai, the tapestry industry arose in connection with cloth-making. Brussels cloth at its height, in 1358, was esteemed by the princely courts as one of the best, for it was commonly known, according to R.H. Bautier, as "the cloth of kings." But in the third quarter of the fourteenth century it began losing this commercial predominance and by about 1390 had disappeared. There seem to be several reasons for this decline, connected first of all with the movements of fashion. Besides the competition of silks, brocades, satins and taffetas, the taste of the wealthy clientele seems to have shifted towards the darker colours characteristic of English and Norman textiles. To these initial causes may be added apparently the scarcity of raw material (English wool) and a loss of quality in the labour available.

The Brabantine weavers are to be found dispersed in England, Germany and throughout Italy, "but one may have doubts about the quality of the luxury stuffs thus manufactured by needy weavers without qualification thereby saved from beggary. The great cloth-making industry was doomed beyond recall" (R.H. Bautier). But while the de luxe woollen cloth industry disappeared, this did not mean the end of all weaving activities. In addition to cheap cloth-weaving which continued throughout the fifteenth and part of the sixteenth century, catering for the markets of central and eastern Europe, the carpet and tapestry industry enjoyed a vigorous growth thanks to the combined skill of weavers and dyers. One may even say that, in Brussels, it was not the extinction of cloth making which brought about the reconversion to another luxury industry, tapestry making. On the contrary, it was the political factors, in particular the accession of Philip the Good to the throne of the Dukes of Brabant in 1430, which by stimulating all artistic activities in Brussels hastened this reconversion, by reason of the high profits to be drawn from the weaving of tapestries. This rapid growth is further evidenced by the fact that the tapestry makers' guild, after being detached from that of the linen weavers in 1418 and closely associated with the wool guild, acquired an independent status in 1447.

The court of Burgundy attracted many artists. "This was the period when the sculptors of Brussels exported their famous carved and polychromed altarpieces throughout Europe, when the architects were completing the tower of the prestigious Town Hall, when the Brussels

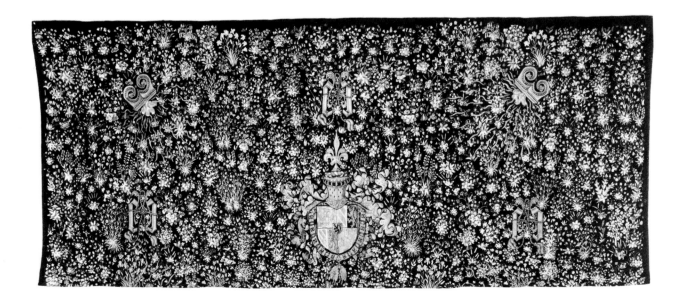

HANGING WITH THE ARMS OF BURGUNDY
Brussels, 1466
Silk, gold and silver thread
Overall size: 10 ft. × 22½ ft.
◁ Entire
▷ Detail

school of painting headed by the brilliant Rogier van der Weyden was inspiring all the painters of Western Europe" (Sophie Schneebalg-Perelman).

Benefiting from these favourable circumstances, the Brussels workshops were solicited by merchants from all over Europe, who supplied the Italian princes and the Pope, the patricians of Cologne, the princes of Spain, and the kings of England and Scotland. Fairs like those of Antwerp and Bergen op Zoom were then considered by the Brussels weavers as the natural outlet of their work. Associated with the tapestry makers of Louvain, Antwerp, Enghien and Ghent, they organized themselves in a merchant guild, the Guild of St Nicholas, and in 1481 hired the yard and galleries of the Dominican monastery in Antwerp as a warehouse for their merchandise. If, by the mid-fifteenth century, this activity achieved such great fame, one is entitled to ask why it remained so long unknown to modern inquirers, and how it is that pieces which may have originated in Brussels have been assigned to other centres.

In order to establish the origin of these tapestries, modern inquiry was for a long time based on analysis of the *Recette générale des finances de la chambre des Comptes de Lille* (Receivership of Finances of the Lille Audit Office), in which figure the purchases made by the Duke of Bur-

gundy, most of them from the tapestry merchants of Tournai. Further, "if the name of the Brussels tapestry makers is not mentioned more extensively, it is because, during the second half of the fifteenth century, up to about 1490, the trade in costly hangings was concentrated in the hands of several rich merchants of Bruges and Tournai who, at Bruges and at the Antwerp fairs, sold hangings woven in all the Netherlandish centres and who supplied all the courts of Europe" (Schneebalg-Perelman). The consequence is–added to the absence of any precise identification of the centres on the hangings themselves–that historians have been led to minimize the activity of other towns in the southern part of the Low Countries: Lille, Louvain and Brussels, for example.

One final cause of this neglect: the loss of the archives of the Trésor de l'Epargne (a treasury office set up by Philip the Good to "serve the private and immediate needs of the court"). These treasury parchments went "to the making of cartridge bags for the artillery of the Revolutionary army of 1793." The one remaining volume of these parchments, rediscovered by Sophie Schneebalg-Perelman, has luckily enabled her to assign to the Brussels workshops, beyond any question, a tapestry in an excellent state of preservation, the *Hanging with the Arms of Burgundy* (Historisches Museum, Berne): "The matter of this verdure,

141

the armorial bearings and mottos decorating it, all correspond to the detailed description of the work which Jean Le Haze, a tapestry maker in Brussels, supplied to Philip the Good in 1466." She has shown beyond doubt that these armorial bearings belong to Philip the Good, and not to Charles the Bold, as all historians had assumed, following Jules Guiffrey. This large piece, over 65 feet square, is of particular interest. Quite apart from its artistic quality, it throws new light on the importance of the Brussels workshops, on the origin of the Flemish verdures and consequently on the origin of one of the most famous pieces of this period: *La Dame à la licorne* or *Lady with the Unicorn*.

This important order given to Jean Le Haze is not the only one he filled, for he is known to have made "eight emblazoned hangings woven with gold and silver thread" and "a chamber with verdure tapestry sown with several foliage scrolls" for Philip the Good, and "four pieces of emblazoned tapestries and verdures" for Charles the Bold. These facts suggest that the Brussels tapestry makers could vie with those of Tournai. Furthermore, from the high

quality of the drawing in the *Hanging with the Arms of Burgundy*, together with the fineness of the weaving and its ground related to a millefleurs, one may infer that the Brussels weavers were past masters in the execution of this type of verdure. This inference is borne out by the ruling of a Brussels magistrate, dated 1476 and recording an agreement reached between the weavers and the painters of cartoons, following a complaint on the part of the latter: "The tapestry makers are authorized to design for each other, without remuneration, anything that may serve for the making of their verdures, that is to say leafage, trees, shrubbery, flowers, birds and other animals"—all the elements characteristic of the millefleurs in their most perfect version. Now these millefleurs hangings, most of which have come to light in France, have always been a matter of controversial attribution. The most interesting case is that of the best known among them: *La Dame à la licorne*.

This hanging was rediscovered by George Sand while it "was lying on the floor, gnawed by rats" (Sophie Schneebalg-Perelman), or in any case it attracted her attention after she saw it several times at the sub-prefect's in the town of Boussac (Alain Erlande-Brandenburg). After repeated efforts begun in 1841 by Prosper Mérimée, it was purchased by the French government in 1882 and placed in the Musée de Cluny in Paris, where it remains. When the *Lady with the Unicorn* set was exhibited at the Paris World's Fair of 1878 (when it was still the property of the Town Hall of Boussac), three of its pieces were attributed to Flanders. In 1882, when it was purchased by the French government, G. Gallier questioned both the traditional attribution to Turkey and the more recent one to Aubusson. The latter attribution was due to a mistake made by Jules Guiffrey, who confused the expression *"tapisserie à la marche"* (treadle tapestry, meaning simply low-warp tapestry), figuring in the 1422 inventory of Charles VI, with the name *"ateliers de la Marche"* (borderland workshops) given to the workshops in the Creuse department of central France, where Boussac is located. As a result of this confusion, Guiffrey assigned the *Lady with the Unicorn* set to the Aubusson manufactory (also located in the Creuse department). This view gained some credence from the fact that this series had been woven on a woollen warp, a traditional practice in the Creuse region; but this was not a telling argument, since Flemish tapestries followed the same practice.

In 1908 J.J. Marquet de Vasselot, keeper of the Musée de Cluny, suggested that the *Lady with the Unicorn* may have been made by itinerant French weavers. This suggestion was at once taken up by Jules Guiffrey, who saw evidence for it in the "French character" of these pieces and in the fact that cultural life had at that time been dispersed in Beaune, Tours, Moulins, Angers, Sens and Lyons–which would permit the assumption that weavers' workshops had been set up around castles and churches in response to local demand. This theory of itinerant weavers working in or near the Loire valley held the field for many years, for there was no evidence to contradict it; on the other hand, there was no sound evidence to support it.

Then, in 1926, Phyllis Ackerman challenged the existence of the Loire valley workshops and assigned the *Lady*

THE LADY WITH THE UNICORN
SIGHT (DETAIL)

with the Unicorn to Tournai. She was followed by W.G. Thomson in the 1930 edition of his *History of Tapestry*, and in 1947 Guillaume Janneau came to the same conclusion "concerning at least two pieces in the series." In 1954 Marthe Crick-Kuntziger suggested Bruges as the possible place of origin, on the strength of a resemblance between *Penelope*, a Netherlandish hanging, and the *Lady with the Unicorn*. One may also note the subsequent attribution to Moulins or the Bourbonnais made in the late 1950s by Pierre Verlet and Francis Salet.

How do matters stand today?

After a long and detailed stylistic analysis, Sophie Schneebalg-Perelman would attribute many millefleurs tapestries to the Low Countries as a whole, while adding: "We do not claim that all the verdure tapestries were

THE LADY WITH THE UNICORN
HEARING (DETAIL)

woven in Brussels, far from it. It is only the finest of them with their highly distinctive aspect, those that were designated by the name of millefleurs in the Loire valley, that we attribute to the Brussels workshops." And in a long article she demonstrates that the *Lady with the Unicorn* can only have been woven in Brussels. But in 1973, after passing the previous theories in review, Geneviève Souchal concluded: "In the prevailing uncertainty, it is no doubt wiser for the present to leave this problem in abeyance and be content with regrouping the works related by their style and execution, in the hope that further discoveries will permit scholars to reach well-founded conclusions." Lastly, in 1978, writing cautiously about the Brussels hypothesis, Alain Erlande-Brandenburg admits that "there is nothing unlikely about it, but it cannot be accepted with certainty until it is based on a document, and as yet we have none."

If the provenance of the *Lady with the Unicorn* has been a matter of controversy, so have its dating and the identity of its designer. Marthe Crick-Kuntziger has related it to two other hangings: the *Famous Women* (fragments in the Museum of Fine Arts, Boston) and the *Story of Perseus* (Private Collection). The first bears the coat of arms of Cardinal Ferry de Clugny and "of families who were related to him," and it shows several figures, including that of Penelope, whose type "both in the proportions and form of the torso and arms as well as in the face and costume and above all the very peculiar arrangement of the fair hair ending in a sort of aigrette, offers some striking analogies indeed with several figures in the *Lady with the Unicorn*." Likewise "the three long slender feminine fig-

THE LADY WITH THE UNICORN
Brussels (?), late 15th century
Tapestry
△ TOUCH (DETAIL)
◁ HEARING
▷ "TO MY ONE DESIRE"

144

ures [in the *Story of Perseus*] are exquisitely graceful and show at the same time the dignity and sovereign ease so striking in the *Lady with the Unicorn*, notably in the panel representing the *Lady with a Parakeet*." As regards Ferry de Clugny, he is known to have been made a cardinal on 15 May 1480 and to have died in Rome on 7 October 1483: so the *Famous Women* must have been woven between these two dates. Despite certain details of clothing (in particular "the presence of slashes in the sleeve of one of the figures") which point to a somewhat later fashion, one may therefore conclude that the *Lady with the Unicorn* was woven towards the end of the fifteenth century. From these stylistic parallels, one is naturally led to raise the question: who made the cartoons for the *Lady with the Unicorn*? Here again there is no shortage of theories.

While Phyllis Ackerman sees him as an "Antwerp master," Marthe Crick-Kuntziger identifies him as "a painter of cartoons... evolving in the wake of the House of Burgundy," Jennyn or Jan Fabiaen, whose designs would have been known to Ferry de Clugny. The views expressed by Sophie Schneebalg-Perelman have varied from time to time. In her thesis she referred to the "collaboration of a French painter." Then she advanced the names of Hans Memlinc and Gerard David. Finally, in 1969, she wrote: "After visiting Lyons it seemed to us that the painter must have been either of Flemish origin, transplanted to this region, as was the Master of Moulins, for example, or a French painter settled in Brussels." In 1976 she pronounced decidedly against the theory put forward in France by Nicole Reynaud and Geneviève Souchal in two elaborate

articles published in the *Revue de l'Art*. For Nicole Reynaud it seemed clear that a filiation should be established between Henri de Vulcop (of whom something has been said in previous chapters) and the Master of Anne of Brittany: "We know that these pattern books remained in the studio, at the disposal of the master and his workmen, and passed by succession to the heir of that studio... That heir..., who designed many stained-glass cartoons, including the rose window of the Sainte-Chapelle ordered by Charles VIII, was also a particularly gifted designer of tapestry cartoons. The most famous of these late fifteenth-century tapestries were woven from cartoons which are quite recognizable, despite apparent differences due to the transposition of the weaving as executed by weavers of different workshops: the *Hunt of the Unicorn*, *Perseus*, the series of *Famous Women*, the *Life of the Virgin* and no doubt also the *Lady with the Unicorn* in the Musée de Cluny and several millefleurs pieces." She bases her reasoning on the many similarities between "certain conventionalisms of Vulcop" and the soldiers in the *Life of the Virgin*; and she points out that a child in the *Hunt of the Unicorn* was borrowed from the initial design of the *Trojan War*. "It is certain," she adds, "that in a general way the Master of Anne of Brittany took over his characteristic figure types from Vulcop, contenting himself with lengthening the proportions in accordance with the canon prevailing at the end of the century, and then clothing them in the fashion of Charles VIII and Louis XII."

Geneviève Souchal, who first noticed the parallel between certain figures in the *Hunt of the Unicorn* and those in the *Trojan War*, refers in turn to this painter whom she

THE HUNT OF THE UNICORN
Brussels (?), late 15th century
Silk, wool, and silver and gilt silver thread
The Attack on the Unicorn Crossing the River (detail)

calls the Master of the Unicorn Hunt. She compares the themes and figures of the *Hunt of the Unicorn* to woodcuts such as the *Passion of Christ* and *St Margaret*, the windows originally adorning the chapel of the Hôtel (now Musée) de Cluny, and the western rose window of the Sainte-Chapelle. For her "this painter, more gifted for gracefulness than forcibleness, contrived on the basis of Vulcop's type of woman to create another, dreamy, measured and elegant, but moving with greater assurance in the world of youth and beauty than in that of ugliness and brutality." She lays emphasis on the duration of his influence, for she finds elements of his handling in the *Life of the Virgin* given in 1530 to Reims Cathedral, without actually attributing it to him. On the other hand, Geneviève Souchal would assign to the Master of the Unicorn Hunt some small patterns for the *Lady with the Unicorn*, a connection which had not occurred to historians, given the differences of weaving in the two pieces, but which she brings out by an accurate stylistic analysis. So that by due sequence one may go on to suggest that other pieces related by their style to the *Lady with the Unicorn*, such as the *Famous Women* and *Perseus*, may also have been woven from this painter's designs.

Apparently born about 1450, this painter "must have been a miniaturist first and foremost, the head of a large workshop no doubt located in Paris, which would explain the fact that not only the printers and the councils of several churches in Paris applied to him, but also some royal officers who are seen to be connected with the city." This French background seems borne out, according to Geneviève Souchal, by some features about which opinions may naturally differ, since they are essentially subjective, "grace, clarity, distinction and that elegant restraint which one may admire in all his works"; and that Frenchness, as she sees it, is accompanied by an "Italian influence" about which, again, opinions may differ. These views, needless to say, are far from meeting with unanimous assent. Sophie Schneebalg-Perelman sees no reason why "the Brussels tapestries... should have gone by way of an untalented but Parisian designer, while these prestigious Flemish painters [Gerard David or Hans Memlinc] could have inspired the Brussels designers themselves."

Margaret B. Freeman (*The Unicorn Tapestries*, 1976) is unconvinced that these two outstanding series, the *Hunt of the Unicorn* and the *Lady with the Unicorn*, could have come "from the imagination and hand of the same designer or designers."

Finally, in 1978, Alain Erlande-Brandenburg found it difficult to believe that this "overwhelming production can be the work of one man of multiple and varied talent."

Going further, he pointed to all the differences that exist between the pieces of the *Hunt of the Unicorn* series and he regrouped them in three different hangings. For him, four pieces belong unquestionably to one and the same series: the *Unicorn at the Fountain*, the *Attack on the Unicorn*, the *Unicorn Defending Itself* and the *Wounded Unicorn Brought to the Castle*. Then two millefleurs pieces seem to be related and posterior to the other four: the *Start of the Hunt* and the *Unicorn in Captivity*. Finally, the fragmentary piece, the *Unicorn Tamed by the Maiden*, would correspond to another series. And he adds: "However, this laudable but hazardous attempt to identify the designer of the *Lady with the Unicorn* has had the merit of throwing light on his artistic background: he was schooled in Paris or in the court milieu and it was there that he executed his designs."

For any answer to the questions raised by the attribution of these tapestries, one last point remains to be examined: the differences of weaving. The colour scheme of the *Hunt of the Unicorn* is much richer than that of the *Lady with the Unicorn*. Shades of red are numerous and impart a gorgeousness to the whole. "There is an unusual amount of orange, and several large areas of pale lemon yellow seldom found in tapestries" (Margaret B. Freeman). Geneviève Souchal adds: "The texture, first of all, is unusually sumptuous: fine wool, many metal threads, silk more abundant still and colour shades much more varied than in the *Lady with the Unicorn*, for example.

Above all, the two sets appear to have been woven on different types of looms. The fineness of execution of the *Hunt* is apparently due to low-warp weaving, while the *Lady*, woven in high warp, suffers from the imprecision caused by this technique. With this imprecision, however, goes a greater freedom in the interpretation of the designs: "the bunches of flowers treated racily and freely are never the same" (Geneviève Souchal), "the flowering plants... are disposed with a freer fancy and more airiness" (Julien

Coffinet), and the low-warp weaving of the *Hunt of the Unicorn*, a point on which all scholars agree, would seem to warrant the assumption that this hanging, or the hangings which it regroups by its theme, were woven in Brussels.

The *Unicorn* hangings have been searchingly studied, and rightly so, but we must not omit to mention other examples whose attribution to Brussels by Sophie Schneebalg-Perelman seems certain. Some are secular millefleurs tapestries: *Semiramis* (Honolulu Academy of Art), *Penthesilea* (Angers), *Verdure with the Arms of Giovio di Como* (Victoria and Albert Museum, London), *Narcissus* (Museum of Fine Arts, Boston), *Concert at the Fountain* (Musée des Gobelins, Paris), *Hercules* (Musée des Arts Décoratifs, Paris), *Neptune and Jupiter* (Detroit Institute of Arts). Some are millefleurs on religious themes: *Angels Carrying the Instruments of the Passion* (Angers) and *Christ on the Cross* (Langeais). There is no space here to discuss all these pieces, but we may pause over two others, the *Annunciation* and the *Adoration of the Magi* (both in the Musée des Gobelins, Paris), which have been carefully studied by Geneviève Souchal, Julien Coffinet and Sophie Schneebalg-Perelman.

At the beginning of this century, on the strength of a composition in the form of an altarpiece, Joseph Destrée saw in these tapestries the influence of the Flemish master Hugo van der Goes. Hulin de Loo, on the other hand, regarded the *Annunciation* as deriving from a picture by Rogier van der Weyden. It seems more likely, however, that its cartoon was designed by Vrancke van der Stockt, one of Rogier's leading pupils, who became dean of the Brussels painters' guild and a municipal magistrate. Among other religious tapestries intended to take the place of altarpieces are the *Nativity*, "one of the earliest tapestries in the royal collections of Spain" (Schneebalg-Perelman), and the *Adoration of the Magi* in Sens Cathedral, bearing the

CONCERT AT THE FOUNTAIN
Brussels, c. 1500
Tapestry
10 ft. × 12 ft.

arms of Cardinal Charles de Bourbon, Archbishop of Lyons, and attributed to the Master of the View of Sainte-Gudule. "The Virgin shows the same type as that in a picture attributed to this painter by various scholars, notably by Max J. Friedländer" (Geneviève Souchal). Comparable to this *Adoration* in the fineness of its weaving, the *Three Coronations* at Sens has been successively attributed to Nuño Gonçalves (H. Bramsen), to a Brussels painter (Geneviève Souchal) and to Memlinc (Schneebalg-Perelman). Two other works may also be connected with Brussels: the *Virgin in Glory* (Louvre), in which festooned clouds reappear, deriving from illuminations and retained for a while yet by tapestry makers; and the *Fall and Redemption of Man* (Metropolitan Museum, New York), received in 1490 by the Queen of Spain, Isabella the Catholic. The latter, rhythmed by gemmed mouldings forming five cusps, has been analysed by Julien Coffinet, who notes that its design has been attributed to Jan van Roome by reason of inscriptions present on the angel's robe. Geneviève Souchal sees in it the hand of a painter in the lineage of Rogier van der Weyden. But Sophie Schneebalg-Perelman thinks it might have been woven by Pieter van Aelst–a name destined to dominate the whole history of tapestry making in Brussels from the beginning of the sixteenth century–before he settled in Brussels.

Pierre d'Enghien, better known as Pieter van Aelst, was born about 1450. He is certainly as fascinating a personage in his day as were Nicolas Bataille or Pasquier Grenier, but unlike them he was not only a man of business; he was also a weaver, and to his personal qualities in this field he owes his European reputation. After settling in Brussels with his son Pierre about 1493, he made several eventful stays in Spain. To him can be assigned a number of hangings mentioned in archival records but no longer traceable. Also known to have come from his workshop are the Gold Carpets of Madrid (*History of the Virgin* and *Mass of St Gregory*), which "are distinguished not only by the profusion of gold and silver thread, but above all by the fineness of the weaving, the accuracy of the line, the expressive delicacy of faces, the great wealth of details and the generalized use of systematic hatchings combined in the flesh tints with a wider range of tones" (Julien Cof-

finet). Also and above all from Van Aelst's workshop is the *Mazarine Tapestry* (National Gallery of Art, Washington). This hanging, in which gold is again prominent, was woven with remarkable fineness either for the marriage of Charles VIII and Anne of Brittany or for that of Philip the Fair and Jeanne of Navarre; it was acquired by Cardinal Mazarin at the sale, in 1651, of the collections of Charles I of England by Parliament. The cartoons were presumably made by Brussels painters schooled in the tradition of Memlinc, Hugo van der Goes and Quentin Massys. Pieter van Aelst is a weaver who played an outstanding role in Brussels, taking financial risks and farming out smaller commissions to other workshops, like those of Van der Tommen or the de Clercks. His great qualities found effective scope because circumstances were favourable to them: the painters of the Brussels school continued to dominate northern Europe, while the rich merchants and bankers of Bruges, Antwerp, Germany and Italy found it profitable to invest in tapestries. While the financial network in which Pieter van Aelst was engaged brought him many commissions, he was also entirely dependent upon it. The loans he contracted involved him in lawsuits. The financial claims on him of Frescobaldi, a Florentine banker in Bruges, were so large that he had to solicit the intervention of King Charles, who appointed an arbitrator to settle the dispute.

Before dealing with the large hangings which ensured his celebrity, we may mention some of his many religious scenes: the *Life of Christ and the Virgin* (Aix-en-Provence), the *Virgin with a Basket* (Museo Arqueológico, Madrid), the *Donation of Fruit to the Virgin* (Musée des Beaux-Arts, Lyons), and the *Combat of Vices and Virtues* or *Redemption of the Human Race* which is known in many versions. Then, to Van Aelst, came the commission from Pope Leo X for the Sistine Chapel: the *Acts of the Apostles*. This being a low-warp weaving, the full-size cartoons were drawn in reverse by Raphael and his pupils (Giulio Romano and Tommaso Vincidor, among others) in 1515–1516. The care with which Raphael foresaw all the problems of reversal raised by a tapestry shows, according to John White and John Shearman, how keenly aware he was of the purpose and nature of this work; it also indicates, on the part

of a painter, a new attitude towards the weavers. The latter, however, as Julien Coffinet observes, could not entirely change their habits; they were not accustomed to copying a cartoon literally, but rather followed a procedure adapted to each element of the models. Here, however, they did keep close to Raphael's cartoons, and discrepancies can be explained by the necessity of supplying a decorative filling for the large surfaces left blank by Raphael, a filling "intended to ensure the solidity of the fabric" (Sophie Schneebalg-Perelman).

Trees, bushes, birds and decorative motifs in the garments of Christ and the Apostles were accordingly added by Pieter van Aelst. The ten pieces designed by Raphael, whose original cartoons, after many vicissitudes, are now in the Victoria and Albert Museum, London, kept the weavers busy for four years. "Displayed in the Sistine Chapel from Christmas time 1519, the first seven hangings aroused a boundless admiration and were hailed as the supreme masterpiece of Christian art" (Sophie Schneebalg-Perelman). But to ease the papal insolvency they were pawned in 1521, dispersed and much damaged before being restored to the Sistine Chapel about 1550, after losing most of their lateral borders. By an analysis of the lower borders, which tell the story of the Medici family (of which Leo X was a member), John White and John Shearman were able to work out the original order of the ten scenes: the *Miraculous Draught of Fishes*, *Christ's Charge to Peter*, *Peter Healing the Lame Man*, the *Death of Ananias*, the *Stoning of St Stephen*, the *Conversion of St Paul*, the *Punishment of Elymas*, *Paul and Barnabas at Lystra*, *St Paul in Prison* and *St Paul Preaching at Athens*.

The success of this hanging was such that at least fifty-five versions of it have been made. The cartoons have repeatedly been copied and used by other Brussels workshops, those for example of Jan van Tieghem, Pieter Pannemaker and Jan Raës. The Mortlake factory in England wove many versions of them. "In France the Paris workshops and the Gobelins and Beauvais factories wove versions of them which were, however, more scarce... The great French collectors of the mid-seventeenth century, like Mazarin, Fouquet, Servien, owned one or several copies of the *Acts of the Apostles*" (exhibition catalogue, *Raphaël et l'art français* 1983).

With this magisterial work to his credit, Pieter van Aelst had no lack of commissions. So it was that, after weaving the *Grotesques* and the *Children's Games* from cartoons by Giulio Romano, Van Aelst received a request from Pope Clement VII concerning another religious subject whose cartoons, sketched out by Raphael, were completed by his pupils: the *Scenes of the Life of Christ*. Even when beset by financial troubles, Van Aelst is known to have begun work on the *Story of Fortunes* and two other hangings which had to be pledged as security to German bankers: *Uriah and Bathsheba* and the *Life of John the Baptist*.

Another work has been tentatively attributed to Pieter van Aelst: *David and Bathsheba*, a splendid, long neglected hanging, no doubt executed in collaboration with Pieter Pannemaker. Acquired in 1847 by the Musée de Cluny, Paris, which for lack of space could not do justice to it for many years, it was exhibited in 1971 at the Grand Palais, Paris, and shown during the 1970s in Amsterdam, New York and Brussels: it is now on display in the Museum of the Renaissance at the Château d'Ecouen, near Paris. Woven about 1515–1525 to designs by Jan van Roome, this set of ten pieces is regarded by all connoisseurs as one of the finest of Western tapestries. Its gorgeousness reflects the luxurious tastes of the courts of that period. But first

and foremost, as pointed out in the catalogue of pre-Renaissance Brussels tapestries (Brussels, 1976) and by Francis Salet (*David et Bethsabée*, 1980), it was conceived as a justification of the divine right of kings: "For who is King David if not the leader, in his sovereign liberty, chosen by God for His people after He had withdrawn His support from Saul?... Moreover David is the young shepherd anointed by Samuel as the token of his election by the Lord. What a reference for the Emperor, the King of France and the King of England who were invested by their coronation with a temporal authority haloed with religious prestige!" After this long career leading him from the Flemish style of Van der Weyden to that of Raphael, characteristic of the Italian Renaissance, Pieter van Aelst went on to collaborate with Bernaert van Orley for the weaving of the *Legend of Our Lady of the Sands*, which marks the supremacy of Italian art in Brussels.

Pieter van Aelst is rightly seen as the weaver responsible for the transition "of tapestry from an autonomous art to an art of interpretation" (Julien Coffinet). In this he was not alone, for the workshops of Michel de Moer, Leon de Smet, Julien Portois, Jan de Clerck, Pieter Pannemaker and Willem de Kempeneere also had their importance. But he personalized this transition with remarkable talent. This is also the reason why, beginning in the second quarter of the seventeenth century, the history of tapestry keeps more closely to that of the painters connected with it. In this sense Bernaert van Orley is the first example, after Raphael, of this predominance of the painters. "Thanks to the wealth of his gifts and imagination, to his sense of the monumental and his thorough knowledge of Raphael's work, probably acquired through Tommaso Vincidor da Bologna, he succeeded in opening new paths to Flemish

THE STORY OF JACOB
FROM CARTOONS BY BERNAERT VAN ORLEY
Brussels, workshop of Willem de Kempeneere, c. 1530
Silk and gold thread
Jacob Blessing Esau (fragment)
Size of the fragment: 14 ft. × 27½ ft.

THE HUNTS OF MAXIMILIAN
FROM CARTOONS BY BERNAERT VAN ORLEY
Brussels, c. 1530
Tapestry
July (Leo): The Lion Hunt (fragment)
Size of the fragment: 14 ft. × 19 ft.

tapestry, without entirely breaking with the Gothic tradition" (R.A. d'Hulst). Van Orley was born in Brussels about 1488. A court painter, familiar with religious subjects, admired by Dürer, he was the designer of the *Legend of Our Lady of the Sands*, *Moralidades*, *Honores*, and *Apocalypse or Revelation of St John*, still very Flemish in spirit, and then of the *Story of Tobias*, the *Life of Abraham* and the *Battle of Pavia*, marked by Italian influence. But his best known cartoons are those for the *Hunts of Maximilian* (Louvre) and the *Story of Jacob* (Brussels).

Woven about 1530 and consisting of twelve scenes, the *Hunts of Maximilian* was inspired by the *Livre du roi Modus et de la reine Ratio*, a French treatise on venery. The sense of detail, both in the garments and the landscapes, shows how intent Van Orley was on keeping to models based on nature. The *Story of Jacob*, woven about 1530 in the workshops of Willem de Kempeneere, is also marked by accurate drawing. "Each of the ten broad compositions is peopled with astonishingly lifelike figures moving in a very decorative architecture and an ever present natural setting. The dynamism of the gestures, which sometimes 'burst through' the woven surface, is emphasized by the movement of the draperies with their deeply hollowed

folds" (J.P. Asselberghs). Following Van Orley, other painters proceeded to acclimatize the Italianizing tradition in Flemish tapestry. One of them is Lancelot Blondeel, who designed a *St Paul* series and a cycle on the *Life of the Virgin*. Another is Pieter Coecke, born at Aelst about 1500, who died in Brussels in 1550: he designed a *Story of Joshua*, a *Story of St Paul* and a set of the *Seven Deadly Sins* in the lineage of the *Acts of the Apostles*. Jan Cornelisz Vermeyen is known thanks to the order he received from the Emperor Charles V for an extensive series celebrating the *Campaign of Charles V against Tunis*. Marthe Crick-Kuntziger also attributes to him the hanging of *Vertumnus and Pomona* (Vienna). Finally, there is Michiel Coxcie, whose life spans most of the sixteenth century. He worked chiefly at Malines. A stay in Italy to perfect his style earned him the sobriquet of the "Flemish Raphael."

During the latter half of the sixteenth century, four names stand out, none however with quite the talent of their predecessors. Pieter de Kempener took over from Michiel Coxcie; he made his reputation first in Italy, then in Spain at Seville. Little is known about the work of Denis van Alsloot and Hans Vredeman de Vries; the latter's name is connected with a canopy dossal of 1566 on the

theme of *Pluto and Proserpine* (Vienna). The personality of
Lucas de Heere is better known. He made the cartoons of
the *Valois* tapestries (Uffizi, Florence). The figures done by
de Heere stand out against landscapes probably executed
by Antoine Caron, painter to the French court. This work
is typical of a trend noticeable at the turn of the sixteenth
and seventeenth century, when the setting becomes increasingly prominent, in particular the landscape treated
more flatly. "The representation becomes flatter and more
confused than in pieces dating to the middle of the century.
The horizon line stands very high. The rendering of life
and movement arouses less interest" (R.A. d'Hulst). The
weaving of tapestries with grotesques, like the *Months with
Grotesques* (Kunsthistorisches Museum, Vienna), provides
further evidence of this purely decorative trend, under
way not only in Flanders but also in France and Italy.

Brussels tapestry of the seventeenth and eighteenth centuries illustrates themes from mythology and from Greek
and Roman history. Also among its chosen subjects are
peasant life and military life, so much so that R.A. d'Hulst
writes: "When churches, monasteries and brotherhoods
wished to order such works [on religious themes] they
were usally obliged to supply the cartoons themselves or
to hand over the order to a cartoon designer."

In the eighteenth century the exotic subjects fashionable in France also spread to Flanders, but to a limited extent. The influence of the major painters was brought to bear so strongly that the works of Rubens, Jordaens, Justus van Egmont and others raised problems of interpretation that proved difficult to solve. "It is certain that the models created by the great master of colour and movement [i.e. Rubens] stand at the opposite pole from the traditional conception of tapestry" (Madeleine Jarry). Cartoons had evolved in a few years' time in such a way that what the weavers were given now were actual paintings. "It often happened that the technical resources at the weavers' disposal were inadequate to vie in wool and silk with the virtuosity of the brush, to render the vigorous musculature

of bodies in all their power, to interpret the stuffs without stiffness. Not without reason did Cattando request Rubens to give his opinion of the *Decius Mus* series when it came from the workshops of Jan Raës and Frans Smeerts" (R.A. d'Hulst). Between 1649 and 1653 the workshop of Jan Raës also executed the *Story of Achilles* (Musées Royaux d'Art et d'Histoire, Brussels).

To Jacob Jordaens are due some cartoons executed in wash: the *Story of Philip of Macedon*, the *Story of Achilles*, the *Story of Ulysses* and the *Scenes of Country Life*. Despite the fame and ability of these painters, such as Rubens and Jordaens, the Brussels tapestry works, and with them Flemish tapestry as a whole, gradually lost their dominant influence. But it was not until 1794 that the last Brussels workshop, that of Jan van der Borght, closed down. Several factors contributed to this decline. R.A. d'Hulst invokes the evolution of taste and changing conditions of life. It is true that walls could more easily be draped with woven silks, with velvets, even with wallpaper, than with costly tapestries; and rooms became smaller and were filled with precious furniture. But most telling of all was the competition coming from other European tapestry factories: Aubusson, Beauvais and the Gobelins in France, Mortlake in England, those of Munich and Rome, and Santa Bárbara in Madrid. These received financial and political support from the reigning sovereigns and were effectively protected against imports. What is more, most of these workshops were set in operation by immigrant Flemish weavers. "From 1591 on, the Delft workshops in Holland were directed by Frans Spierinck, a very good tapestry maker from Antwerp. The Fleming Daniel Pepersack, called in by the Duke of Mantua, installed the workshop at Charleville. In 1603 Jan van der Biest, of En-

ghien, took charge of the Munich manufactory, and at the same period some Brussels weavers were working at Nancy. More important still was the arrival in Paris in 1602 of the Flemings Marc de Comans and François de La Planche, first directors of the workshops out of which grew the great royal manufactory of the Gobelins" (Madeleine Jarry).

But after all any centre that has known a great commercial success may be overtaken by time and events. The predominance of ever larger painted cartoons, and therefore more difficult to interpret, confronted weavers with problems of speed of execution, not to mention the question of hangings which could not reconcile resistance to light with multiplication of colour shades. With the result that in Brussels (and elsewhere) it became customary to paint on the tapestry such details as could not be woven. On 24 April 1525, following a complaint for fraud lodged by the merchants, the Brussels magistrate decreed that: "Any member of the tapestry-makers' guild undertaking to make a hanging worth more than 20 *sous* the ell, shall be obliged to design and weave in the cloth the heads, nose, eyes, mouth, etc. without retouching them with any liquid substance, on pain of being expelled from the guild for good and condemned to be never allowed out of the town in order to prevent him from practising his fraud elsewhere." This decree must have proved insufficient, for it was followed in 1528 by another stipulating that the Brussels mark and the maker's mark must appear on each tapestry.

When further scandals occurred in 1539, not only in Brussels but also at Oudenarde and Enghien, some tapestries were confiscated. This led to a new decree in 1544 running to ninety articles. After a firm reminder of the previous measures, the craft of retoucher was carefully defined: "It is here stipulated that any tapestry shall only be glazed in the town where it is woven, and that this operation shall be carried out only by a sworn and specialized glazer or by the master maker of the hanging itself. The retoucher shall make use of no liquid colours save ink and wild-grain colour, and these materials shall only be used to mark the contours of fruits, verdures, naked limbs, etc., but not to add anything that is not wrought in the weave of the tapestry. The use of white, red and black chalk is authorized, provided that only dry sticks of chalk are used and nothing added that is not in the weave."

One point here is worth emphasizing. While these decrees were intended to raise the ethical standards of a profession in which the weavers could still take great liberties with the cartoon, one realizes, in reading between the lines, that the liberties taken in the matter of retouching were due to the increasing unsuitableness of the cartoons. So that one is not surprised to find a retoucher, in 1621,

bringing an action against two weavers, whom he accused of employing painters instead of professional retouchers.

From the ordinance of 1476 regulating the rights of weavers and painters to the quarrels between retouchers and painters in the seventeenth century, one feels, as Sophie Schneebalg-Perelman notes, that the masters of painting had gained the upper hand. "In 1476, when the history of tapestry weaving in Brussels begins, it was the painters who reproached the tapestry makers for encroaching on their professional ground by making their own cartoons. A century and a half later, it was a tapestry maker's turn to complain about 'the undue role assigned to painters'."

Apart then from the emigration abroad of the best weavers, one cause of the decline of Brussels was this ineluctable transition towards the tapestry-picture, which in turn, just as ineluctably, "transformed these concerns into State manufactories or privileged works" (Julien Coffinet), which alone could afford the time necessary to work from increasingly complex cartoons.

PAINTER'S TAPESTRY: THE GOBELINS, BEAUVAIS AND THE WORKSHOPS OF LA MARCHE

The history of Western tapestry, from the foundation of the Gobelins manufactory (1662) to the beginning of the Third Republic in France (1871), has often been described

as the inexorable trend of tapestry towards a decadence characterized by its progressive subservience to painting, first under the influence of Flemish weavers who staffed the workshops of the main European manufactories, then under the influence of the painters who directed these workshops or were associated with them: Nicolas Poussin, Simon Vouet, Jean Berain, Charles Le Brun, Charles-Antoine Coypel, Pierre Mignard, Jean-Baptiste Oudry, François Boucher, and Goya.

HANGING AFTER THE FRESCOES IN THE GALERIE FRANÇOIS I, FONTAINEBLEAU
Fontainebleau, 1541–1550
Silk, gold and silver thread
Danaë, after Primaticcio (fragment)
Size of the fragment: 10'10" × 20'6"

THE STORY OF ARTEMISIA, AFTER ANTOINE CARON
Paris, Faubourg Saint-Marcel,
workshop of François de La Planche,
first half of the 17th century
Silk and gold thread
Soldiers Carrying Vases (fragment)
Size of the fragment: 15'10" × 9'8"

from Claude Babouin and entrusted the weaving to Jean Le Bries and Pierre Blasse; the latter was also commissioned in Paris to weave a *Story of St Mammas*. These tapestries have been carefully studied by Julien Coffinet, who sees in them a perhaps unique example of the efforts of high-warp weavers to equal in quality the Flemish low-warp work of the period, while at the same time doing their utmost to retain the traditional workmanship. As noted in the introduction, it was at this period that high-warp weavers were trying to devise the procedures which would best enable them to transfer the design to the warp. "The men who wove the hanging [for François I] seem to have been a small group of competent weavers, of others less well trained or specialized, together with a few apprentices who, one cannot help thinking, must have been hastily trained for the needs of the workshop. It looks as if these apprentices, or would-be apprentices, had been deliberately set to rendering in a coarse technique, with grey monochrome tones, the stuccoes of the originals in the Galerie François I, the better to set off the main pieces" (Julien Coffinet).

Between the mid-sixteenth and the mid-seventeenth century, a number of workshops were established in Paris, and the regrouping of them was to lay the basis of the royal manufactories. In 1551 Henri II founded a tapestry workshop in the Hôpital de la Trinité, in the Rue Saint-Denis. Little of its work remains, but the head weaver, Maurice Dubout, was to play an important part. For it was to him and to Gérard Laurent that Henri IV applied in 1597 to set up a tapestry factory, located first in the professed house of the Jesuits, then transferred to the Galerie of the Louvre in 1606. In 1601 the two Flemish weavers François de La Planche of Oudenarde and Marc de Comans of Antwerp arrived in Paris and settled in the Faubourg Saint-Marcel, at the king's invitation, eliciting a protest from the high-warp weavers: "The high-warp tapestry that has hitherto flourished in this city... is much better and finer than that of the treadle, which is what they use in the Low Countries, and which is what they want to establish here." To no avail. In 1607 letters patent conferred privileges on the Flemings and recognized their importance. Among the privileges were the right to open breweries and the exclusive right to sell tapestries in France. R.A. Weigert comments on "this famous clause about the opening of breweries which figures in so many records, so that one is entitled to say that, but for that beer, the Gobelins might never have existed." The factory retained the right to work for private customers, should royal orders be insufficient. So it is that the *Story of St Crispin and St Crispinian* was woven in 1634–1635 by the children of Dubout and Laurent for the cordwainers' guild of Paris. Of middling quality, these pieces cannot compare with the *Old Testa-*

While on the whole this view cannot be disputed, it needs to be considered more discriminatingly. The fact is that in the late sixteenth and early seventeenth century the French workshops resisted Flemish influence and tried to maintain the freedom of high-warp weaving. Moreover the quarrels between painters and weavers in the seventeenth and eighteenth centuries testify to a resistance against the controlling power of painting. Finally there is the recent analysis made by Pierre Vaisse of the ideas that gained ground in France at the beginning of the Third Republic: he shows that a more original approach to tapestry–too often supposed to be characteristic of the twentieth century–was already being made in artistic and political circles from the time when Louis Lacordaire became director of the Gobelins in 1850.

We have some evidence for the maintenance of high-warp weaving in France during the later sixteenth century: a *Life of St Peter* (Saumur) woven in the workshop of Jean Duval at Tours, and a *Life of St Stephen* woven at Toulouse. It is known with certainty that François I (1515–1547) was responsible for a revival of high warp at Fontainebleau, near Paris. This king, who ordered many tapestries from Flanders, decided to have one made from the frescoes in the Galerie François I in the Château de Fontainebleau, probably with the idea of taking it with him when he travelled. For this hanging (now in the Kunsthistorisches Museum, Vienna) he ordered designs *ment* ordered by Louis XIII from Simon Vouet about 1630; one piece, *Moses Saved by Pharaoh's Daughter*, is an example of particularly finished weaving. A third high-warp tapestry factory was set up in Paris about 1648 by Pierre Lefebvre, summoned back from Florence where he was in charge of the workshops founded by the Grand Duke of Tuscany. This third factory was also housed in the galleries of the Louvre, but Cardinal Mazarin granted Lefebvre and his son Jean the right to set up a large stall and a workshop in the garden of the Tuileries. Finally there was a carpet factory, also in the Louvre, founded in 1608 and directed by Pierre Dupont. The latter took over and perfected the technique worked out by Jean Fortier: "for the tools and the true method of setting children to work, with facility, on Turkey carpets and on needlework." This factory moved in 1626 to Chaillot, to the Hôpital de la Savonnerie founded in 1515 by the regent Marie de Médicis, and the children given asylum in this poor-house became the workmen of Dupont and his associate Simon Lourdet. Among the most interesting of these early seven-

teenth-century works is the *Story of Artemisia*, woven from cartoons which had been made in the sixteenth century for Catherine de Médicis. These designs, attributed to Antoine Caron, have been woven more than fifty times. In the Mobilier National Français is a version of it from the workshop of François de La Planche. In addition to the *Old Testament*, Simon Vouet designed the *Trials of Ulysses*, the *Story of Rinaldo and Armida* and the *Loves of the Gods*.

Outside Paris, to complete the productions for which the Parisian high-warp weavers had been granted privileges, workshops sprang up in different regions of France. So François de La Planche and Marc de Comans were able to employ weavers at Tours and Amiens. The workshop at the Château de Cadillac, property of the Duc d'Epernon, was run by a pupil of the Faubourg Saint-Marcel. But most important of all for the history of tapestry, in view of the personality of its director, Charles Le Brun, was the factory set up at Maincy in 1660 by Nicolas Fouquet, the Surintendant Royal. In 1661, after Fouquet's disgrace, the looms and tapestries at Maincy were

THE OLD TESTAMENT, AFTER SIMON VOUET
Paris, workshop in the galleries of the Louvre,
first half of the 17th century
Wool and silk
Moses Saved by Pharaoh's Daughter (fragment)
Size of the fragment: 16'3" × 19'4"

confiscated and the first work to be done in the Gobelins Manufactory consisted in completing the projects undertaken at Maincy. For this purpose, on 6 June 1662, Louis XIV acquired the town house of the Gobelin family, descending from Philibert Gobelin, merchant and dyer of scarlet stuffs, at Saint-Marcel-les-Paris on the banks of the Bièvre. By the king's orders this house, the future Gobelins factory, was fitted up. This work lasted until 1667, when the factory received letters patent as the Manufacture Royale des Meubles de la Couronne (its official title). The painter Charles Le Brun was appointed director, all designs to be supplied by him. As Jules Guiffrey has written: "His style at that period was distinguished for the admirable harmony of all the parts. Each part contributes to the common aim, and from the grand architectonic lines to the least details the same spirit and purpose presides over the execution of the whole. To him, to his influence and taste, must be given the credit for the fine hangings executed during the first half of the reign of Louis XIV. Practised artists consented to be the interpreters of his conceptions, and so it was that the immense task of decoration at Versailles could be rapidly carried through."

Tapestry making at the Gobelins was marked by Le Brun's respect for the traditional workmanship. There high warp triumphed. Of the four original workshops,

three practised this technique under the respective direction of Jean Jans the Elder, Jean Lefebvre and Henri Laurent; the one low-warp workshop was headed by Jean La Croy who came from the Faubourg Saint-Marcel. Two hundred and fifty weavers, partly of Flemish origin, were employed at a wage per ell varying from 200 to 400 livres, and they were entrusted with the work according to a fairly strict hierarchy. Some fifty painters attended to the cartoons. Thus Van der Meulen worked on the *History of the King*, the *Royal Houses* and the *Months*, in collaboration with Anguier, Baudouin Yvart, Boels and Monnoyer: these hangings celebrate the apotheosis of the French monarchy at its height. The *Portières des Renommées* or "Door-Hangings of Renowns" with the arms of France, done from cartoons made by Le Brun for Maincy, and the *Story of Alexander* answered the same purpose. In 1687 began the weaving of the *Ancient Indies*, a hanging after Van der Eeckhout which marks a change of style by its emphasis on documentary and exotic aspects. So great was the success of these pieces that no less than eight hangings were woven up to 1730. "Exoticism triumphed in a profusion of 'Indian' plants and animals, interpreted by the Gobelins artists in tapestry, no doubt from live models provided by the famous menagerie set up by Louis XIV at Versailles" (Madeleine Jarry).

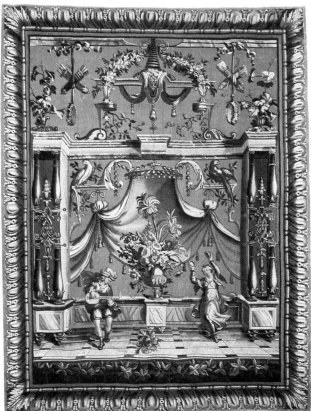

The parallel creation of the Royal Manufactory of Beauvais, under Louis Hinard, took place in 1664. "Colbert's determination to develop artistic production in France, to avoid purchases abroad which drained away currency, was, as we know, at the origin of the creation of this factory in which he never ceased to take an interest" (Jean Coural). After a period of financial uncertainty, lasting until 1684, Beauvais was put in charge of Philippe Behagle who, after working at the Gobelins, had settled at Oudenarde. He found a privileged clientele among the princes of the blood (*Chinese Hanging* or *Story of the King of China* for the Duc de Maine, *Story of the King's Conquests* for the Comte de Toulouse). "But the greatest success (some 150 pieces being woven between 1689 and 1732) was had by the tapestries of *Grotesques* from cartoons by Monnoyer and Vernansal, after a composition engraved by Jean Berain" (Jean Coural). In Weigert's words: "Their sumptuousness is reminiscent of the settings which Berain devised for the operas of Lulli, in his capacity as designer to the Royal Academy of Music." In 1690 Le Brun was succeeded by Pierre Mignard, then seventy-six years old, but the Gobelins had to close from 1694 to 1699. Then came a succession of artistic directors: Robert de Cotte, Jean-Baptiste Oudry and François Boucher. In this period of seventy years, the most notable painters, apart from

them, were Charles-Antoine Coypel and François Desportes. It was Coypel who designed the *Old Testament*, the *Iliad* and the *Story of Don Quixote*, from which most European workshops took inspiration. Nine hangings of this last theme were made at the Gobelins from 1714 to 1794, and many variants of the decoration surrounding the principal scenes (the *alentours* or woven frames) were prepared by Blain de Fontenay, Claude III Audran and Louis Tessier. Audran, in 1735, followed up the success of the *Ancient Indies* with a hanging of like inspiration, the *New Indies*. Executed in low warp, it is much more decorative in aspect than its predecessor.

Louis XV ordered from the Gobelins a *New History of the King*, a set of hangings which includes the *Hunts of Louis XV* designed by Oudry. "Style and execution had evolved at the Gobelins. The very spirit of this hanging is quite remote from that of the *History of the King* done in the previous century... The person of Louis XV, surrounded by the throng of huntsmen, is only a very distant pretext for some delightful hunting scenes set in the midst of the forests of Compiègne and Fontainebleau" (Madeleine Jarry). At Beauvais, the hanging of *Russian Games* from cartoons by Jean-Baptiste Le Prince, a painter who had travelled in Russia, Finland, Livonia and Siberia, went to popularize a Slav exoticism which lasted down to the Revolution.

Throughout this period the predominance of painting became ever more pronounced, founded as it was on the evolution of technique. An invention by the engineer Vaucanson, devised at the prompting of Neilson and Soufflot, effected a remarkable unification of the two types of loom. "The [low-warp] loom was made to tip up, so that the low-warp weavers were able to follow their work more easily, almost as well as their high-warp colleagues"

(Julien Coffinet), while the generalized use of tracing permitted an accurate transfer of the cartoon to the high-warp loom. Much has been made of the allegedly baneful influence of Oudry, who from 1726 was artistic director at Beauvais, and then exercised his power at the Gobelins "progressively and by stages over a period of more than thirty years" (H.N. Opperman). He was blamed by Mérou, the Beauvais director, for the fact that the workmen had great difficulty "in executing their work from the composition of paintings by Oudry, which are very much lighted and finished like cabinet pictures." This has obscured the fact that after Mérou's departure Oudry did much to set the Beauvais works on a firmer footing. But similar complaints were made by the Gobelins workmen after 1748, when Oudry was appointed chief inspector of the workshops. The quarrel seems to have borne more on the problem of rapidity of work than on a purely aesthetic question, though the two were necessarily connected. Paid by the amount of work they accomplished (rapidity therefore being a matter of concern to them) and often living in wretched conditions, with scarcely enough to eat, the weavers were restive under the management of a man unsympathetic towards their problems, who demanded finer, more complicated and therefore slower weaving and did not hesitate to cut out any weaving he did not like. Then there was the rivalry between the two factories: "The Gobelins workmen did not want to have the 'inferior' methods of Beauvais foisted upon them by Oudry, and most of all they did not want to see their craft secrets stolen by Oudry and imitated at Beauvais" (H.N. Opperman). When Boucher was appointed director of the Gobelins in 1765, the workmen extended thanks to him; yet he professed no very different aesthetic from that of Oudry. The *Story of Psyche* woven at Beauvais for the

THE ANCIENT INDIES, AFTER VAN DER EECKOUT
Paris, Gobelins, workshop of De La Croix, 1689
Silk thread
The Dapple-Grey Horse or The Indian Rider (fragment)
Size of the fragment: 15½ ft. × 12 ft.

kings of Sweden, Prussia and Naples, or the hanging of the *Loves of the Gods*, are tantamount to woven paintings — which would tend to show that the weavers were prepared to accept the domination of painters, and even to forestall their wishes, provided that the latter sympathized with the difficulties of their craft and showed themselves more human. As Julien Coffinet has pointed out, a similar conflict arose between Goya and the weavers of the Santa Bárbara tapestry factory (set up in 1720 under the patronage of Philip V of Spain), who were called upon to execute the forty-five cartoons supplied by Goya between 1776 and 1791.

As Phyllis Ackerman has written, "Goya's genius was put to the service [of these workshops], enabling them to produce the only tapestries of the eighteenth century which, as tapestries and as works of art, are of primordial importance." But one feels, in examining the pieces woven throughout this period, that a point of no return had been reached, and that what mattered most of all was a hyperrealistic fidelity to painting. In France, during the troubled period of the Revolution, the administration settled the issue for good by providing the Gobelins and Beauvais weavers with stable employment and permitting them to work at a pace imposed by the complexity of the design. "This change may have slowed down the weavers' output, but on the credit side it kept the manufactory in existence, for all the contractors were ruined and about to abandon their workshop" (Madeleine Jarry).

Among these "private" workshops, those of La Marche (Aubusson and Felletin) had received letters patent, granting them the title of Royal Manufactory, between 1665 and 1689. But it was not until 1732–1737 that Joseph Dumons, a painter dispatched to this region in central France by Louis XV, together with a dyer trained at the Gobelins, undertook to reform the work of these family workshops on the spot. Their private clientele accepted coarser weaving, and designs from Beauvais or Paris (*Hunts of Louis XV*, *Fables of La Fontaine*, *Chinese Scenes*, works by Boucher) were regularly interpreted.

THE HUNTS OF LOUIS XV,
AFTER JEAN-BAPTISTE OUDRY
Paris, Gobelins, workshop of Monmerqué,
1743-1745
Silk threads
The Stag Hunt (detail)
Overall size: 14'3'' × 26'

THE STORY OF DAPHNIS AND CHLOE
Aubusson, mid-18th century
Tapestry
The Grape Harvest Where Daphnis and Chloe Are Admired (fragment)
Overall size: 6′10″ × 10′6″

THE KITE, AFTER GOYA
Madrid, Santa Bárbara,
late 18th century
Tapestry

Workshops in other French provinces depended on the changing will or whims of princes and local authorities. Those, for example, of Nancy, Lunéville and Lille (all influenced by Flanders and the work of Teniers), also those of Valenciennes and Strasbourg. After the period of the Directoire (1795–1799), when some 180 pieces from the Gobelins collections were burnt, the Empire and the Restoration failed to produce any hangings of a high artistic standard. In the matter of tapestry, the Napoleonic era had no painter comparable to Le Brun, and from 1824 on two technical innovations were to bring tapestry still closer to pictorial accuracy. At the Gobelins factory the chemist Eugène Chevreul reformed the dyeing works by devising 72 colour scales of 200 tones, while the weavers took to twisting together threads of different colours in order to obtain intermediate shadings. Things were set moving in the same direction by the Deyrolle process, in which "any tone whatsoever was made up of two shades of equal value, alternating from every second weft-thread" (Julien Coffinet).

Significantly, one finds that even before the advent of the Third Republic (1871) the problem of this subservience to painted subjects was being canvassed. On this matter: "There exists nothing absolute, unless it is the latest theories, more or less belied by the experience of centuries: it is not absolutely necessary that a painter should have offered to make a tapestry design for his work to have

the qualities required by this manufacture," declared Louis Lacordaire in the 1850s. And a report on the Gobelins, in 1848, states that "the art of tapestry should be considered solely from the decorative point of view, as a means of adorning public monuments, and these trompe-l'œil hangings made in imitation of pictures depart utterly from the principle of utility which created this factory, a principle which must be reverted to without delay."

In 1875–1876 Alfred Darcel, the first administrator of the Gobelins under the Third Republic, set in train a *St Agnes* whose weaving was much simplified. "All the modellings, both on face and hands and in the folds of the dress, are rendered by a system of broad hatchings, and all the forms are systematically contoured by a redrawn outline. Perfectly successful as an attempt at textile simplification, the work is less satisfying on the artistic plane," writes Pierre Vaisse, and he adds: "Unique technically, here an unquestionable success, this attempt was not followed up; or rather, despite its example, the trend continued slowly and not without misgivings and backward turns. So it is that *Innocence*, woven from a picture by Urbain Bourgeois, was undertaken nearly ten years later." This spirit of reform, called forth by the faded colours of tapestries woven over the previous decades and by the growing conviction that woven painting served no useful purpose, met with a response in England when, with William Morris, the history of contemporary tapestry began.

◁◁ St Agnes, after Louis Steinheil
Paris, Gobelins, 1875–1876
Tapestry
6′5″ × 2′8″

◁ Innocence,
after Urbain Bourgeois
Paris, Gobelins, 1884–1886
Tapestry
7′10″ × 4′1″

163

THE WOODPECKER, AFTER WILLIAM MORRIS
Tapestry
Woven by Morris and Co., London, 1885

THE LATE NINETEENTH AND TWENTIETH CENTURIES

To understand the situation of tapestry in Europe in the second half of the nineteenth century, it is enough to quote two complementary remarks, one by William Morris commenting on his visit to the Gobelins in 1854, the other by Jules Guiffrey, author of a history of tapestry published in 1886, who was appointed director of the French manufactories in 1893. Morris condemned what he saw as being harmful to creative art as a whole: "It would be too polite to say that what they are doing is not worth the effort of doing it. It is much more serious. Their influence on all the minor arts in France is disastrous." Guiffrey lamented the absence of any clear idea about the nature of tapestry cartoons: "We certainly have no lack of distinguished painters, but how many of them have studied the laws of decoration? How many understand that tapestry in particular can on no account lend itself to all the virtuosities of the brush?"

These two comments go to indicate the basis on which thinking about this subject was to stand for a little over a hundred years: the search for ways of restoring originality to tapestry by drawing on its own resources, and the attempt to strike the right balance between the pictorial and the mural on the one hand, and the specific features of the material and the technique on the other. From this point of view, the work of William Morris in England and its repercussions on the Continent, in Germany and Scandinavia; the relations of modernity that Marie Cuttoli, Jean Lurçat and Pierre Baudouin successfully established with the Aubusson workshops; and the recent taking up of this art form by weaver-designers who execute their own tapestries outside the big workshops–these mark the three high points of an evolution which has had nothing linear about it. These innovations and the guiding ideas behind them are by no means free of ambiguities, and they have been constantly counterbalanced by the defenders of pictorial tapestry based on copies or using multiple forms of adaptation. What we find here is a dialectical interaction or conflict made all the sharper for us by the fact that it is so recent. Actually it is no more than an extension, broadened and magnified, of the conflict that we have evoked in dealing with earlier centuries.

WILLIAM MORRIS AND ENGLAND

It would be difficult to overestimate the vital contribution made by William Morris to the revival of the textile arts, and the momentous influence his work exerted on the renewed awareness of the historical background which has characterized the twentieth century. But, where textiles are concerned, Morris is perhaps best known for the tapestries which he designed towards the end of his life in collaboration with Burne-Jones. Needlework and tapestry had always been of the keenest interest to him, and he was instrumental in the acquisition by the South Kensington Museum of two very famous pieces, the *Trojan War* woven at Tournai between 1475 and 1490 and *Pity and Justice* woven in Brussels in the first quarter of the sixteenth century.

Linda Parry has suggested that, if Morris waited so long before designing his own tapestries, it was because he held this technique in such high esteem and wished to gain beforehand a thorough knowledge of its history and requirements. While Ruskin and the Pre-Raphaelites admired the Middle Ages as more in keeping with their aesthetic ideas, it was rather the tapestries of the late fifteenth century that inspired the productions of Morris & Co. Trying to break the stranglehold of painting, Morris, long before Lurçat, called for a return to a very limited range of colours, the use of well-marked hatchings for the modelling, and the abandonment of perspective effects: this, in effect, was a reversion to the original means of tapestry. Moreover, he left a certain freedom to his weavers. The result is that certain details, the flowers in particular, are thought to have been reproduced from nature. The design was photographically enlarged to the size of the actual weaving, the photograph being then retouched and serving as the tapestry cartoon.

The subjects always stand out against a background of verdure comparable to the millefleurs or to an orchard. However, as Julien Coffinet notes, this verdure is closer to the flowering plants of Brussels tapestries than to the genuine millefleurs which preceded them. Morris actually made complete designs for only three tapestries. But he supplied many background details against which stand out the figures designed by Burne-Jones. One of his earliest original works is the *Woodpecker*, set in a garland of flowers and leaves; it is also one of his most attractive.

After Morris's death in 1896, his Merton Abbey looms continued a production strongly influenced by Brussels tapestries of the sixteenth century.

In Scotland it was the personality of William George Thomson that stimulated the further development of modern tapestry. He directed the Dovecot Studio, founded in 1912 on the initiative of the Marquess of Bute, and still active today. Thomson was a scholar and traveller who took the trouble to learn Flemish and Basque in order to translate the early records he needed to write his *History of Tapestry* (London, 1906). Beginning with the *Lord of the Hunt*, the first piece woven there before the First World War, the Dovecot Studio has commissioned designs from many painters and sculptors, such as Sir Cecil Beaton, Louis Le Brocquy, Henry Moore, Louise Nevelson, Robert Motherwell and David Hockney. Since 1963, under the management of Archie Brennan, with the collaboration of Fiona Mathison and Maureen Hodge, the in-

fluence of this pictorial and often humorous approach to tapestry making has spread through the English-speaking countries, to Australia in particular.

GERMANY AND SCANDINAVIA

Something will be said later about the characteristics of textile art as it developed in Europe in the context of Art Nouveau. As regards warp tapestry, it was in Germany and the Scandinavian lands that William Morris's influence made itself felt immediately. So true is this that,

THE ALPS, AFTER ERNST LUDWIG KIRCHNER
Cover of a lounge chair
Woven by Lise Guyer, 1928
8'6'' × 5'8''

166

after the First World War, when Jean Lurçat set out to explain his principles of tapestry reform to the management of the Nuremberg factory, "the lady in charge expressed her surprise at hearing him describe as a novelty the only method that she had ever applied" (Pierre Vaisse).

We cannot however agree with Pierre Vaisse when he writes, concerning the style of these works: "In Germany and Scandinavia, the almost mystical attachment to the traditions of folk arts and crafts kept tapestry to the status of an applied art, ruling out any creative vitality. The cartoon designers felt obliged to adopt a sham naïve style, with deliberate clumsinesses, a style which is still rife today in Germany." On the contrary, the works woven in the Scherrebek workshops, and the creations of artists like Frida Hansen or Marta Maas-Fjetterström, are signal examples of the renewal of contemporary tapestry.

It was in 1896 that Justus Brinckmann decided to set up a school of weaving in a North Schleswig village–Scherrebek. There he drew on the resources of regional styles, but also succeeded in interesting Otto Eckmann, Hans Christiansen and Alfred Mohrbutter in the art of weaving. Owing to the simplified technique which Brinckmann advocated, and the limited knowledge of the weavers, the textile design was emphasized by broken contours and therefore adapted itself easily to the Japanese influence then prevailing. Otto Eckmann's *Five Swans* (1897) and Alfred Mohrbutter's *Flamingo* (1901) answer perfectly to a type of highly contrasted composition in which the birds ensure the development of the motif over a background simplified to the utmost by the mark of the rippling waters or the unmodelled leafage. Effects of depth are avoided. The decorative design is well thought out: conceived in terms of the technical resources of the medium, it is quite free of any "sham naïveté."

Although this German workshop only lasted for eight years, these Scherrebek tapestries deserve to be remembered. They stand out among all those woven around the turn of the century with a view to singling out anew the specific features of this art. They were equalled in Germany only by those woven in the 1920s by Lise Guyer from designs by Ernst Ludwig Kirchner. Since then–apart from the important work done at the Bauhaus–the revival of German tapestry has been centred in Munich and Nuremberg. Among the best known artists are Herbert Bayer, who has done much to elucidate the question of the visual impact of colours, and Dirk Holger, who has been an ardent propagandist in Germany for Jean Lurçat's theories.

Scandinavia is best known for its federative activity, characterized by the creation in the late nineteenth century of associations for the purpose of improving the quality of domestinc weaving by providing weavers with cartoons suited to tapestry making–cartoons designed by such varied personalities as Alf Wallander and Nils von Dardal in Sweden, and Frida Hansen and Gerhard Munthe in Norway. The name of Frida Hansen deserves special mention for her all-round activity in favour of textile art and for such works as the *Dance of Sirens* and the *Milky Way*, which have their due place in the context of European Art Nouveau. Her *Milky Way* is remarkable for its effective repetition of female figures over a blue, star-sprinkled ground. Not enough emphasis has been laid on the extent to which this work, even more than those of William Morris, approximates to the treatment of the woven surface that we find in the Angers *Apocalypse*.

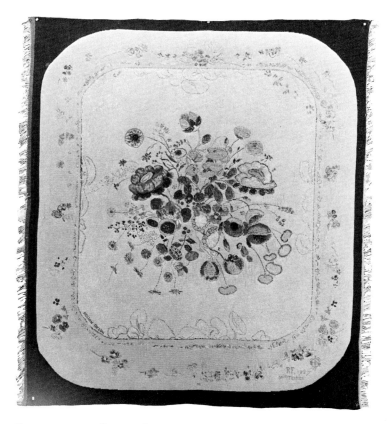

FLOWERS, AFTER ODILON REDON
Panel of a screen
Paris, Gobelins, 1909
39½″ × 32½″

THE FRENCH NATIONAL MANUFACTORIES

Jules Guiffrey made some pertinent and far-sighted criticisms of the attitude to tapestry prevailing at the French national manufactories, but it is not to him that goes the credit for attracting the painters destined to renew their style. Apart from the large tapestry by Jean-Paul Laurens, *Une descente de tournoi à la fin du XVᵉ siècle*, which answers his call for a return to the great subjects of tapestry, but without attaining the level of style distinctive of William Morris and Burne-Jones, the outstanding work of Guiffrey's period as administrator of the Gobelins (1893–1908) is Gustave Moreau's *The Siren and the Poet*, which came from the looms in 1899, was exhibited at the Paris World's Fair of 1900, and then figured in the Musée du Luxembourg alongside its painted model.

The Siren and the Poet shows a certain effort in the choice of the stitches, in particular the use of *crapeautage*, indicating a purposeful attempt to emphasize the texture of the weave. But its composition, heavily bordered with a frame, takes no account of the preoccupations expressed by Jules Guiffrey; indeed, it is at the farthest possible remove from them. In the words of Pierre Vaisse: "The nineteenth century failed to produce a good cartoon designer; that is, an artist attracted by wool. Hence the necessity for the Gobelins to produce absurd facsimiles of pictures, to the extent of conscientiously copying Gustave Moreau's *Siren and Poet*, and trying to render the impasto which catches light on the canvas by highlights of silk and gold thread!" As one studies the production of the French manufactories from the late nineteenth century to the present day, the most striking thing about it is seen to be the conflict between the administrators, more or less intent

THE LOGE, AFTER PIERRE BRACQUEMOND
Paris, Gobelins, 1925 (cartoon before 1914)
9'4" × 8'6"

on finding solutions peculiar to tapestry, and the dead weight of the institution, its traditions, and above all the quality of the cartoons commissioned from painters or artists and the problem of adapting them to tapestry.

After the failure of Guiffrey's efforts, it fell to Gustave Geffroy to make a fresh attempt to renew the spirit of tapestry by turning away from the official painters and applying to his impressionist friends. Among the pieces which have retained a lasting interest are *The Loge* by Pierre Bracquemond and, even finer, Odilon Redon's *Flowers*, a high-warp tapestry executed at the Savonnerie carpet manufactory. It must be noted that during his administration (1908–1926) Geffroy called on illustrators like Jules Chéret and had tapestries made after pictures by Claude Monet and Vincent van Gogh. Some of these works retain at least a certain nostalgic imprint, so that Julien Coffinet's judgment may seem over-severe: "Gustave Geffroy, an art critic who had distinguished himself by defending the impressionist painters, appears to have felt that the question of cartoons could be solved very simply by substituting his friends for the academic painters. He took no thought of technical questions, which apparently had little interest for him. Except dyeing: it was he who, to keep more closely to the tone of the Impressionists, caused natural dyes to be given up and replaced by synthetic products. A reform that would have become inevitable, but was then premature and proved disastrous for many tapestries of that period. There can be no question that a tapestry, as it was understood by Gustave Geffroy, was the copy of a painting, but a copy interpreted much more freely by the weavers."

The third influential personality at the head of the Gobelins was Guillaume Janneau (1935–1944). He shared the views set forth by his predecessors: "Our workshops are not going to devote their talent any more to counterfeiting paintings: they are going to make tapestries... We

shall provide an equivalence to the effects which the painter aims at, but from the resources of our craft, not from those of the painter." Unlike his predecessors, he put them into practice by reverting to natural colours, to 120 colour scales of seven to nine tones only, and to greater freedom for the weaver. Janneau called upon Gromaire and Lurçat for two cartoons, the *Illusions of Icarus* and *Forests*, and in 1939 he sent Gromaire, Lurçat and Dubreuil to Aubusson for the purpose of "studying the possibility of a renewal of local art" (Madeleine Jarry). Since the Second World War, the French national manufactories have been influenced in turn by the evolution of tapestry characteristic of the private workshops and by the revival of textile art.

THE FOUR ELEMENTS, AFTER MARCEL GROMAIRE
EARTH
Paris, Gobelins, 1948
11'10" × 16'7"

There have been some remarkable achievements on these lines, like *Polynesia*, a hanging in two pieces, *Sky* and *Sea*, woven at Beauvais in 1946 from Matisse's paper cutouts, and *The Woman and the Farrier* by Le Corbusier, or *Flagstones, Sand and Water* by Henri-Georges Adam, all perfectly in keeping with the craft of tapestry weaving. As against these, we find many reproductions of modern, often gestural paintings like those of Mathieu or Hartung, which as textiles have little or no interest.

However, the freedom of some transcriptions executed in independent workshops has had a certain influence on the use of varied textures in the making of tapestries from designs by James Guitet, Etienne Hajdu, Alicia Penalba, Pierrette Bloch and Thomas Gleb. On the initiative of Jean Coural, the present administrator of the Gobelins, an experimental workshop has been exploring a specific type of approach to the works of such artists as Alicia Penalba, André Messagier and Nicolas Schöffer, for a construction in space or the use of plastic tubes. Jean Coural has also taken the initiative of organizing exhibitions at which the French manufactories have displayed other forms of "textile identities," in Paris in 1969 on the invitation of the Fourth Tapestry Biennial of Lausanne, and in a series of one-man shows by textile artists held at Beauvais since 1982. The fact remains that in France, as in Europe generally, the cartoons recently purchased for weaving reflect all too clearly the almost total lack of interest which the painters of the 1980s have shown for tapestry.

THE WOMAN AND THE FARRIER, AFTER LE CORBUSIER
Beauvais, 1967
7′2″ × 11′11″

POLYNESIA, AFTER HENRI MATISSE
THE SEA
Beauvais, 1946
6′5″ × 10′4″

AUBUSSON

In the space of fifty years the Aubusson workshops passed from a state of profound crisis to a revival whose importance was appreciated throughout the world. Now again, in the past few years, there has been a loss of interest and a commercial decline.

Several names were associated with the revival of Aubusson, those of Marie Cuttoli, Marius Martin, Elie Maingonnat, Jean Lurçat and Pierre Baudouin. The public at large was familiar with only one: that of Marie Cuttoli. She began as a collector, attracted by the painting of her time. She was led to take an interest in textile art in a traditional context, in Algeria, where her husband's political career had taken her. There, at Sétif and Constantine, she set up some embroidery workshops and a carpet workshop. For the latter she employed four Algerian women and applied to Jean Lurçat for cartoons. Her influence on tapestry is better known, and rightly so, for it was at her prompting, under her patronage, that pictures by some of the greatest living painters were woven at Aubusson—Rouault, Léger, Braque, Picasso, Dufy, Miró, Derain, Matisse, Lurçat. Acknowledged as a moving spirit by historians of modern tapestry, she did not however bring about any innovations on the part of the Aubusson weavers who executed these works. On the contrary, what she required of them was fidelity to the pictures, to the point of having the picture frames woven as well. Here one is justified in speaking of trompe-l'œil weaving, such as has had no equivalent since—except for certain tapestries

woven under the guidance of Yvette Cauquil-Prince or from photographic cartoons in the United States.

At the same time some reforms were undertaken at the Ecole Nationale des Arts Décoratifs, founded at Aubusson in 1884 to train weavers. When Marius Martin was appointed director of the school in 1917, he began promoting a new approach. These efforts were continued and extended by his pupil Elie Maingonnat, who succeeded him in 1937. "Their purpose was not simply to revert to a big warp and a limited colour scale. These two imperatives were only the starting point for long researches intended to define the means of translating into this simplified language the forms utilized in the composition: human body, animals, leafage," writes Pierre Vaisse. And he adds: "Future historians of tapestry will have to analyse and define the contribution of these two men, but one point is certain: but for them, Lurçat would never have produced the works he did produce." We share this view, wholeheartedly, for apart from works by Elie Maingonnat like his *Ferns* which cannot compare with those of the painter designers grouped around Lurçat, the Aubusson archives contain some technical experiments by Lurçat which are extremely responsive to textile art and sometimes foreshadow textile works executed in the United States and Eastern Europe twenty-five years later. These experiments made no attempt to reduce tapestry to a set formula; such was, however, the case with Lurçat's colour-coded cartoon.

Jean Lurçat is one of the artists who has written most about tapestry, and his are the works which have been most often reproduced. He owed this success to the fact

THE BIRTH OF THE LANSQUENET, AFTER JEAN LURÇAT
Aubusson, Tabard workshop, 1945
7′4″ × 9′2″

THE APOCALYPSE,
AFTER JEAN LURÇAT
Aubusson,
Tabard workshop, 1955
14 ft. × 39½ ft.

that, apart from his personal qualities as a painter, he embodied and voiced untiringly a spirit of reform which has been at work in tapestry since William Morris. Defending its mural function, proficient in all the simplifications already arrived at before he went to Aubusson, he laid stress on one principle essential to textile art: keep in mind the colour of the material, before referring to the colour of the painting. This primary concern is already evident in a personal statement in his book *Le bestiaire dans la tapisserie du Moyen Age*, touching on the canvas tapestries he made before the First World War or had his mother make: "Owing to the poverty of my equipment, I was prohibited, whether I liked it or not, from having any wish to cast a guilty glance at my own easel paintings or making any attempt to reproduce them in fabrics."

The method that he developed was the colour-coded cartoon. On this, Jean Lescure commented in 1963: "The range of colours was set for him as easily as if by a colour merchant. And no mixing was possible, except by juxtaposition. It is true that the juxtaposition could be so subtle, close and varied that it became a particular mode of mixing; true, too, that by its exigencies the play of colours was governed by strict rules. The tone could be prepared to any extent desired, before being dipped in the dye. But once it was dyed the wool became a pure tone which had to be used as such without any possible mixture. This way of thinking opened an unexpected prospect on an art wholly new, fairly revolutionary and almost mathematical. If the samples of dyed wool supplied to the artist are correctly numbered, one can in fact, after a short apprenticeship, bear in mind a series of numbers corresponding to colours, to these tones made pure in the manner I have described. Henceforth the painter has no need to seek out on his palette the harmony of a blue and red, but from a cartoon as abstract as he may desire he can carry out the juxtapositions of A3 and J7, of B2 and V6. His eye, practised in the light of the different wools, will have connected them with the numbers corresponding to an exact value."

However exact it may be, this procedure has one serious drawback: it narrows down the part played by the weaver. As Julien Coffinet aptly writes: "Contrary to what was often said, Jean Lurçat's method did not represent a return to the procedures of the medieval weavers. Actually it marked one further stage on the way towards eliminating any autonomy in the interpreter, who was turned into an almost automatic machine. Jean Lurçat's method, adopted by many painters, leads to industrial techniques." It nevertheless appealed to many painters, who in 1947 joined together in Paris to form the Association of Painters of Tapestry Cartoons, under the joint chairmanship of Jean Lurçat, Marc Saint-Saëns and Jean Picart Le Doux. One of the most active members of this association was Denise Majorel, who with Madeleine David opened the Galerie La Demeure in Paris which, until her recent retirement, was the place where this form of tapestry was best promoted. She has also collaborated with some creative weavers of the younger generation, such as Pierre Daquin, Josep Grau-Garriga, Jagoda Buic and Jacques Brachet. Some of the Aubusson workshops, like that of François Tabard, Raymond Picaud, the brothers Pinton and Camille Legoueix, were open-minded and intelligent enough to welcome this movement and contribute to its commercial success.

FLAGSTONES, SAND AND WATER,
AFTER HENRI-GEORGES ADAM
Paris, Gobelins, 1964
13 ft. × 19½ ft.

In 1977 Mario Prassinos paid tribute to the qualities of the colour-coded cartoon, pointing out that it leaves, in his words, a "veritable imprint" from which an accurate weaving can be made even after the painter's death: "The wools being referenced, their colours coded and the weaving procedures thought out and named, the painter accordingly lays down an actual programme for the weaver, whose role, while it may seem reduced since the painter denies him the 'interpretation,' is fully assured in the intelligent application of the design and the quality of the execution. There are sensitive hands, chilly hands, wandering hands, diligent hands. There are foolish hands and fairy hands... The painter has to cope with all these hands, of which he is at once the master and the slave. He is the conductor of this orchestra." The work of Jean Lurçat is based on a style of emphatic contrasts: colours shaded over three or four values, dog-tooth hatchings, contrasty backgrounds setting off figures, animals and plant life and creating symbolic time and space relationships between them: cocks, fish, owls, interacting with the fundamental elements, earth, air, water and fire. Lurçat's *Song of the World*, covering 400 square metres and now displayed in the Hôpital Saint-Jean at Angers, was intended as a contemporary equivalent of the Angers *Apocalypse*. In sheer size it vies with the tapestries of the Middle Ages. In the workmanship of the weavers, on the other hand, it cannot bear comparison with them.

Jean Lurçat must be credited with attracting to tapestry such important artists as Jacques Lagrange, Robert Vogenski, Emile Gilioli, Michel Tourlière and Mario

ROMEO AND JULIET, AFTER MARIO PRASSINOS
Aubusson, Goubely workshop, 1961
5′2″ × 7′8″

POPPY WITH BLUE HEART, AFTER MICHEL TOURLIÈRE
Paris, Gobelins, 1984
14′4″ × 22′6″

Prassinos; and with successfully propagating his ideas throughout the world, in Belgium by way of Anne Deglain, in Germany by way of Dirk Holger, in Spain at Sant Cugat del Valles, in Portugal through the Portalegre manufactory, in Brazil through that of Genaro de Carvalho. The fact remains that a certain academicism due to technical constraints gained ground in the course of time, in spite of the work done for Aubusson by some abstract painters since the 1950s. It was fortunate, as Pierre Vaisse has observed, that "in 1948 Pierre Baudouin, professor at the workshop school at Aubusson, undertook in collaboration with Raymond Picaud the weaving of some tapestries from prints by Henri-Georges Adam... Thus was opened a path which might have been blocked by the clear-cut theories set forth by Lurçat, a path which has led to successful work and will lead to more."

For all tapestry lovers Pierre Baudouin has become a legendary figure. The recent homage paid him in Paris through an exhibition of works, in particular several acquired in the last few years by the Fonds National d'Art Contemporain Français, has helped the public to understand the indispensable role that can be played by a personality acting as intermediary between painters and weavers. Outside the great precision afforded by the colour-coded cartoon (and, it must be admitted, the dryness of this approach), there is no other solution but to work out a formalized vocabulary of transcription. The painter has an idea: it has to find its intermediary (paper cutout, photograph, tracing) before it can take its place behind or beneath the loom. The painter has his colours: they have to be intelligently made up into samples, and their equivalents in threads and fibres have to be found. No easy task, and a thankless one, for the transcriber's personality disappears once the work has been executed. (Pierre Baudouin mentions, however, that in the contract of assignment for Le Corbusier's cartoon *Woman and Farrier* "the state of it on 25 May 1967 acknowledges my part as co-author.") A thankless task but an essential one which has been performed, and still is, by the directors of some private workshops: Pierre Daquin, Yvette Cauquil-Prince, Denise Mornet and her colleagues in the Angers workshop.

Pierre Baudouin's work with Beaudin, Calder, Lapicque, Masson and Picasso is important, but his position as intermediary was seen at its most remarkable on three particular occasions. First with Henri-Georges Adam just after the Second World War: "His prints raised a problem of shadings which the grey tints could not solve. Dumontet [professor of weaving at the National School of Aubusson] proposed to proceed by a mixing of threads in order to obtain the intermediate values. The question of transitions was thereby relegated to the background (whereas the art of hatching had long been held to be the essence of the tapestry craft). On the other hand, the forms and design, long thought of as a straightforward matter, came again to the forefront. Which is confirmed by the *Lady with the Unicorn* and the Angers *Apocalypse*."

VIOLET HEAD ON WHITE GROUND, AFTER GEORGES BRAQUE
Aubusson, 1961
10¼″ × 13¾″

The second occasion was highlighted by the exhibition of small tapestries held in 1961 at the Maison de la Culture in Le Havre: among them, a Georges Braque which deserves to rank among the finest achievements in the field of painter's tapestries. Thirdly, Pierre Baudouin's collaboration with Le Corbusier, which was the subject of a complete exhibition over ten years ago at the Musée d'Art et d'Histoire, Geneva, and the Musée des Arts Décoratifs, Paris. François Mathey's catalogue notes give a good account of the closeness and imaginativeness of the working relationship established between the two men, in their mutual esteem and devotion. It was an unqualified success, and together they created a set of tapestries which stands out as one of the most coherent of this century.

GUADARRAMA, AFTER LUIS FEITO
Workshop of Saint-Cyr, 1971
6′3″ × 8′6″

INDEPENDENT WORKSHOPS

There are other workshops in which independent weavers have taken a personal pleasure in interpreting the work of painters through the rich medium of the textile vocabulary. One of the most lyrical of all these interpreters is Plasse Le Caisne, who with a frame loom has interpreted Zack, Rouault, Bazaine and Manessier. He writes: "In the painter's cartoon you will find the diapason and pitch of sound. If the cartoon is an oil, you have to set the grand organ playing. A gouache, and it's the piano. A water-colour, and it's the harp, it's Debussy."

These interpreters have rediscovered the delight of coloured fibre as a substitute for transparency, opacity and glazing; and the delight of their mastery of weave as a substitute for a coat of paint, a cracking, a tapering, a laceration. J. de la Baume-Dürbach, wife of the sculptor René Dürbach, made adaptations of Léger, Villon and Picasso in their lifetime, of Delaunay and Van Doesburg after their death, working in a highly architectured manner, but without making play with texture. Proceeding on the same lines Yvette Cauquil-Prince has adapted Max Ernst, Roberto Matta, Fernand Léger and Marc Chagall, going even as far as hyperrealism with Brassaï. In contrast, Pierre Daquin and Marie Moulinier have expressed a personal vision in which the role of the weaver is inseparable from that of the painter. Daquin has interpreted works by Fichet, Morin, Feito, and the American artist June C. Wayne; his skill has attained its full scope in his collaboration with Raoul Ubac in which the roundings-off marked on the right side of the tapestry go to render the reliefs of Ubac's work. As regards Marie Moulinier, her use of the *lirette*–that is, weaving done on strips of cloth–enables her to extend the range of her colours, which are brought into play as much as texture.

Two other names must be mentioned. Alain Dupuis has worked out an original technique of collage stitching which achieves an equivalence of painting in the same spirit as woven tapestry. Julien Coffinet, a former weaver at the Gobelins in Paris, has settled on the Lake of Geneva with his wife Aimée Collonges: there, in addition to his twofold activity as a writer and teacher, he has made weavings from works by Hans Erni and Jean Arp.

SHOCK WAVE, AFTER JUNE C. WAYNE
Workshop of Saint-Cyr, 1978
10 ft. × 6½ ft.

GRAFFITI II, AFTER BRASSAÏ
Cauquil-Prince workshop, 1971
6½ ft. × 12½ ft.

INDEPENDENT CREATORS

One of the most striking features of tapestry in the past twenty years is that some weavers, unconnected with national or private factories, have felt the need to carry out a work of their own which, while keeping to traditional of lettuce. Denis Doria has woven a set of tapestries which are like an emblem picture of modern society. For him a Métro ticket, a calendar page, an identity card, are so many symbols of present-day life, capable of recording history of today, just as battle scenes and Nativities once acted as symbols of the divine right of states. Frédérique Petit has within a few years acquired a position of her own as one of the foremost creators in this field. She stands for experiment and renewal with due respect for traditional techni-

SYMBOLS DESIGNED AND WOVEN BY URSULA PLEWKA-SCHMIDT
1978
Wool and linen
9′10″ × 29′6″

techniques, has achieved some novel results. These weavers have had no share in the renewal of textile art, for their aim is not to bring back into perspective the constituent elements of the fabric, but on the contrary to accept the constraints and even the history of Western tapestry, while renewing the traditional imagery in a contemporary context.

Among the forerunners of this movement was Manzana Pissarro, the direct heir of the Arts and Crafts movement and Art Nouveau. His gold-thread tapestries, woven in the workshop he set up with his wife in 1913, were much influenced by Oriental imagery, common to both the fashions and the illustrations of his period. The layout of his works is distinctively illustrational, bringing the frame into play with effects of symmetry and featuring a simple central subject whose curves lock the figures in a spiral movement which carries the eye towards a centre occupied by the symbol of the work. His *Nativity*, exhibited in 1914 at the Musée des Arts Décoratifs, Paris, is one of the most representative works of this independent venture.

In more recent years several names have gained prominence in France: Marie Moulinier, Denis Doria and Frédérique Petit. In addition to her skill at transcription, Marie Moulinier, using the *lirette* technique, has admirably rendered her impressions of days spent at Nice, on the French Riviera, where she has made frequent stays. Her woven miniatures evoke the times of day in the form of small poetic landscapes in a highly personal style. In collaboration with Denis Doria, she exhibited at the Lausanne Biennial a *Salad* which made play with textile materials so effectively as to create the likeness of a freshly picked head

FRANZ KAFKA DESIGNED AND WOVEN BY JAN HLADIK
1978
7′6″ × 4′9″

176

ques. Her works usually consist of a sequence of scenes in which the subject, whether landscape, interior or sky, dissolves into the monochrome weaving. Her technical skill is never virtuosity for its own sake. It establishes a felt relation between the elements of a fully mastered execution and a setting which, despite its reduced size, retains a thoroughly theatrical spirit. In Canada, the United States and Eastern Europe too, in recent years, some talented tapestry makers have come forward who have pursued a tradition challenged by international textile art.

Marcel Marois, of Quebec, has chosen to illustrate ecological and topical themes. His large panels, with their alternation and overlapping of uniform surfaces and narrative spaces, lay stress on the massacre of wild animals. Ruth Scheuer and Helena Hernmarck also make use of photographs of landscapes and flowers. Working with the high-warp technique in her Greenwich Village studio, Ruth Scheuer starts from colour slides in which the main subject stands out against a hazy background. Helena Hernmarck is a Swedish artist who works on a low-warp loom; her weaving is characterized by emphatic textural effects. Among the younger artists, Sheila O'Hara has developed a distinctive imagery derived from advertising: suspended motorways and computers go to make up landscapes peopled with small stylized figures taken over from video games.

THE MOON DESIGNED AND WOVEN BY MARIE MOULINIER
"Lirette" tapestry, 1982
12″ × 10″

PROGRESSIVE TENSION DESIGNED AND WOVEN
BY MARCEL MAROIS
High warp, natural wools and linen
1981
6′ × 10′4″

In Poland, Ursula Plewka-Schmidt and Stefan Poplawski have done much to make the renewal of tradition better known. *Symbols,* exhibited by the former at the Lausanne Biennial of 1979, brings face to face the emblems of the two opposed worlds of the West: Marilyn Monroe and a Polish Madonna. The hyperrealistic weaving makes use of a very distinct mixture of materials and brings the history of tapestry into fresh focus. The squaring, which enabled her to transfer the cartoon design to the warp, is here displayed in the actual weaving, while certain ele-

CLOUDS
DESIGNED AND WOVEN BY FRÉDÉRIQUE PETIT
1983
Mini-tapestry

THE PONTIAC CURTAIN
DESIGNED AND WOVEN BY GERHARDT KNODEL
1982
Cotton, mylar, wire, linen
8 panels, each 5′7¾″ wide

ments are offset in relation to each other, bringing to mind the montages of Polaroid photographs exhibited in recent years by Stefan de Jaeger and David Hockney. Stefan Poplawski also illustrates some of the picture symbols which belong to the common stock of the West: topical photographs from newspapers or films (like *Death in Venice*) are woven in sisal hemp, following the principle of a highly contrasted weave combining two opposing colours.

But the richest personality is certainly that of Jan Hladik. Drawing directly from tradition, from Mantegna or from Raphael's *Acts of the Apostles,* he has renewed its workmanship by simplifying weaving procedures and colours. He also makes use of photographic portraits, successfully working out his operative relations with these images of tapestry's past. Like Ursula Plewka-Schmidt, he marks out a fresh line of thought for an art which can thus pursue a dialogue with history by drawing on its prestigious tradition.

If tapestry has been a "mirror of civilization" (Phyllis Ackerman) and a "mirror of history" (W.G. Thomson), it may be through these independent artists that it can best renew this dialogue with the past, unthought of and unheeded so long as the painters had dominated the scene. The way thus pointed out is one to which the tapestry manufactories should not remain indifferent.

THE REVIVAL OF TEXTILE ART

Elsi Giauque (1900)
Gilded Colours Column, 1978
Personal technique, silk, wool, gold thread
7′2″ × 11″ × 11″

THE SOURCES OF CONTEMPORARY TEXTILE ART

WOJCIECH SADLEY (1932)
MISSA ABSTRACTA, 1965
11′10″ × 6′7″
Wool and linen
Tapestry and knotted stitch

Although it is only quite recently that the consciousness of a renaissance in the art of textiles may be said to have dawned with a dazzling effect, owing to the impact of the great international exhibitions, it would be wrong to consider the phenomenon as spontaneous.

It is thanks to creators particularly involved in the artistic and social thought of their time, almost without interruption since the close of the nineteenth century, that the art of textiles has enjoyed a new wave of popularity in the West. Not only have the creations of these artists been based on a revival of the techniques and formal elements belonging properly to textiles; they have often been accompanied by a militant and pedagogic intention.

To reduce to its simplest expression a chain of events spanning a century, we can say that contemporary textile art sprang from a strange, *a priori* confluence of the Bauhaus with non-Western textile traditions.

On one hand there was a rigorous spirit in pedagogic form attained after the reflections of William Morris on the fresh impetus given to the Applied Arts, the Arts and Crafts Movement and Art Nouveau. It was a frame of mind in which everything had to be achieved by elaborating an approach that, in textiles, aimed at showing to advantage the grammatical importance of the running of the yarn and the texture of the fabric: the influence of this approach came to be felt in Western and Central Europe as well as in Japan and the United States, particularly following the diaspora of teachers after the general break-up of 1933.

On the other hand there were miraculously preserved cloths enabling archaeologists to piece together the puzzle of societies for whom textiles were a language, a vehicle of thought, the image of, and sometimes the field in which to exercise, their powers; fragments of stuffs that enabled ethnologists studying techniques still used today to compare those textile structures with the representation of the world and the social structures of certain communities; fabrics, in short, permitting contemporary artists to draw upon a diversified vocabulary offering them new, extra-pictorial material and a chance to work in the dimensions of space, bringing suppleness or tension into play–in other words, to adopt approaches no longer aimed solely at figurative representation, but which allow the expression of textile qualities and values.

Nevertheless, it is clear that a concrete appreciation of the full extent of this rediscovery of the past had to wait until the 1960s, when designers formed a movement known as "Textile Art" or "Fiberart" as a reaction against traditional tapestry, which had gained recognition down through the centuries as the most important textile expression.

The International Tapestry Biennial of Lausanne, Switzerland, was founded in 1962, thanks to the efforts of Jean Lurçat, who managed to persuade the municipality to create a permanent centre known as the International Centre of Ancient and Modern Tapestry (ICAMT). This body, whose statutes were not adopted until 6 June 1966, included in its objectives the creation of a library, a repository for tapestry cartoons and a card file of designers, the possible setting up of a weaving workshop and, lastly, the organization "of international tapestry exhibitions, in principle Biennials." It is worth noting that it was the

MARIA LASZKIEWICZ (1892-1981)
WHITE LADY, 1979
5'11" × 2'7"
Sisal, tapestry

attainment of the last of these goals which caught world-wide attention and made Lausanne the city of tapestry.

From these facts it may be concluded, therefore, that a confrontation had become historically necessary to achieve the recognition of the diversity of textile art; and that the success of the Lausanne Biennial was rooted in that historical necessity. But at the same time it is noteworthy that this event, which Jean Lurçat hoped would act as a seismograph in recording the evolution of tapestry, accommodated the strongest protest since the post-war years against the viewpoint defended in France by the painter-designers of tapestry cartoons.

In fact, although there were seven French members on the "Sponsoring Committee" which, under the presidency of Jean Lurçat, prepared the first two Biennials; and although in 1962 French painters formed the largest numerical group of exhibitors (14 out of 57); and although, finally, the works were for the most part woven in France, on the other hand, beginning with the second show in 1965 some new approaches in weaving and certain off-the-loom techniques were accepted that opened the door to designers from Eastern Europe (Magdalena Abakanowicz, Jagoda Buic, Maria Laszkiewicz, Wojciech Sadley), from Spain (Josep Grau-Garriga, Aurelia Muñoz) and from Holland (Wilhelmina Fruytier, Herman Scholten), who succeeded in creating an alternative to the leadership of the French school of tapestry design. The following Biennial of 1967 would confirm that loss of hegemony still more closely by the presence of Olga de Amaral, Maria Teresa Codina, Sheila Hicks and Elsi Giauque, who was to create her *Column of Singing Colours*, one of the first spatial works shown in Lausanne.

The press release issued by ICAMT in May 1965, "New Techniques in Tapestry at the Second Lausanne Biennial," in fact explained: "For some years we have witnessed a sensible change in the procedures of traditional tapestry. Some artists have not hesitated to break with the 'classical' technique of the Gobelins (high warp) and of Aubusson (low warp) by using new materials and turning some of the laws of tapestry upside down. These innovations were given a reserved welcome by purists of the arts of the heddle, but an enthusiastic one by all those who sought to depart from beaten paths and translate into 'tapestry' the poetic language of our time. It was for this reason that the jury of the Second Tapestry Biennial accepted woven works which had not been created and carried out by traditional technical methods. The programme was expanded and embroidery, for example, was not excluded from this international festival of woolcraft."

This press release, together with a personal article by André Kuenzi emphasizing the high quality of participation by Polish artists, touched off violent reactions from Jean Lurçat and the French artists in general, which assumed the proportions of a veritable diplomatic incident.

Marie Frechette, who devoted her thesis in 1976 to "The Renewal of Tapestry from 1960 to 1975 through the Lausanne Biennials," quotes some of these reactions from the archives of ICAMT, often addressed to Pierre Pauli, chief commissioner and friend of Jean Lurçat, who succeeded in attracting to Lausanne these artists who approached the art of fibre in a new spirit.

To cite only two of the most significant statements, there is the one by Jean Lurçat of 12 May 1965: "Now the ideas this circular puts forward are at the opposite extreme from the position taken by several members of the French Committee and the International President"; and that of 25 May by Mario Prassinos: "On one hand it seems to me that this publicity granted to one section of your Biennial shows prejudice against others, particularly the French section, which in our eyes is relegated to the rank of 'traditional' old hat... What you have stirred up resembles something of a press campaign against the French section. You will understand that we take a rather dim view of it."

The first wrathful reaction by Jean Lurçat was followed by a more humorous challenging of the quality of the Polish and Yugoslav entries. "Let us salute in passing those charming feminine comrades, formerly fabric designers, who, passing lyrically from tweed to Greek tragedy, press themselves so tightly against the tragic spirit of 1965 that we feel at last made fruitful and ready to bear. The candied fruits inserted into the body of the cloth have, from another angle, achieved this miracle. But at least it has relieved the tension in the atmosphere; our bad temper has given way to laughter." Such a remark, apart from its antifeminist character, has the merit of demonstrating, by its very extremism, that what scandalized most was the act of revealing beneath the image of tapestry the hidden language of textiles.

AURELIA MUÑOZ (1926)
MACRA ROSA, 1972
27½″ × 10″
Sisal, macramé

HERMAN SCHOLTEN (1932)
KNOOP, 1966
5′11″ × 6′7″
Wool, weaving, appliqué work

"Watch out for those little girls who knit," Lurçat had further warned. Those artists, men or women, whom Pierre Pauli and René Berger, Curator-Director of the Cantonal Museum of Fine Arts of Lausanne, had succeeded in attracting to the Biennial, brought a new approach which Marie Frechette summed up with striking clarity by forging a new term to describe them: "The weaver-creators, producing their own object from start to finish, perceived that their material was not colour, paper or canvas but in actual fact the fibre; that the tool of their trade was not the drawing pencil or paper, but in the first place the loom, the crochet hook or the needle; that the laws governing their creations were not the formal laws of the organization of coloured designs on paper or canvas but before all else the special procedures of the technique they were using. This meant the conscious rejection of a legitimacy of painting in tapestry. The weaver-creators were aiming no longer at reproducing a pictorial image in wool, but instead at producing an autonomous object telling of the specific qualities of the materials and techniques that went into its making. The signifier once again was playing an active role."

Twenty years after these impassioned reactions, with a large collection currently being assembled at Lausanne by the Pierre Pauli Association, presided over by Dr Pierre Magnenat, it is possible, with the benefit of some hindsight, to observe that the surprise of the painter-designers was in fact due only to a too-imprecise statement of the aims of the exhibition. If the Lausanne Biennial had been conceived with the aim of promoting tapestry through the different pictorial tendencies of the designers who had shown an interest in it, those designers' disillusionment may be legitimately understood. If, on the contrary, the seismograph was meant to record the whole of the development of textile art, it may be said that there was nothing surprising about the entry of "new approaches and new techniques."

Beyond the fact that these techniques were not really new–some even preceded the beginnings of warp tapestry–, the approaches to textiles made by the artists selected at Lausanne, coming together at the same time from all the corners of the globe, amounted only to the public revelation of a deep-rooted movement arising in the late nineteenth century.

Therefore, even before examining the tendencies and evolution of that movement, we must go back to the personalities and institutions that were capable of influencing this renaissance of textile art in the West.

WILLIAM MORRIS

The hangings of William Morris marked an essential stage in the rereading of tapestry characteristic of the past hundred years in the West, but his creations in the fields of embroidery, printed fabrics, weaving and rugs made him an equally original forerunner of the renaissance in textile art. In his approach Morris combined revivals of interest in several areas: rediscovery and fresh promotion of cottage-industry techniques; research into and contemporary adaptation of historical examples of Western and Eastern textiles; scrupulous matching of a creation with the specific characteristics of its technique.

He was born in 1834, shortly before the publication of Pugin's *True Principles of Christian Architecture*. His adolescence was coming to an end when Ruskin brought out *The Seven Lamps of Architecture* (1849), and in 1861, at the age of twenty-seven, he started his first business venture (Morris, Marshall, Faulkner & Co.) with Rossetti, Burne-Jones, Madox Brown and Philip Webb, the architect to whom he entrusted the designing of his home, Red House, at Upton, Kent. This became the meeting place of the community of artists which gathered around him. Not all of them, in fact, were artists; Marshall had been trained as an engineer and Faulkner was a mathematician. But all these men, whether closely or distantly involved in the Pre-Raphaelite movement, subscribed to the idea of a

WILLIAM MORRIS (1834–1896)
ARTICHOKE, 1877
Wool over linen, embroidery
Created for Mrs Ada Phoebe Godman,
Smeaton Manor, Yorkshire

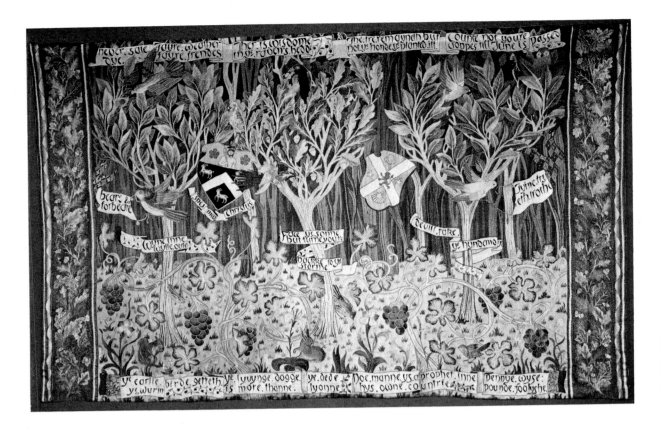

MAY MORRIS (1861-1936)
THE BATTYE EMBROIDERED
HANGING, c. 1900
Silk over linen
Created for the
Battye family

necessary return to the Christian values that had led to the creation of the noble buildings of the Middle Ages.

Their thought processes were thus characterized not only by the return to a previous style of architecture, furniture and pictorial representation, but also by an attraction to a way of life in which the artist-craftsman practised his craft with joy as part of a collective purpose.

William Morris's preface to Ruskin's "The Nature of Gothic," a chapter from *The Stones of Venice* (published separately by the Kelmscott Press, 1892), clearly shows how closely this romantic vision of the Middle Ages is related to the socialist beliefs inspired by Robert Owen and Charles Fourier. Morris involved his family and friends closely in his work, in a community spirit. Henry James, reporting a visit to Queen Square in 1869, mentions that Morris was assisted by his wife Jane and his two small daughters, aged seven and eight. It was in fact his eldest daughter May who, following in his wife's footsteps, took over the management of the embroidery workshop in 1885. She was helped by John Henry Dearle, an assistant to Morris, who became the artistic director of the firm on Morris's death in 1896.

It is noteworthy that although tapestry formed one of the strongest poles of attraction for William Morris, embroidery was for him, as it was for Jean Lurçat, the initial testing ground in the textile arts. From 1857 onwards he relaunched the study of medieval embroideries, in particular of English pieces known as *opus anglicanum*.

His first embroidery, *If I Can*, was the only one he did entirely with thick woollen yarn coloured with an aniline dye. The recurrent motif of bird and tree was highly stylized, and by its strongly pronounced texture and considerable thickness sought to imitate the effects of woven tapestry. Subsequently, however, thanks to his personal rediscoveries, he advised his embroiderers to use couched-down stitches, more in keeping with the spirit of the technique, and also utilized yarns dyed with vegetable pigments, brought to new perfection according to his instruc-

tions by Thomas Wardle. Then, abandoning medieval inspiration, he turned his hand to the silks and velvets of the sixteenth and seventeenth centuries from the Middle East and Italy. The most celebrated design of this period was the "Artichoke." First commissioned in 1877 by Ada Phoebe Goodman for wall panels worked in wool on linen for Smeaton Manor, a house designed by Philip Webb, this design was afterwards to be repeated in silk embroidery for Margaret Beale.

The embroideries by May Morris remained, on the contrary, in a completely medieval style, playing upon the alternations and intertwinings of stylized trees, flowers, fruits and birds, and incorporating stanzas chosen from her father's poems or the armorial bearings of the patron commissioning the work, as in the case of the panels for the Battye family.

It was in the field of printed fabrics and weaving, however, that Morris best achieved an original creation of textile designs and an intention to come as close as possible to the truth of traditional techniques of handicraft industry. His philosophy regarding techniques and materials admirably heralds the attitude of many designers today: "I have tried to produce goods which should be genuine as far as their mere substances are concerned, have tried, for instance, to make woollen substances as woollen as possible, cotton as cottony as possible, and so on; have used only the dyes which are natural and simple because they produce beauty almost without the intervention of art." Elsewhere he adds: "Never forget the material you are working with, and try always to use it for doing what it can do best: if you feel yourself hampered by the material in which you are working, instead of being helped by it, you have so far not learned your business, any more than a would-be poet has, who complains of the hardship of writing in measure and rhyme. The special limitations of the material should be a pleasure to you, not a hindrance: a designer, therefore, should always thoroughly understand the processes of the special manufacture he is dealing with, or the result will be a mere *tour de force*. On the other hand, it is the pleasure in understanding the capabilities of a special material, and using them for suggesting (not imitating) natural beauty and incident, that gives the *raison d'être* of decorative art."

This search for the genuine was based on socialist political convictions which led William Morris to oppose the whole range of products and techniques of the industrial society of his day. The dyeing industry, for example, was in his view more interested in boosting its profits than in serving original designers. It was for this reason that he engaged in long and costly research on indigo dyes. It is not merely anecdotal to mention that the embroidered panels decorating Red House were done on the usual material of work-clothes, blue serge; and that William Morris systematically wore clothes of wool, cotton or linen that were dyed indigo.

The technique of block printing was among the most interesting of those revived by Morris. It consists in taking a fabric which has first been dyed all over to a uniform colour and, with a wooden block, applying to those parts meant to appear white or pale blue, or subsequently to be dyed yellow, a bleaching reagent of greater or lesser strength.

"Wandle," a chintz fabric of 1883 designed in the spirit of seventeenth-century silks, or "Tulip and Willow," based on an 1873 design, are good examples of this technique. The designs of this period are always of a large size, making an especially masterful use of the mirror effect, and are spread over the entire width of the cloth. It was surely this feature that made the printed stuffs of William Morris best known, for he told designers: "Do not be afraid of large patterns; if properly designed they are more restful to the eye than small ones: on the whole, a pattern where the structure is large and the details much broken up is the most useful... Very small rooms, as well as very large ones, look best ornamented with large patterns."

In the field of weaving, William Morris, starting with only four looms, was to reintroduce a variety of weaves and a richness of design practically unequalled since the seventeenth century.

After 1877, thanks to technical assistance from a French brocade-weaver named Bazin, he used a steam-powered Jacquard loom. Apart from Jacquard weaving, which provided great freedom in the adaptation of designs, this highly diversified technical vocabulary included serge, gauze, damask and the "three-ply tapestry" used, for

WILLIAM MORRIS (1834-1896)
TULIP AND WILLOW, 1873
Indigo chintz
Designed for Morris and Co., London

WILLIAM MORRIS (1834-1896)
BIRD, 1878
Wool, double cloth weaving
Designed for Morris and Co., London

example, in the "Bird" woollen cloth created in 1878 for the drawing-room at Kelmscott House. The "Bird" design offers a striking example of the fusion of oriental and Middle Eastern influences. In addition to the unbroken chain of foliage patterns of the ground, the mirrored animal stylizations reappear in perfect proportion and alternation.

Morris's studies of Middle Eastern fabrics, begun under the influence of John Henry Middleton, an archaeologist whom he met in Iceland, led him not only to become a collector and consultant valued for his choice of acquisitions by the South Kensington Museum, but also to take over the colour schemes of Middle Eastern textiles. Weavings such as "Peacock and Dragon" or "Ispahan," and above all the carpets of the 1880s, are perfectly in keeping with the spirit of his assertion: "On the whole, in designing carpets the method of *contrast* is the best one to employ, and blue and red, quite frankly used, with white or very light outlines on a dark ground, are the main colours on which the designer should depend."

THE ARTS AND CRAFTS MOVEMENT AND ART NOUVEAU

The work of William Morris moves us today by the originality of its designs and the breadth of its scope; but it also derives all its significance from the questions it raises, some of which are still of interest today in textile creation.

How can art and handicrafts be brought together? How can artistic creation find a common ground with industry? The movement to restore a privileged status to handicrafts and to secure the fusion of the arts traces its origin to Ruskin, whose analysis comparing the status of craftsmen down through the centuries culminates in the idealization of Christian society: "The Greek gave to the lower workman no subject which he could not perfectly execute. The Assyrian gave him subjects which he could only execute imperfectly, but fixed a legal standard for his imperfections. The workman was, in both systems, a slave. But in the medieval, or especially Christian, system of ornament, this slavery is done away with altogether; Christianity having recognized, in small things as well as great, the individual value of every soul. But it not only recognizes its value; it confesses its imperfection."

It is obviously a vision of this kind, making possible a reconciliation between artist and craftsman, which enabled England, at the close of the nineteenth century, to become the world's chief centre of attraction in the applied arts. As Gillian Naylor writes: "British architects and craftsmen had broken free from the tunnels of the past, and had created a new art, a personal aesthetic that would embrace architecture and design as well as the 'fine' arts." This Art Nouveau was to spread throughout continental Europe and to the United States, with characteristics peculiar to each country; but during this period the influence of English creators was remarkable. Some of them exerted that influence by forming themselves into guilds or by carrying out reforms in teaching: for example, A.H. Mackmurdo, the founder of the Century Guild and initiator of the Art Workers' Guild, managed by Walter Crane and W.R. Lethaby, who founded the Central School of Arts and Crafts in London.

WILLIAM MORRIS (1834–1896)
A HAMMERSMITH RUG, c. 1890
Wool and cotton, handmade

Henry van de Velde (1863-1957)
The Angels' Vigil, 1893
Embroidery on felt ground
4'7" × 7'8"

Others were influential through their personal talents as writers and teachers: C.R. Ashbee, founder of the Guild of Handicrafts, whose dialogue with his fellow architect Frank Lloyd Wright was extremely fruitful; Lewis Day and Walter Crane, both textile creators highly esteemed throughout the rest of Europe. It was also the period when the Arts and Crafts Exhibition Society, formed in 1888, and the London magazine *The Studio*, launched in 1893 to propound its philosophy, drew the aesthetic adherence of Louis Comfort Tiffany in the United States, of the architect Victor Horta in Brussels (especially after the 1891 Exhibition) and above all of Henry Van de Velde. Within the Brussels group calling itself "La Libre Esthétique" (The Free Aesthetic), Van de Velde equally strove, on his side, to unify all the arts. It was Belgium moreover, no doubt because of the socialist convictions of the leaders of the artistic movement, which would succeed in establishing a necessary relay for the Arts and Crafts Movement by forging an alliance for continental Europe between English ideas and those originating in France (in the Union Centrale des Beaux-Arts appliqués à l'Industrie), Germany (around Hermann Muthesius, Peter Behrens and Walter Gropius) and Austria (in the Wiener Werkstätte).

This transmission of ideas, however, was marked by a noteworthy purification. Although the ideal of handicraft was preserved, it was disburdened of its Gothic idealism, as being too simplistic, and of its hard-line rejection of mechanization. Indeed, although the English creators succeeded in imposing Art Nouveau, they nevertheless failed in their aim of turning it into a popular style. Ashbee alone was capable of exposing this contradiction between social aims and the elitism inherent in cottage-industry creation: "Modern civilization," he wrote at the dawn of the twentieth century, "rests on machinery and no system for the endowment or the encouragement or the teaching of art can be found that does not recognize this." It cannot be denied that such an observation sprang from the reading of texts by Frank Lloyd Wright, but it very quickly became general throughout all of Europe.

Henry Van de Velde, although he desired that painters and sculptors should become handicraftsmen, advocated the acquisition of the practical skills of industrial design by the craftsman himself. In his view, the first thing to be done was to reunify architecture, the decorative arts and industry. Hermann Muthesius developed similar ideas in Germany beginning in 1904, and it was the Deutscher Werkbund, formed in 1907, which gave a concrete shape to the basic ideological movement out of which the Bauhaus was born.

From this standpoint, the manifesto of the Weimar Bauhaus, drawn up by Walter Gropius in 1919, has remained famous: "There is no difference between the craftsman and the artist. The artist is a craftsman inspired. In rare moments of inspiration, transcending his conscious will, his work, by the grace of heaven, blossoms into art. But competent craftsmanship is essential to every artist. It is in craftsmanship that the primary source of creative imagination lies. Let us therefore create a new guild of craftsmen freed of class distinctions that raise an arrogant barrier between craftsman and artist. Let us desire, conceive, create together the new structure of the future that will unite architecture, sculpture and painting into a single

189

unity from which, produced by the hands of millions of workers, will rise heavenwards the crystal symbol of a new faith."

A parallel but lesser known movement that grew up in Russia must also be mentioned. The principles of Suprematism and Constructivism were transmitted to the applied arts, and in particular to textiles and clothing, even before the Revolution of 1917. Vladimir Tatlin shared with William Morris the conviction that social and economic problems could be solved through art. Rodchenko, Popova and Stepanova, as well as many other lesser known artists of revolutionary Russia created woven and printed stuffs as well as professional clothes. Their approach seems to us perfectly in keeping with the

general philosophy of the Arts and Crafts Movement: Walter Crane, Lewis Day, A.H. Mackmurdo and Arthur Silver. Their patterns made the Liberty firm a success, so much so that Art Nouveau English textiles are often identified with this company, and that the Italian equivalent of Art Nouveau was to be named "Liberty Style."

In the next generation, Charles Rennie Mackintosh equally deserves to be mentioned. Between 1915 and 1923, indeed, he collaborated with his wife on designs for fabrics and appliqué work highly stylized and perfectly suited for either wall panels or the furniture of his own design.

In Belgium and Germany the personality of Henry Van de Velde was naturally pre-eminent in this field. The *Angels' Vigil*, a transposition in appliqué embroidery of a

HENRY VAN DE VELDE (1863-1957)
EMBROIDERED BODICE, 1896-1898

remark by Brick published in the review *Lef* in 1924: "Artistic culture is not confined to objects displayed in exhibitions and museums... Painting is not the framed picture but the whole pictorial ensemble of everyday life experience. The Indian woman is a product of artistic culture as much as a painting is; there is no reason to draw a distinction between them."

The cluster of ideas developed by English Art Nouveau, French Modern Style and German and Austrian Jugendstil, ending with the opening of the Bauhaus, is expressed above all, of course, in architecture and furniture. But a number of creators also became interested in fabrics, to the point where textile creation became, as for Morris, essential to their interest in applied arts.

In England, the personality of William Morris somewhat eclipsed the other textile creators adhering to the

painting which he sent to the Salon of Les Vingt in Brussels in 1893, forms a veritable statement of aims marking the reconciliation of painting and textiles.

This work, made of pieces of felt in complementary colours, is both of Japanese inspiration and close to comparable textile works of the Pont-Aven school. It aims at keeping as close as possible to the truth of the material it uses. A creator of models and designs for soft furnishings with sinuous, strongly marked lines, at times going back to the technique of batik, Van de Velde also ventured with his wife into the garment world, creating embroidery designs of which the finished executions are preserved in the Zurich Kunstgewerbe Museum. But this interest in clothing which gives freedom to the body, a forerunner of the work of the French *couturier* Paul Poiret, remained confined to a small circle of friends. Cécile Lemaire recalls: "In conclusion, it seems to us that the authentic Art Nouveau style was limited to Van de Velde creations alone. If the will to beauty in the minds of the creators which presided over the birth of their creations depends on a social ethic, their aestheticism places them rather in a *fin-de-siècle* atmosphere. On the other hand, their ornamentation is unquestionably an aesthetic expression of the beginnings of Art Nouveau, that privileged moment in which, as Dr Steinberger has said, line took possession of form."

Apart from the creations of the Austrians Koloman Moser and Josef Hoffman, carefully constructed and flirting with Japanese style, there must also be mentioned those of Hermann Obrist in Germany. After leaving Florence, where he had already done some pioneer work in textile

used. All these workshops were perfectly able to work from folkloric inspiration as well.

Other centres, founded in the same spirit, would be established in Sweden and close to Oslo, where the Norwegian Frida Hansen worked starting in 1887. Madeleine Jarry has emphasized the precursory nature of this artist's work: "More, perhaps, than by her Art Nouveau compositions, which today seem somewhat outmoded, Frida Hansen is ahead of her time in her weaving technique. She furnishes specially conceived models: the idea and the execution are as one. She innovates by inventing her transparent portières, the culmination of research on textures very close to the concerns of artists today."

In the Nordic countries we must mention, finally, the

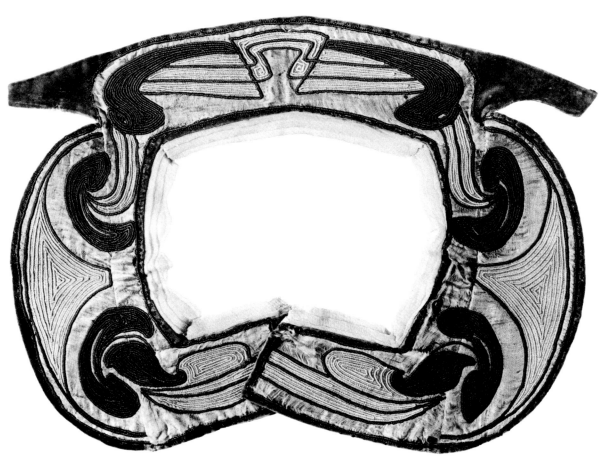

HENRY VAN DE VELDE (1863-1957)
EMBROIDERED COLLAR, 1896-1898

art, Obrist set up his embroidery workshop in Munich in 1894, and in 1895 exhibited *The Cyclamen*, embroidered in golden thread on a silk banner. Like Van de Velde, he also worked with appliqué cloths.

As in Berlin and Munich, Art Nouveau enjoyed public promotion in Hamburg, thanks to the efforts of Justus Brinckmann, Director of the Museum of Arts and Crafts. He contributed to the establishment of weaving workshops at Scherrebek, in North Schleswig, which was active from 1896 to 1903. These, already mentioned in connection with tapestry, but producing cushion covers and rugs, formed a school in Kiel in Germany and at Ljubljana in Yugoslavia (then Laibach and a part of Austria). Whether in tapestry or other textile pieces, there is the complete sense of renouncement of pictorial quality in favour of the quest for a correspondence between forms and materials

Swedish artist Marta Maas-Fjetterström, who drew her inspiration both from local peasant traditions and from Persian carpets; Gerhardt Munthe and above all Loja Saarinen, the wife of the architect Eliel Saarinen, who wove carpets and tapestries by going back to the *rya* technique of the people in a spirit of integration with the architectural creations of her husband.

If the study of plants provided a source of inspiration for William Morris, French Art Nouveau equally took its cue from plant life. The writings of Eugène Grasset *(The Plant and its Ornamental Uses)* or of M.P. Verseuil *(Study of the Plant: its Application to Art Industries)* had an appreciable effect on the printed fabrics of Félix Aubert as well as on those of Alphonse Mucha. Aubert's water irises and Mucha's flower-women make up two of the symbolic themes of *fin-de-siècle* decoration in France. But besides the

adherents of Art Nouveau, a number of painters have shown interest in textile techniques close to tapestry.

The Nabi painters, such as Jan Verkade, were, like William Morris, influenced by the tapestries of the Middle Ages, but also by the *Lady with the Unicorn*. If this influence flowed from tapestry towards painting in the work of Vuillard, in Gauguin's circle, on the contrary, there was a rediscovery of the decorative arts, textiles, tapestry, embroidery and appliqué ornament. In this movement Paul Ranson stands out as one of the major figures carrying out embroidery designs with many arabesques, executed by his wife. He was influenced in this pursuit by Aristide Maillol, who organized an embroidery workshop at Banyuls, in the Eastern Pyrenees, which aimed at quality yarns as well as the best formulas for vegetable dyeing.

Except for Manzana Pissarro, of whom we have already spoken as regards woven tapestry, years had to pass before the advent of artists uncommitted to Art Nouveau, whose contact with fabrics produced works of absolutely amazing feeling for cloth, and which were often used in fashion.

The two famous examples in France are those of Sonia Delaunay and Raoul Dufy. Between Robert and Sonia Delaunay the discussions, or to put it better, the shared experience of colour, led each to translate simultaneous colour contrasts. Robert, who was more of a theoretician, reread Chevreul's scientific studies of colour. Sonia, on the other hand, created simultaneous objects: collages, book bindings, caskets, cushions, waistcoats, lampshades, which imparted concrete form to colour awareness. In 1913 she perfected the first simultaneous

RAOUL DUFY (1877–1953)
THE JUNGLE, 1919
Damask on satin ground
4′9″ × 4′1″

Sonia Delaunay (1885–1979)
Fabric, 1924
Crêpe de chine and silk
18½″ × 9″

dress, for, as Jacques Damase writes: "Dresses for her are like architectural structures of colours playing like a fugue: a dress, a coat, is a portion of space ordered and conceived both by the material and by the dimensions."

Fabric creation, opening a boutique, a fashion atelier, the simultaneous boutique at the International Decorative Arts Exhibition in 1925 and collaboration with Jacques Heim would lead Sonia Delaunay during the inter-war period to manage with success a firm numbering as many as thirty workers. The French poet René Crevel remarks of her: "Familiar, everyday objects were like poems to her, and she took as much interest in them as in paintings." A global approach to fabrics, entirely along the lines taken by William Morris and Henry Van de Velde and which at the same time heralds that of many contemporary artists working towards portable art: "art to wear."

With Dufy, the approach is less global. It was a fashion designer and patron, Paul Poiret, a collector of paintings by Derain, Vlaminck, and Dunoyer de Segonzac, who introduced Dufy to the world of fabrics. From this contact were born sumptuous hangings and, from 1912 until 1927, silk stuffs brought out by the fashion house of Bianchini-Férier.

◁ Raoul Dufy (1877–1953)
Seashells, 1922
Crape
3′5″ × 6′7″
Designed for
Bianchini-Férier, Paris

Paul Iribe (1883–1935)
Fabric, 1929
Brocade
8′2″ × 2′8″
Designed for
Bianchini-Férier, Paris

Apart from the fabrics of Lepape and those from the workshop of Michel Dubost put out by the firm of Ducharne after 1920, there have been no comparable examples since in France between painters and industrialists, at least of creations so perfectly adapted to the spirit of fabrics and textile rhythms.

In Switzerland, lastly, but also subsequent to Art Nouveau, the example of Sophie Taeuber-Arp ushers in the textile-based approach of contemporary creators. Like the Russian Constructivists and Sonia Delaunay, she brings a structured rigour into the creation of embroideries and woven stuffs. Her teaching at the Arts and Crafts School in Zurich from 1916 to 1929 had a considerable influence on several generations of creators, of whom Elsi Giauque is the best known; an influence comparable to that of the analogous workshops of the Bauhaus, but which worked rather towards the formal rigour of simple geometric forms and pure colour confrontations.

THE BAUHAUS

Ludwig Mies Van der Rohe well described the essence of the Bauhaus by saying that it "did not involve an institution with a clear programme—it was an idea, and Gropius expressed that idea with great precision. I think that the very fact that it involved an idea accounted for the enormous influence of the Bauhaus on all the progressive schools of the whole world. A result like that cannot be obtained with an organization or by getting up an advertising campaign. Only an idea can spread so widely."

It was actually as much through the educational methods of its workshops, adapted to different stages in the development of the school, as by the dispersal of its teachers all over the world after 1933, that this experiment exerted an important influence on contemporary textile creation.

SOPHIE TAEUBER-ARP (1889-1943)
CUSHION EMBROIDERY, C. 1916
20″ × 21″

194

One feature of the Bauhaus idea lay in the partnership between a master of design and a master of technique. For the weaving workshop of the Weimar Bauhaus, it was between Georg Muche and Helene Börner, a weaving specialist who had been part of the team set up by Van de Velde in his pre-war School of Applied Arts in Weimar. Because she herself furnished the looms for her Bauhaus workshop, it was able to get started faster than the others, which were drastically short of equipment. During the first few years, of the Bauhaus, in the early 1920s, the influence of Johannes Itten's introductory courses in forms and colours was very appreciable. It is particularly evident in the tapestries of Ida Kerkovius and Margarete Köhler, who did an enormous amount of work in the alternation of materials (wool, cotton, silk and viscose) helped by contrasts of black, grey and white. But Georg Muche and Paul Klee were also responsible for certain features peculiar to a textile production of carpets and mural works that were not lacking in folkloric influences besides. The hangings of Hedwig Jungnik, for example, are more convulsive, the alternation of stitches more marked, the textile vocabulary of tapestry much richer and more colourful. Nevertheless,

it must not be forgotten that the work undertaken by Itten on textures was to make a huge contribution to all the workshops, and thus to weaving first of all.

After 1922 the discussions over the need to produce industrial models became intensified, both for commercial reasons and as an outgrowth of Gropius' original concerns.

In 1926 differences with students too deep to resolve drove Georg Muche to resign from the workshop and then, in 1927, to leave the Bauhaus. Gunta Stölzl took over running it, assisted by Lilly Reich, and soon to be replaced by her in 1931. But Gunta Stölzl's influence had already been active from the time of her entry in 1919.

When the Bauhaus moved to Dessau in 1925, she was already in charge of technical supervision of tapestry, carpets and the Jacquard method. In her textile approach she passed on the artistic concerns of Paul Klee and above all of the introductory course of Moholy-Nagy; and in a highly systematized way she tried out experiments with new materials such as cellophane. Gunta Stölzl was to make the pupils aware of the specific physical and tactile properties of textile fibres (sound absorption, light reflection) in relation to their possible use in industry.

ANNI ALBERS (1899)
Woven Fabric, 1926

It was during this period that Otti Berger, Anni Albers, Lis Beyer and Helene Nonné-Schmidt also introduced a mood of discussion, making the workshop a hub of communications virtually unique at the Bauhaus. This appreciable movement away from the one-off item towards the mass-produced object was very well described in Gunta Stölzl's essays of 1931: "Our conception of the house in 1922–1923 was very different from that which we have today. Our textiles could be poems full of ideas, of floral décors and personal experiences. They rapidly received the approval of a wide public, even outside the walls of the Bauhaus; being more accessible, and owing to the nature of their subject matter, they were the most appreciated items among the radically revolutionary productions of the Bauhaus. Progressively, a shift occurred. We began to notice the pretentiousness of these unique and independent objects: fabrics, curtains, wall panels. Their richness of colour and forms began to appear far too autocratic to us; they were not integrated into the house. We tried to become simpler, to discipline our methods and attain a greater unity between the materials utilized and their function. In this way, we managed to produce textiles by the yard, capable of clearly responding to the needs of the rooms and the problems of the house. The slogan of this new field was launched: prototypes for industry."

After its final move to Berlin in 1932, the political pressures that had always weighed on the Bauhaus became intolerable. The financial position of the school, already difficult, became catastrophic. The best teachers who had not yet left Germany, like Ludwig Hilberseimer or Wassily Kandinsky, were denied the right to teach. It was Ludwig Mies Van der Rohe who signed the information circular to students announcing the official closing on 10 August 1933.

That closing in no way signified the end of the Bauhaus adventure. The instructors emigrated, spreading the philosophy of the school, creating new teaching centres or being invited by existing schools and universities.

Walter Gropius emigrated to London, where he remained until 1937 before going on to Harvard in the United States. Josef Albers settled with his wife Anni at Black Mountain College, North Carolina; then, beginning in 1950, he taught at Yale. Marcel Breuer moved to London, then went on to Cambridge, Massachusetts. Mies Van der Rohe settled in Chicago and Kandinsky in Paris. Only Moholy-Nagy attempted to set up a new Bauhaus in Chicago in 1937, but it had to close for financial reasons. Architectural and pictorial experiments, and those with furniture, thus found a welcome and possibilities of development throughout the world.

As far as textiles were concerned, it was principally in Switzerland, Holland and the United States that the Bauhaus teaching was able to continue. Johannes Itten directed a school and a museum in Zurich, after having taught in a technical school for textiles at Krefeld. Gunta Stölzl had already set up her private workshop at Krefeld, in the Rhineland, in 1931.

Grete Neter, a Bauhaus pupil, moved to Nunspeet in Holland. There she was joined by Kitty van der Mijlle Deker, Hermann Fisher, Frans Wildenbaum and Trude Guermonprez, who herself emigrated to the United States, replacing Anni Albers, who had left to study archaeological textiles in South America. Grete Neter afterwards settled in Amsterdam in 1945, and directed the textile department of the Arts and Crafts Institute, which later became the Gerrit Rietveld Academy: she taught there for twenty-five years.

In Holland, too, Betty Hubers, a pupil of the Arts and Crafts School of Stuttgart, joined "Het Paapje," a workshop founded by the Czech Hans Polak. Her weaving, until the closing of Het Paapje in 1941, would also be the forerunner of contemporary textile research and deeply influence young Dutch creators.

Liesbeth Crommelin typifies this influence by emphasizing her extremely fertile union with the De Stijl movement and the ideas of Theo van Doesburg. It must be said that the conflict-ridden exchanges between the latter and the Bauhaus professors (especially Itten) had not been foreign to the reorientation towards industrial prototypes begun in 1922: "The principles of functionalism of the Bauhaus, in association with the principles of drawing and colour of De Stijl, laid a stable foundation for reflection on the independent treatment of threads and the structure of the fabric. Taken together, these elements constitute the seed-bed from which new trends grow in the visual arts."

In the United States, Anni Albers and Trude Guermonprez gave a new impetus to textile studies, which found an echo in Ed Rossbach, Lenore Tawney, Claire Zeisler and Sheila Hicks. Anni Albers' impact was all the more forceful in that her books *On Weaving* and *On Designing* were read all over the world, and for the most part retain their topicality to this day. She was probably the one who best expressed a primordial element of the Bauhaus philosophy on the specific characteristics of the construction of a fabric and its tactile nature: "The establishment of a structure/function relationship appeals to our intellect for its construction or its decoding by analysis. Matter, by contrast, is essentially non-functional, non-utilitarian, and for these reasons–like colour–it cannot be the object of an intellectual experience... It must be perceived instinctively... Our task today is to exercise that sensitive faculty so as to recover a faculty that was once natural to us. We must learn again to use grain and lustring, softness or roughness, relief, mixtures of coarse and fine materials. These formal elements that belong to our tactile aesthetic experience must be utilized on an equal basis with drawing and colour..."

ANNI ALBERS (1899)
Woven Fabric
7'3" × 4'

HELEN FRANKENTHALER (1928)
Left to right:

TANGERINE, 1964
Oil on canvas. 6′4″ × 5′6″

COOL SUMMER, 1962
Oil on canvas. 6′ × 10′

ACRES, 1959
Oil on canvas. 7′9″ × 7′10″

As exhibited at the Centre d'Arts
Plastiques Contemporains, Bordeaux, 1981

TEXTILE MATERIALS AND MODERN ART

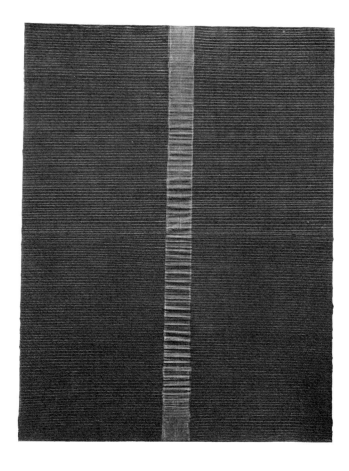

JEAN DEGOTTEX (1918)
TRANSFER LINES 1/1, 1978
Acrylic on canvas
9'6" × 6'8"

Looking at the whole range of textile experiments and creations between the mid-nineteenth century and the period just before the Second World War, we are struck by the degree of renewed attention given to the specific qualities and historical past of textiles, as if, after several centuries of neglect, the worldwide impulse to recombine the techniques of handicraft industry with artistic expression had restored to textiles the foundations of a language. It was from this starting point that the artists born in the 1930s or just after the war built up–from contact with their predecessors or works by them–a varied creative output, taking over, detail by detail, all the data which textiles provided.

The attraction, not to say at times the fascination of textiles, and of soft materials in general, not only made itself felt in the representational field, but found expression in material and sometimes even conceptual integration. Between the rope encircling Pablo Picasso's 1912 collage *Still Life With Chair Caning* and the rope installed by Magdalena Abakanowicz in various museums since 1973 or the cloth heaped, knotted or unfolded by Sheila Hicks in exhibitions throughout the world, lies all that is problematical in the entry of textile materials into modern art. If the art of textiles has broadened its domain by recognizing and putting names to its constituents and its history, painting has also stepped outside its frame in recognizing and identifying its component elements. The canvas has once more become a meaningful support in the eyes of painters and in their artistic practice.

We do not wish to imply that for centuries the canvas had remained an unknown quantity for painters, made up with paint that turned it into a mirror. Before Cézanne, before Matisse or Pollock, there were artists who utilized the ambiguity inherent in the depiction of a fabric; others had allowed the fibre of the canvas to show through so as to draw attention to the materiality of their painting, to the nature of their support.

To be convinced of this we have only to take another look at Louis Marin's descriptions of the *Veil of Veronica* as treated by Domenico Feti or Philippe de Champaigne, or those by Leo Steinberg of the *Menippus* of Velazquez, where the mystery of the philosopher is captured between the thick impasto of the foreground and a background of canvas barely veiled with paint. What distinguishes a particular type of contemporary painting is not its ignorance of its sources but the intensification of its analysis of the canvas. It is a diversified movement, spreading through an area of American and European painting, of those who have been grouped , or have grouped themselves, under the label "Support/Surface." In this movement, the most obvious characteristic is the changed status of the painted canvas, both in the method of work and in the final installation, and thus its perception by the spectator. The canvas is a nomadic space, and is treated accordingly.

Secondly there is the problem of the figure. The liquid pigment becomes the medium of figuration. It is the colour itself that creates the image, with the artist thereby transcending the traditional dualism of line and colour. As

Michel Butor writes, the canvas "blots," once more becoming an area to be dyed.

The third point involves the instruments. They are manufactured to be receptive to an impression or a mark; and the canvas itself once more becomes a tool of the trade. To get an idea of the status of the canvas, we need only consider the photographs taken by Hans Namuth of Jackson Pollock at work. The canvas is walked over and around, from side to side: its possession is the object of a ritual dance. Its impregnation no longer follows a preferred course; although it is placed back in a vertical position when hung, its status changes in nature through the preparation itself: so-called "all-over" or "action" painting, in which the raw canvas is substituted for the painting and body of the picture; where space is no longer defined, but without limit.

Indeed, Pollock's canvases, before being stretched on the frame, are quite often cut into pieces. The work then becomes a random account, the fragment of a vaster continuity, an open area. The frame no longer encloses anything.

This new working space opened up by Pollock was to attract, as into the eye of a whirlwind, a whole group of painters to which the American art critic Clement Greenberg lent his support and the benefit of his analysis. Helen Frankenthaler discovered Pollock's *Brown and Silver* series,

in which the enamel paint impregnates the textile fibre of the unprimed cotton duck canvas. In 1953 Greenberg introduced her to two older painters: Morris Louis and Kenneth Noland. He drew their attention to Frankenthaler's painting *Mountains and Sea*, in which the paint is spread in thin layers, circulates through the fibres of an unsized cotton duck canvas, and lets its furthest advanced edge, its chromatographic front, become apparent.

The radicalization in Morris Louis of an awareness of colour area was given physical expression by Helen Frankenthaler. In both artists, however, the appearance of something genuinely new needs to be understood. Each colour is kept discrete from the other, not by simple dispersal or juxtaposition, but by transparent veiling. The canvas, the fabric, is the support for the transparency, since the colour does not sit on the canvas, but is stained in the weave of the visible threads.

Kenneth Noland carried this exploration further by targeting: adopting a restrictive formal geometry that nevertheless harmonizes with its support because the colour is visible as form and the form as stained colour. This unfurled path of colour travelling through the canvas and permeating it is to be found also in the work of Sam Gilliam and Judith Reigl: dance, walk-through, direct action, union of the painting with the painted, regained freedom of canvas and gesture, reconquest of elastic space.

SAM GILLIAM (1933)
CAPE II, 1970
Oil on canvas
5′7″ × 10′

SIMON HANTAÏ (1922)
INSTALLATION
Centre d'Arts Plastiques
Contemporains, Bordeaux, 1981

In the case of Sam Gilliam, the final hanging of the painting helps to restore to the canvas this status of nomadic space; causes it to participate fully in the surrounding space and the space which it surrounds.

The French painter Mazeaufroid has emphasized in a glaringly obvious way this surfacing of memory by bringing back to visibility the distinguishing feature of the canvas: the warp-weft pattern written and repeated over the whole of the painted surface. At the head of his work he quotes this phrase from Hubert Damisch: "A matter of painting, to borrow Marxist language, ceasing to pretend that the sublime reality which dress confers upon canvas may be considered separately from its more or less rigid and filamentous body."

To apply make-up to canvas or to stain it. To stretch the canvas or sew it. Two such opposed choices arising from the memory of the material cannot fail to strike all those fascinated by the art of textiles, past and present. What is involved is a vast recognition of a subject/object of work in terms of its qualities: flexibility (folding, wrapping, crumpling), wovenness (ripping, cutting, unravelling), porousness (pigmenting, dyeing, printing), texture (scraping, rubbing, coating) and airiness (stretching, honeycombing, airing).

Alan Shields, Noël Dolla, Simon Hantaï, Marcel Alocco, Chacallis or Max Charvolen have each chosen a different angle from which to grapple with the problem. Alan Shields cuts up the canvas, reconstructing it into rit-

ual grids or shelters. Noël Dolla hangs torn rags on a stretcher frame and pierces holes in them, rebuilds cruciform monochromes with a trace of colour or superimposes tarlatans with dyed borders. Hantaï folds his canvas and sets it aside. Alocco cuts it up, recomposes and unweaves. Chacallis pleats and crumples, shaping his canvas into ritual arches. Charvolen reassembles it from fragments and strips around its body, which remains stationary during the work and leaves its mark in the final object.

Following in their wake, Anne-Marie Pêcheur perforates and assembles fragments; Jean-Baptiste Audat fashions make-believe objects; Dominique Gauthier produces oscellated flags; Joël Desbouiges hides what is painted from the eye beneath a fold-out monochrome.

With regard to the new instruments available to the painter, there are two opposed tendencies. First, that of Pollock and Morris Louis, which may be stated as follows. Contrary to the tradition which regards paint as a mirror, I do not touch the canvas with any tool. It then becomes its own master, receiving the dripping of paint at random, it drinks in the colour according to the laws of its own nature, even if the dripping movement is controlled.

The opposing camp is that of the imprint painters, or those of the studied affirmation of gesture: Viallat, Jaccard or Degottex. Viallat's choice of tool has now passed into the mythology of contemporary painting, as has the plaiting work of Jaccard preparing his tools: lengths of string, rope ladders of braided canvas. In their regard we may

Christo (1935)
Valley Curtain, Grand Hogback, Rifle, Colorado,
1971-1972
Nylon and steel cables. Span 1250 ft., height 185-365 ft.

recall Viallat's remark concerning the first act of the painter: "In the beginning the mark of the hand on the wall of the cave; but before that, the slime on the hand and the mark of the hand in the slime, existing before the gesture."

There is also control over gesture in the work of Degottex, whose *Transfer-Lines* constitute one of the clearest manifestos of the meeting of the painter's work and the textile material of the canvas. His monochromatic canvas, freshly painted, is folded in two. A gestural line-tracing follows the thread of the weave, strongly pressing the fibering of one half of the canvas onto the other, leaving an impression on its texture of veins, creases and parallel lines. The painting rises of its own accord from the interior of the canvas, yielding the instant reading of a space, of the transitoriness of a gesture, of the memory of the act and of the pleasure which produced it.

To reconsider the individual gesture of the painter by testing it against the mark on the wall of a cave; to reconsider it by setting it against the textile pattern in a combining that is complex but with a repetitive spread. To reconsider the support by treating it once more as a nomadic fabric. The designers who wished to relearn and re-use the vocabulary of textiles equally relied on these commitments. A remark by Pierre Francastel on the connections between painting, sculpture and relief acquires general applicability that is equally valid for textile materials: "The source of contemporary plastic inspiration is the abandonment of the principle of inertia. Previously, the influence of materials on art was shown in methods capable of achieving the superficial transformation of surfaces. From now on, the artist assigns qualities to matter instead of exploiting them."

The introduction of matter for its own sake into the art of contemporary sculpture and therefore, in the same movement, textile materials, fibrous and flexible, originated with artists for whom assemblages were a first principle. At the very moment when collage was resolving the problem of perspective, and "primitive" art was deconstructing the Western artist's way of seeing, a group of creators were turning to assemblages to find the way to pure abstraction. The most radical artist in this field was undoubtedly Vladimir Tatlin. Relatively little known for want of examples of his work (most of the originals have been destroyed), he took relief further out into three-dimensional space than Picasso had done, eliminating the frame and treating the form roughly with unconventional materials.

By virtue of this very fact, Tatlin ushered in the most up-to-date aspects of contemporary sculpture: "Real materials in real space–such was his programme as a sculptor. Faithful to his principles, he proceeded to study the special behaviour of each material, persuaded that the renovation of sculpture had to begin with a veritable 'culture of materials,' the rudiments of which he proposed to establish... He had to break away from his usual material in order to

Liberated by its materials, the assemblage took directions as different as some of Max Ernst's collages, the object paintings of Miró, the sculptures of Anthony Caro, the paintings of Antoni Tápies, the boxes of Joseph Cornell, the black wardrobes of Louise Nevelson, the combine paintings of Robert Rauschenberg and Jasper Johns, the junk heaps of Arman and Spoeri, the strange machines of Jean Tinguely, the aluminium sheets of Frank Stella and the simple assemblages of juxtaposed pieces of wood by Carl André or of metal plaques by Richard Serra or of felt strips by Robert Morris. It is striking to observe that the softness of certain materials has further made it possible to define a particular category of these sculptors.

At the moment when textile designers were bringing fabrics out from the wall, "soft art" was taking off in quite a special way. To speak of "soft art" or "soft sculpture" means necessarily giving pride of place to the work of Claes Oldenburg. "He who wants to be loved, desires a soft world. Rigid materials resist being approached, reject

COLETTE (1947)
REAL DREAM, 1975
Installation-performance
Silk, satins fluescent, audios

maintain, by modifying them, his relations with the space that surrounded him" (Dora Vallier).

Equally, it is to Kurt Schwitters, later on, that we must look for another pioneer whose influence continues in contemporary textile art, especially on artists working with paper. Linked with the Dada movement, Schwitters used a very personal form of collage. Around 1925, he began building in his Hanover house a Merz environment (Merzbau), assemblages starting from a column and invading first the ground floor, then, after perforation of the ceiling, the floor above.

Along with Picasso, Tatlin and Schwitters, it is equally important to mention Pevsner, Gabo, Rodchenko, Van Doesburg, Jean Arp and Sophie Taeuber-Arp, El Lissitzky, Domela, Christian Schad, Torres-Garcia and Oskar Schlemmer, who, if they did not all use textile or fibrous materials, influenced contemporary textile artists by their attitudes.

contact; their hardness raises a wall of indifference. But if I press on a rubber ball it yields, welcomes me and responds by reassuming its shape. A friendly dialogue is established." If on reading this statement we sense the frantic attempt to come to terms with the world, these objects equally give a shape to the desire for a technological delusion, thereby demythicizing the idols of the modern world: household appliances, telephone...

Such objects were in dialectical relationship with the works of Robert Morris and Eva Hesse, who were to push the form/material relationship to its maximum identification. Indeed, it is too often forgotten that if Robert Morris has strong ties to minimal art in the use of pre-restricted materials, his use of soft materials is not entirely a substitution of one field of exploration for another. Just as metallic objects frequently in serial arrangement posed the problem of the well-built, and therefore of a remnant of aesthetic concern, so did soft materials offer themselves as

GÉRARD TITUS-CARMEL (1942)
BLACK CHALK IV
"NARWA SERIES," 1977
Pencil and charcoal
5'3" × 4'

a field for the application of chance: "In the recent object-type art the invention of new forms is not an issue... Rigid industrial materials go together at right angles with great ease. But it is the *a priori* valuation of the well-built that dictates the materials... recently, materials other than rigid industrial ones have begun to show up. Oldenburg was one of the first to use such materials. A direct investigation of the properties of these materials is in progress. This involves a reconsideration of the use of tools in relation to material. In some cases, these investigations move from the making of things to the making of material itself. Sometimes a direct manipulation of a given material without the use of any tool is made [as formerly by Pollock and Morris Louis in painting]. In these cases considerations of gravity became as important as those of space. The focus on matter and gravity as means results in forms which were not projected in advance. Considerations of ordering are necessarily casual and imprecise and unemphasized. Random piling, loose stacking, hanging, give passing form to the material. Chance is accepted and indeterminacy is implied since replacing will result in another configuration. Disengagement with preconceived enduring forms and orders for things is a positive assertion. It is part of the work's refusal to continue aestheticizing form by dealing with it as a prescribed end" (Robert Morris).

These words apply entirely to Eva Hesse, who was influenced by Oldenburg and who produced a remarkable body of work over a few years in an atmosphere which her biographer, Robert Pincus-Witten, describes as particularly propitious to the development of an art conceived on the watershed of ideas: "Neither painting, nor sculpture... I remember wanting to achieve non-art, the non-connotative, the non-anthropomorphic, the non-geometric, non-nothing, everything; but of another sort, another vision, another kind, from a point of reference totally other, is it possible?"

It is in the unexpectedness of its forms, but also in their link with the ideas of pliancy, of gracility, often of entangling, that this strange work of rare force inscribes itself. "Eva Hesse," Pincus-Witten adds, "found support among a small group of like-minded artists. A series of disparate works was born, resistant to the architectural and sculptural ambitions of minimalism. To get away from the atmosphere of minimalism these artists tried not to take themselves seriously. The change in sensibility expressed itself in the increasing use of vividly coloured materials with emotional associations and by the rejection of the geometric tradition of constructivism. Everything flexible, pliable, cheap was at a premium; everything hard, pretty, expensive became suspect. The accent was placed on unexpected methods of stitching and assemblage, sewing, netting, stumping. Rags, vinyl, street refuse, became prized materials, superior even to welded stainless steel."

Beyond these very strong statements of purpose must not be forgotten those artists who focused all eyes on the fabrics which formed their environment. Colette dared to display an intrusion into her inmost self: an entire room covered with fabrics, a grotto of softness offered to the eye like a body turned inside out. Christo, by contrast, introduced fabric into the external social world: ephemeral barriers running over hills; soft prisons cutting off a slope; a curtain drawn across a valley; a rug covering the walks of a park; a shifting surface encircling islands. Fabric that substitutes yieldingness for hardness, softens outlines, suggests them as by an unvarying garment effacing differences of style if not of forms.

One last dimension cannot pass unremarked: that of the mass introduction of primitive figures into contemporary art. With Picasso, Max Ernst or Brancusi, the entry is both formal and conceptual; a renewed awareness of the primitive gesture, its social significance and mythological roots. The installations of Richard Long or Nancy Graves, the felt-work of Joseph Beuys, show a desire to go back to primary symbolic elements. Beuys's statement, "Insulating materials: felt, cardboard, foodstuff-based wood; fat, honey and the primordial bases on which passing life leaves its marks, clay and sand; the sculptor constitutes a symbolic location, in which all that remains for him to do is place his voice," gives a concrete shape to this vision by which artists forging new links with archaeology or ethnography cannot remain unmoved.

By drawing, too, some contemporary artists have tried to suggest how far a new look is needed at a textile image of life and death. Gérard Titus Carmel shapes textile objects in which the splicings, the ligatures of the stuff play a primordial role, and goes on to draw them. Wolfgang Gäfgen focuses his gaze on the folds of stretched or pleated stuffs, fabrics that allow the naked form to be guessed: a fascination of designers that links up with the reflections of philosophers like Michel Serres. In this expanded context of reawareness in contemporary art of the softness of textile materials, the art of textiles, rediscovering its language, may hear the philosopher's enquiry: "I suppose there is a science today, but perhaps it deserves another name, that requires entanglement and wrapping and veil and knot. Building it is also taught and learned. A science that requires folding, that calls for coding, that piles cipher on cipher, that ties knot onto knot."

SHEILA HICKS (1934)
THE FAVOURITE WIFE OCCUPIES HER NIGHTS, 1972
Nylon, silk, gold and linen, wrapping
Diameter 13'4''

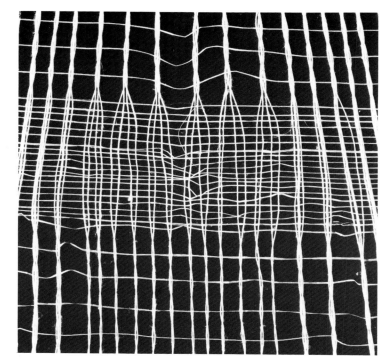

Techniques and Materials

While the revival of textile materials has touched all the disciplines of modern art, there is one in particular, textile art, which has thereby experienced a deeper stimulus, a deeper stirring of memory.

The rediscovery of the forerunners, combined with a favourable artistic context in general, has exerted a very particular influence on artists who have focused their efforts on a fresh understanding of textile functioning, on the elements of its handwriting, on its materials and techniques, on its positioning in space and its historical concepts.

Anni Albers' statement about the need to rediscover the values peculiar to textile found an unmistakable echo among the artists who, in the late 1960s, moved away from traditional tapestry and in doing so released textile techniques and materials from their subjection to representation.

To return to the researches of Marie Frechette, another quotation from her will illustrate this state of mind: "The tangible qualities of texture, grain, colour and textile malleability, the procedures of interweaving, knotting, etc., the maker's handling, the leaving bare of thread or warp or weft in all their variables, all these are no longer the mere accompaniment of information to be conveyed, they are themselves agents of information, then actual information. One may say now of this object, that it is no longer an object of reproduction, but that its 'sense' is worked out at all levels of production."

A structural analysis of this kind answers perfectly to the historical facts, in so far as one may say that the autonomy of textile art involves the working out and setting up of a sort of primer. An initial step in this direction consisted in laying claim to the weaving tools for their own sake and showing how they can be used in specific ways of their own unknown to tapestry. A second step, in laying claim to all the tools outside the loom which are connected with textile techniques. A third step, inclaiming the autonomy of the fibre qualities, whether spun, knotted, crocheted or simply felted. From that point on, the manipulations of the soft textile could be accompanied by a passage from the wall to space and by a rediscovery of the close relation between textiles and the human body. Through the breach opened up, could then come back the past of textiles and their history. And textile artists did indeed lay claim to their past, stretching back beyond the origins of Western tapestry to all the centres of textile art that we have described.

Instead of illustrating these developments by a series of portraits of the artists who have marked the past two decades, we prefer to evoke their innovations in relation to the most significant works illustrating different trends. We do not thereby overlook the importance of those ten or a dozen of them who were recognized by the early Biennials at Lausanne and have continued their work along the lines best suited to the further enrichment of textile art. Where they have transgressed the techniques of tapestry, they have done so deliberately. So true is this that Magdalena Abakanowicz could confide to Marie Frechette: "I have chosen this medium of expression [i.e. weaving] perhaps because I was attracted by a craft which is so full of rules and set procedures. When one has to depend so much on norms and regulations, one is tempted to go on and see whether it really has to be like that or whether there is not some way of bypassing what everyone expects you to do." Among these elemens of transgression, the free handling of the relations between warp and weft stands out as one of the main points of attack against tradition. For in traditional weaving the warp remains a fixed element, like a hidden armature to which the design of the weave is applied. Contemporary textile artists have proceeded otherwise, intently making play with the combined wealth of vocabulary to be drawn from the two constituents of the fabric. This autonomy is clearly felt in the works of Lenore Tawney *(The River, The Egyptian, The Whisper)*, an American artist born in 1925, who studied sculpture with Archipenko and weaving with Marli Ehrman. The greater or lesser tightening of the weft threads, their more or less marked bunching together to constitute the fabric (from actual tapestry to Peruvian gauze), the varying treatment of the warp threads, now independent, now interwoven—these elements together amount to the conquest of a new freedom of weaving.

A like freedom of treatment has been achieved by Peter Collingwood, an English artist born in 1922, who has written three technical treatises on weaving and sprang. In his work the warp threads cross and uncross from zones of tighter weaving, sometimes turning the fabric inside out.

This same outlook, linked with the transition to volumes, has also influenced the work of Kay Sekimachi and Sherri Smith. Transparency often arises not only from the technique, the weft threads being less tight than in tapestry, but also from the nature of the fibres employed. Certain plastic materials thus permit the artist to let the underlying warp threads show through; such is the case with Pierre Daquin's *Oblique Nylon Fold*. Novel as it may seem, this procedure is in many cases only a rediscovery of earlier weaving techniques, in particular of those practised by Peruvian weavers—techniques which, however, by being applied on a much bigger scale, thereby gain a new plastic value.

PETER COLLINGWOOD (1922)
MACROGAUZE 3D2, 1980
Linen and steel rods, weaving
5'10" × 2'9"

The Colombian artist Olga de Amaral could not help responding to this rich past of South America. Among her earlier works, *Entrelazado en blanco y negro* (1965) stands out as almost a paradigm of this new spirit. The artist handles the warp threads in bunches, but shifts them from one level to another, laying emphasis on these zones of interchange by a sudden shift in the colour of the weft. The result is a work whose optical impact is very forceful, but arises naturally from the interplay of threads and not from a pre-existing pictorial image. On the strength of this virtuosity, combined with the use of varied materials (wool, horsehair, and more recently metal), and with weaving which unrolls from top to bottom and undergoes during the work a change of tension and direction, she has created a body of work particularly rich and dense.

Freedom of warp may be said to act in itself as a theme of reference for contemporary textile art. The warp has become visible in many works, so that it is no longer interdependent with the weft except at certain precise points which go to form so many descriptive marks (*Spatial Element* by Elsi Giauque or *Red Dots* by Désirée Scholten); so that indeed it even appears as the only element of the work, liberating its own weight under the effect of gravity (as in the art of Masakazu Kobayashi) or marking out the design of the textile by the previous work of spinning (*Homage to Lenore Tawney* by Susan Weitzman). And, in addition, it is from the concerted manipulation of the warp that arises a form or design.

Particularly demonstrative in this respect is the work of Pierre Daquin, a French weaver-designer born in 1936, of whom something has already been said regarding his adaptation of pictures into tapestry. Influenced both by minimal art, in which feelings give way to the natural expression of the materials themselves, and by Coptic and Peruvian fabrics, Daquin set forth all the specific values of the expressive means of weaving in a sequence of mostly monochrome tapestries done from 1965 to 1974. Among them, the duplication of the warp enabled him to treat several chains of thread independently and so to double the fabric, gravity coming into play afterwards and disengaging an oblique or transversal fold in the finished work. This "fold-action" was pursued on other materials of

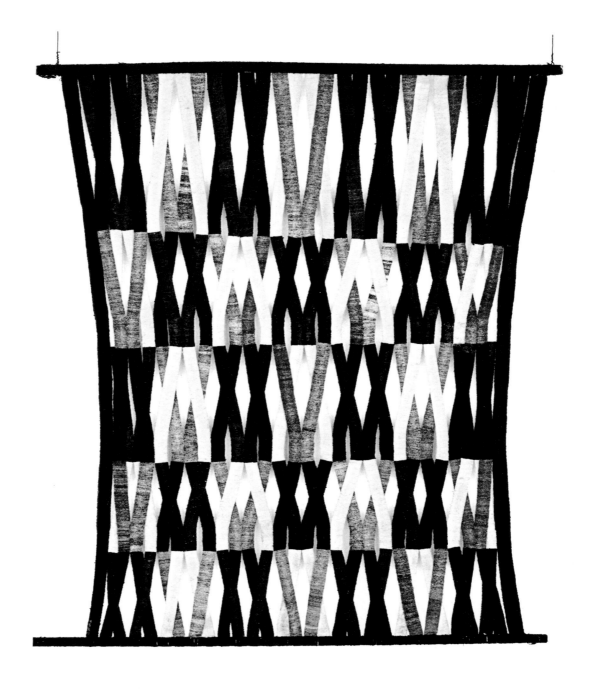

complementary qualities (plastic, leather, metal, paper, rubber), extending the range of expression by an approach similar to that of Robert Morris.

In 1981 Daquin set out on another line of work, carefully controlling the gesture of weaving in order to obtain a disordering of the fabric. One of the weaver's greatest difficulties is to maintain a constant tension of the hand on the weft thread, whether the latter moves to right or left of the fabric. Unless this tension is kept steady, one warp thread out of two has a tendency to sink down, creating what are known as organ pipes. By making concerted use of this defect over one half of the fabric, but not on the other half, Daquin has produced works in which (to use his own words) "the visible relief form emerges directly from the interior, 'induced' by the gestural option chosen beforehand." The notion of "defect" is also to be taken into account when we remember that the artist's purpose is to find significance in the technique by an obvious misuse of it.

Some technical sources concealed in traditional tapestry have again come to the fore. The *relais*, for example, a slit

OLGA DE AMARAL (1932)

◁ ENTRELAZADO EN BLANCO Y NEGRO, 1965
Wool and cotton, interwoven bands
7'10" × 6'

▽ ALQUIMIA XIX, 1984
Gesso, linen, gold, mixed media
4'11" × 6'

in the fabric between two colours juxtaposed vertically, which for a long time was reinforced by a seam, to make the tapestry resemble a painted surface in so far as possible: it has regained an expressive value which the Copts, the weavers of the fourteenth and fifteenth centuries, and the weavers of Turkish kilims had all made skilful use of.

The Swiss artist Moik Schiele has often made play with these expressive rhythms. So has Lenore Tawney. But it is probably Marguerite Carau, in her *Horizontal-Vertical* (1969), who has made the most striking use in minimal terms of this line traced over the void. Also Swiss, born in 1928 and living now in the South of France, she has gained a thorough mastery in the careful manipulation of stitches of different size to produce a highly contrasted textile design, arising naturally out of the actual weaving.

Another example of it is provided by the driadi or round-off. This is a traditional stitch which consists in winding the weft thread successively around all the warp threads, in contact with a form which it is desired to limit with precision. Invisible on the right side of the tapestry, this stitch shows through in relief on the other side. Pierre Daquin and especially Jagoda Buic, by considerably increasing the size of the round-off and reversing it to make it appear on the visible surface, have adopted this technique, using it to achieve a specific textile handwriting.

With Buic, whose textile art is based on the folk tradition of her native Yugoslavia, this stitch has become a major stylistic feature, setting the rhythm of her enormous monochrome surfaces, in black, white or red, often conceived as stage sets. The resulting relief arouses a desire to reach out and touch them. She has commented on this sensuousness: "I find the essential features of weaving in the intellectual developments required by the possibilities of tying the threads, in the tactility and intimist eroticism of the warm surfaces and their flexibility. And I project them into space. Then the imagination of the material exists."

When one weaves a tapestry, the thread cannot be continuous from one end of the fabric to the other. For the shuttle or spindle can only take in a certain length of a given thread. So the course of the weft is regularly broken off and resumed by the use of a new length, the end of the previous thread often being knotted to the beginning of the next one, to maintain the stability of the weave.

In traditional tapestry, which is meant to be seen only on the right side, these threads and knots are allowed to show on the other side. This "defect" has also been taken up and emphasized as a further means of expression. For example, in Maria Teresa Codina's *Primitive Song*, a tapestry whose right and wrong sides may be said to be on a par; in Sadley's *Missa Abstracta* and also in Sheila Hicks's *Reincarnations of the Prayer Rug*, which take over the knotted stitch and the guimping of free threads to recreate a carpet in a thoroughly contemporary spirit.

Sheila Hicks, an American artist who stands out as the major figure in contemporary textile art, lays stress on this notion of equal surfaces, front and back: "Pre-Inca textiles have always fascinated me, but more and more I'm studying and enthusiastically collecting the textile art of all periods. I have often noticed that the back of a tapestry or cloth raises as many questions as the front. Analyzing and defining the infrastructures and superstructures of textile art is one of the most absorbing activities I know of." With Sheila Hicks, whose textile art is one of the most exemplary of our time, the notion of continuity in the thread concept probably accounts for the dominant expressive value. This continuity has been developed in a long series of works: miniatures in wool, cotton, silk and vicuña's hair, alternating the elements of the formal vocabulary on a scale no bigger than a man's hand; *The Favourite Wife Occupies Her Nights*; *Memory*, a huge macroweaving, with bunches of nylon threads, set up in the IBM building at La Défense on the west side of Paris; the *Cristobal Triangle*, based on the same principle; and, by way of culmination, the circle of *75 Handkerchiefs* (1976).

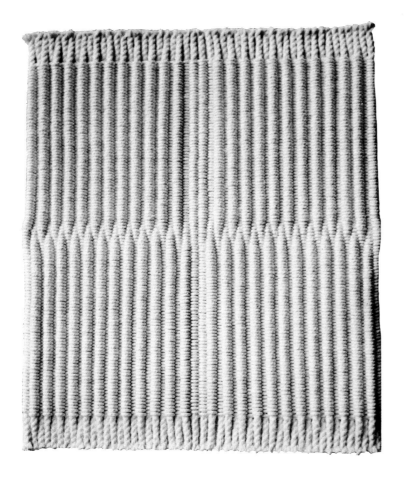

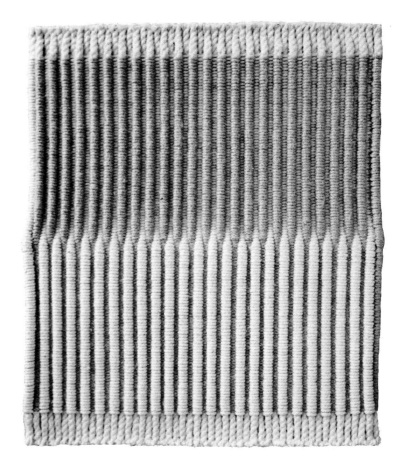

The thread, even figured by a sort of padded bolster, is the link in the memory of the work. It is the link within the artist's memory. Lastly, it is the link which ensures a direct insertion into the memory of civilizations.

But even before it is locked into the fabric or into an embroidery (one thinks of the splendid embroidered wall in the auditorium of the Ford Foundation, New York), the thread is a pliant element having its own plastic value as it falls in skeins, in the manner of a prayer rug, in its evocation of liana, in the moment when it unwinds off the spool or reel or takes the shape of a knot.

Here again, like Daniel Graffin in *Six States of a Metamorphosis*, Sheila Hicks brings the form into being by enlarging the scale or emphasizing the structure. Fibre combined with fibre creates the strand, and strand combined with strand gives the thread, and the threads bound together form the cords of the rope, and the ropes appear to bind the space they stand in. The artist thus opposes closed compositions, in which the thread is caught up in the movement of the fabric, to open compositions in which the thread comes into play by its own weight, by its shiftings and curves. But the work regains its unity in the notion of pattern, which sets up a to-and-fro movement between the two categories. The thread works free of the rope to create a swelling in the *Lianes nantaises* or sinks into the material to create the mend which goes to mask the absence of cloth, where wear and tear has broken the surface. An immense task of innovation which Sheila Hicks is continuing towards the quotidian and social dimension of the textile. The fabric is again designated and described, and its structure again becomes the primary element of the work. The tool that makes it is intrinsically present.

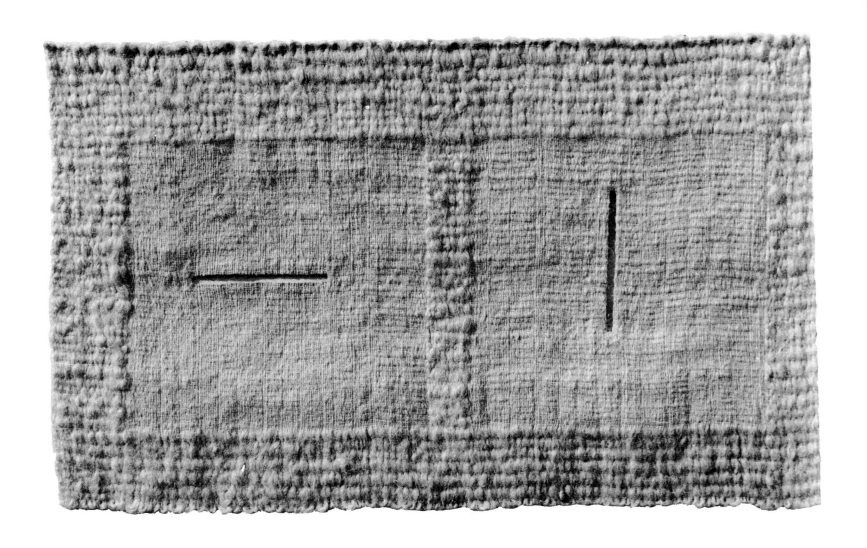

Marguerite Carau (1928)

△ Horizontal-Vertical
Sisal, high warp
5'11" × 9'5"

◁ Incised Composition, 1970
Sisal high warp
6'7" × 7'

212

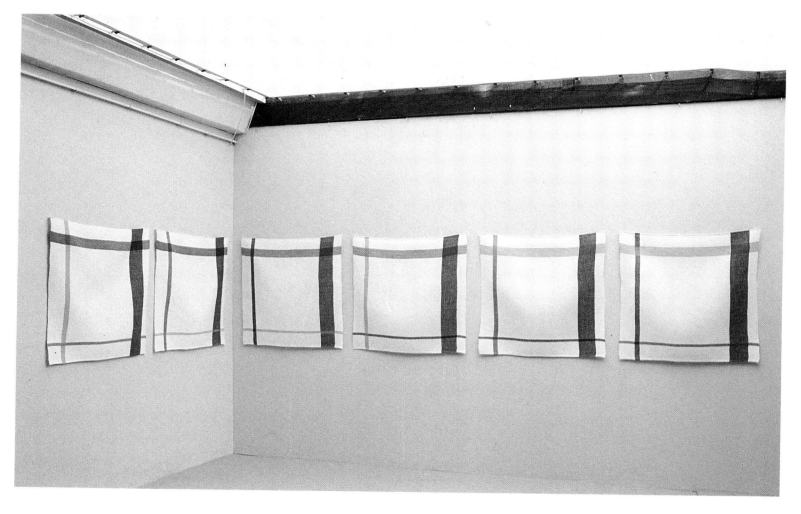

MARGOT ROLF (1940)
STARTING FROM 4 COLOURS XXXIX No. 13-18, 1981
Linen weaving
6 times 31½″ × 31½″

Mildred Constantine and Jack Lenor Larsen have des-cribed this textile paradigm as the pursuit of a "new classi-cism," as opposed to the romanticism or expressionism of the fibre. Based on the Bauhaus tradition, this classicism is particularly marked in Holland, with such personalities as Herman and Désirée Scholten, Loes Van der Horst, Mar-got Rolf and Madeleine Bosscher; also in the United Sta-tes, with Warren Seelig, Ed Rossbach, Lia Cook, Anne Wilson, Richard Landis and Nancy Guay. All these artists, often proceeding with great technical skill, lay emphasis on the rhythms and patterns of the thread in the fabric.

Warren Seelig, who is thoroughly familiar with textile technology, has taught at the Cranbrook Academy of Art in Michigan and now gives courses in Philadelphia. He has developed the simple principles of double-cloth weaving: the regular folds formed by pieces of cardboard inserted in the fabric during the work enable him to create pleated forms closing over each other, and then, more recently, his ribbon folds, an emblematic pleating in which the right and wrong side of the fabric again assume an equal value. Two comments by Warren Seelig and Herman Scholten may help to show the extent to which, in all these works, the true nature of textile is at stake.

Warren Seelig: "When you have understood it, the structural language of cloth becomes a way of thinking.

It's a language made up of mathematical systems and a uniform alphabet of symbols which describe the move-ment of line, the formation of motifs and the construction of the cloth surface. The fabric may be its own symbol. I realize now that, from the start, my interest was focused on the textile as image, rather than on the textile used as a means of image-making."

Herman Scholten: "At the start of my career I loved the work of Fernand Léger, Robert Delaunay, Stanton Mac-donald Wright, Alberto Magnelli, Piet Mondrian and Bart Van der Leck. As the years passed, I fell in with the work of American artists like Frank Stella and Ellsworth Kelly. But painting doesn't suit me. I don't like to work on a surface, I prefer to realize objects whose process is based on a construction element." For some years now Herman Scholten has been weaving pieces which emphasize the spreading out of colour within the fabric by the inter-related tension of warp and weft threads, each of them becoming predominant in turn. The triangular, diamond-shaped, sometimes rounded forms are often integrated into each other quite naturally by the continuous thread pattern.

The warp is made up of thread held on the wall by nails arranged in the desired form, and the crossing of threads may be carried out along oblique lines—which breaks the

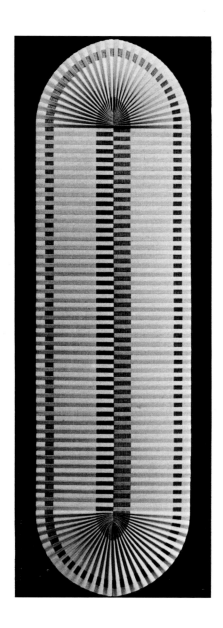
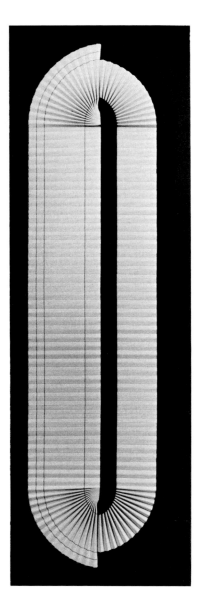

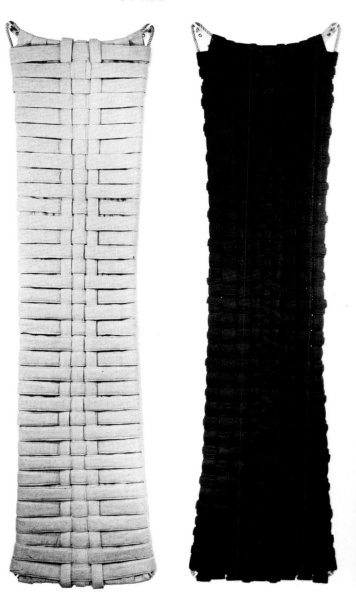

habit the eye has acquired of perceiving the fabric as the outcome of simple perpendiculars. Also making play on a monumental scale with the weaving stitches, these pieces, in the words of Herman Scholten, "look as if they were cut out of a great length of cloth, showing off a design that one might come across in a warehouse."

Margot Rolf also explores the thread pattern, but taking her stand on repeating forms which refer quite explicitly to fabrics of everyday use. Taking over the traditional primary colours found in Mondrian and in the furniture of Gerrit Rietveld, she creates sequences of square linens in which the colour is developed in accordance with the modular processes of mathematics. For some months now, the mural pieces with their simple forms have been accompanied by double fabrics designed to clothe the body in the manner of highly geometric tunics, which have something in common with the clothing designed by Sonia Delaunay. One is also reminded of the work of Marisa Bandiera Cerantola, an Italian artist of whom more will be said in connection with the data-processing developments which have characterized textile art in recent years.

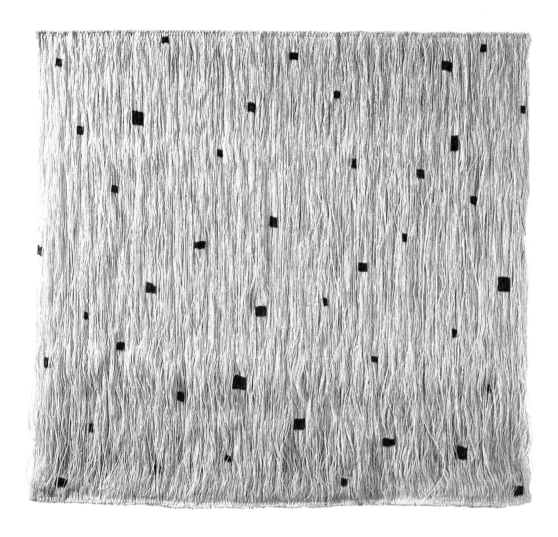

DÉSIRÉE SCHOLTEN (1920)
RED DOTS, 1976
Weaving, wool, linen, silk
4'3" × 4'3"

HERMAN SCHOLTEN (1932)
MUD, 1976
Weaving, wool, linen, sisal, cotton
4'7" × 3'9"

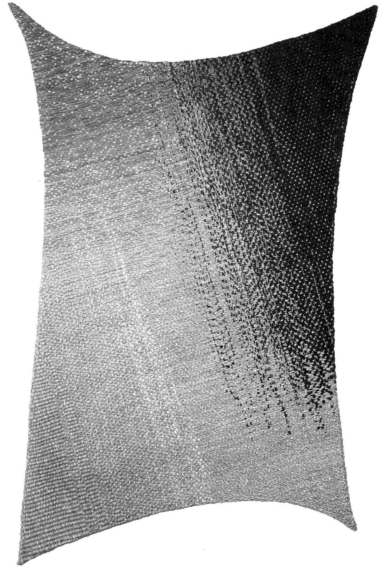

Even apart from weaving, which represents a marked broadening out of tapestry, practically all the textile techniques practised today owe something to a reconsideration of past methods and practices. Among the artists who have made much of them is Ed Rossbach, an American born in 1914, who has taught at Cranbrook, Seattle, and the University of California; he was represented at the Milan Triennial in 1964. He is certainly the one who has gone furthest in this deliberate attempt to take over one by one all components of the techniques practised in the traditional centres of textile art.

Rossbach has written books on basketry and the Indian shawls of Paisley. Together with his wife Katherine Westphal, he has re-explored the potentialities of weaving, lacework, dyeing and basketry; he has also tried out photocopying on fabrics. His work is a mixture of fragments drawn from different civilizations and brought to life by their new cohabitation. "In this private world a piece of plastic dividing off a cake box naturally takes its place alongside a piece of Coptic fabric... I hope to approach the objects and materials of our time with the same freshness as a savage in the Brazilian jungle."

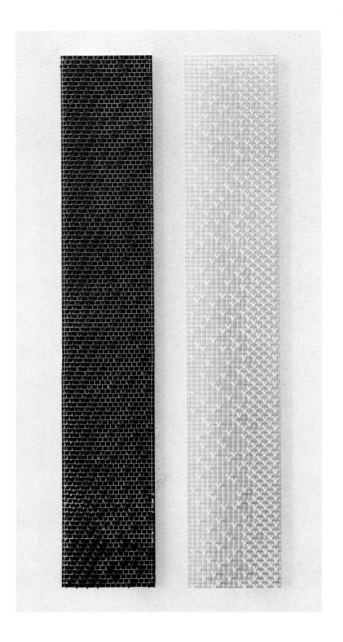
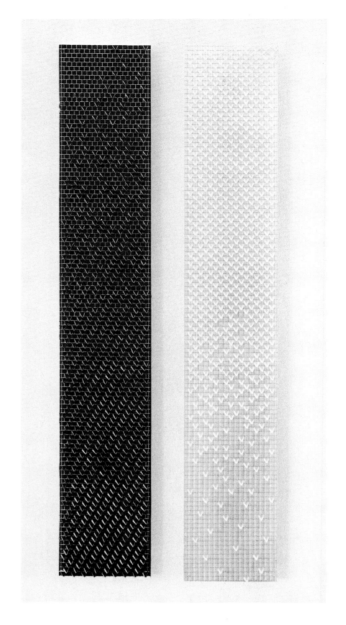

Although Rossbach is represented at the Museum of Modern Art, New York, his unassuming work remains too little known to the public. On other creators, however, indeed on several generations of them, it has exerted a major influence. Among them is Lia Cook, who has rediscovered and followed up all the potentialities of dyeing. Giving new life to the *ikat* technique, by using weaves of variable thickness, she creates modulated surfaces in which forceful optical effects arise from within the fabric. She makes skilful play with the ambiguities of the image, manipulating a rayon fabric, woven by herself, and passing it through a hand-press. She then goes over each twill weave with paint, creating new motifs on a large scale. Into the surface she sometimes inserts freely sewn threads which seem to limit the underlying design by describing a new figure: a coverlet, a drapery. "In other words, the intensity of the work also springs from its ability to multiply the gaze, as it were, and make it diverge" (Rémy Prin).

Besides Lia Cook, there are many other artists who have revived and re-explored the dyer's art: Marian Clayden, Ethel Stein, Kris Dey, Karen Chapnik, Yoshiko Wada, and Rémy and Monique Prin, all of them referring back objectively to the statement by Elsi Giauque: "What distinguishes textile from all other materials is that it consists of threads, that is, of a line in which colour is immanent through its infinite variations."

There are many techniques which draw on the thread's expressive resources and permit its colour effects to be modulated without reference to painting: the breaking up of the dye on the thread before weaving, the mixing of strands of different shades, etc. But by the working of the thread a great creative power can be drawn from embroidery, lace, crocheting, netting, macramé and knitting, all of them too long neglected and dismissed as leisure pastimes. Liselotte Siegfried and Lissy Funk have renewed lace-making and embroidery. Marie-Rose Lortet has led knitting and lace towards naïve forms of expression sometimes related to Art Brut. In a recent series this French artist has designed what amounts to miniature cities of great architectonic power, which develop a poetry of space all the more telling because the scale is so small. This continual play of scales is equally striking as handled by Aurelia Muñoz, a Spanish artist, or by Françoise Grossen, a Swiss artist now living in New York: both have imparted a monumental dimension to macramé. With the braiding of synthetic film so turned as to form pointed shapes in relief on a monochrome ground, Roland Jung has also made use of a very minimal handwriting effect on a variable scale.

216

◁ ROLAND JUNG (1941)
TRANSMUTATION DIPTYCH, 1981
Sheets of polyester woven and reversed
Each sheet 6′ × 1′

LIA COOK (1942)

△ SPACE DYED PHOTOGRAPHIC WEAVING, 1975
Photograph printed on cotton
and polyurethane foam
8′ × 10′ × 1′

▷ TWO POINT FOUR, 1980 (DETAIL)
Pressed and painted rayon
Entire 5′ × 4′

But it is by a systematic working out of methods, practices and evidencing codes that these textile techniques have linked up with the renewal of tapestry. The stitches of embroidery constitute the coded elements of a strictly grounded language. The patterning of machine-embroidered lines by the Polish artist Emilia Bohdziewicz yields so many virtual possibilities, in the form of textile books or successive panels. With Lisa Rehsteiner, the variations of this vocabulary are concretely demonstrated by the stitches set over wire netting.

Finally, Rolf and Elisabeth Brenner have laid stress on knotted and braided structures. In a large panel done in 1978, *Kunchina African Structures*, they rendered an account of all possible types of African headdress, carrying out what amounts to an ethnographic survey. Even industrial knitting has revealed some new possibilities. By overlaying some tight-stretched jerseys, the Hungarian artist Judit Droppa has produced watered effects and distortions which bring out the qualities of extensibility inherent in the fibres. That no technique, not even the most elementary ones, has been left untried is shown by the netting of Wojciech Sadley and Joanne Segal Brandford, the large sprang panels of Karen Hansen and the split ply twining of Kay Sekimachi's textiles. These techniques have been utilized in order to revive and re-explore the specific nature and workings of textile, and also because their formal elements afford a fresh line of research into rhythms and space.

ROLF BRENNER (1948) AND ELISABETH BRENNER (1944)
KUNCHINA AFRICAN STRUCTURE (DETAIL), 1978
High warp, wool, cotton, linen
Entire 10′2″ × 6′5″

KAY SEKIMACHI (1926)
VARIATION ON A CAMEL'S GIRTH 7, 1977
Split ply twining, natural cotton
and cotton braid
30″ × 10″

Another important extension of contemporary textile art lies in the exploration of materials—of everything, that is, which may go to the making of a textile fibre.

In this field, too, the contrast with traditional tapestry is striking. If in the course of centuries some materials have been constantly preferred (wool, cotton, hemp, silk, gold and silver thread), contemporary artists have extended this range of materials to include not only those used in other civilizations, but also those invented by modern technology. An exhaustive listing of the latter would be pointless; their use answers chiefly to purposes of experiment with new textures and specific qualities of flexiblity and malleability.

With some artists, practical reasons have determined their choice; sisal, for example, is cheaper than wool. With others, reasons of a philosophical order: a desire to emphasize the importance of waste in contemporary society or to bring out the nobleness of vegetable fibres, in relation to cosmic rhythms. Here again one may say that their use is not actually new, when one remembers the basketry, the carpets, the raffia fabrics, the feather weavings, that were referred to in the first chapter. But the interest attaching to them has been renewed by the declaratory value of these works.

Materials are expressive in and by themselves, without being enlisted in the service of any external expression. Such is the message or statement of Elsi Giauque's *Corn* (1945) and of comparable works of Lenore Tawney from

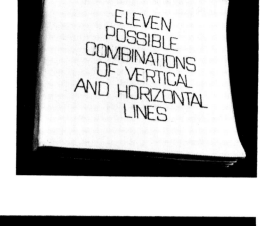

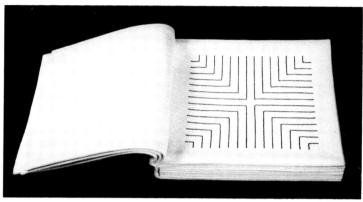

Emilia Bohdziewicz (1941)
Eleven Possible Combinations
of vertical and horizontal lines, 1978
Book, machine sewing
25½″ × 25½″

Lissy Funk (1909)
Composition in White, 1977
Embroidery on cloth, linen, silk, cotton
54¼″ × 73¼″

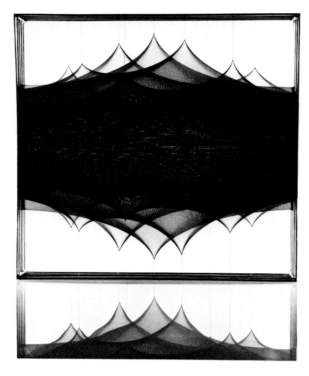

JUDIT DROPPA (1948)

△ TENSION IN RED, 1978
Polyester mesh
39½″ × 39½″ × 4″

▽ STRATA II, 1979
Polyester mesh
23½″ × 23½″

the late 1950s, in linen, nylon and feathers. In this they hark back to the preoccupations already expressed by William Morris in the late nineteenth century. Vegetable fibres, and sometimes even plants and herbs taken over whole, have attracted artists who in using them have rediscovered the traditional gestures of peasant society.

Thus Maria Teresa Codina, an artist of French extraction who has memorably asserted the values attaching to the Catalan soil, bases her whole work on one ruling idea: "True tradition does not mean doing over again what our ancestors did, but doing what they would do if they were living now." For her: "A fibre should never be dyed, for that would be to hide what it has to say in its own right.

The unspun fibre should be used, in order to respect its vital force. For the stem and leaf of a plant possess a polarity. Their cut base is the reflection of death, the extremity signifies growth, and the middle which enters into the weaving constitutes the dynamic zone, the centre of life... The fibre speaks of man, it reflects his work, whether tillage or breeding, and in its use it manifests a social reality. The fibre is an element of political struggle. An element rooted in human culture, it helps man to face cultural levellings and resist them... The textile fibre offers a means of resolving the contradictions between the rigour of structuralism, that of minimalism and the poetics of artistic creation. Because if one does not 'use it,' if one does not 'apply it,' it reveals—even and indeed above all in a minimal

MARIE-ROSE LORTET (1945)
THREAD HOUSE, 1983-1984
Stiffened lace
10″ × 21¾″ × 4¾″

presentation—the expression of an age-old cohabitation with man."

Work done with grass is necessarily frail and ephemeral. Knotting and weaving grass, Marinette Cueco performs simple gestures, like an endless activity, applying them to a material which springs from the earth every year. She works with a sampling of it, imparting to her cut grass an unusual plastic value. Expression is immediate, without the intervention of any extraction of fibres or spinning. Smell, handwork, texture, all are brought together in a discreet setting whose force lies in that very discretion. This reversion to elementary matter is of course part of a broader movement of contemporary art which we have already evoked, but it is certain that the artists who have focused their efforts on textiles have emphasized the sensuous aspect of the fibre. An impression of sumptuousness is conveyed by the large baroque works of Josep Grau-Garriga, another Catalan artist, in which the threads seem to flow out of the work, while the austerity cultivated by Magdalena Abakanowicz tends to suggest a notion of the body's proximity, standing between life and death. The matter is offered up not only for seeing, but also for touching. And it is offered up for seeing just as it is, somewhat the worse for wear. The ropes of Magdalena Abakanowicz are worn and frayed by the hands that have tugged at them, by the stones they have rubbed over and the salt spray they have been exposed to.

It comes as no surprise to find that many American artists have also extended the range of materials, making up the body of their work with the waste products, torn wrapping paper, strips of cloth, lengths of rope, which are thrown away every day in the city. The baskets of Ed Rossbach consist of old newspapers, the grates and jewelry of Debra Rappoport consist of paper, thread, splintered wood and scrap metal re-used before their inevitable disappearance.

Sometimes these creators leave it to time to intervene and act upon the finished work. Karen Hansen's metal grates are meant to stand and rust, and the artist seeks, expects and sometimes provokes this attrition: "The wrought iron necessarily bears the dampness of the hand, so in the end it becomes oxidized. I want the rust to be present in certain pieces right now, and I want further rusting to occur with no other interference but the touch of the hand in the making of it."

In this fashioning of matter, the fibre records passing time in a privileged way, lending itself to any proceedings calculated to arrest it or evoke its flight. But these notions

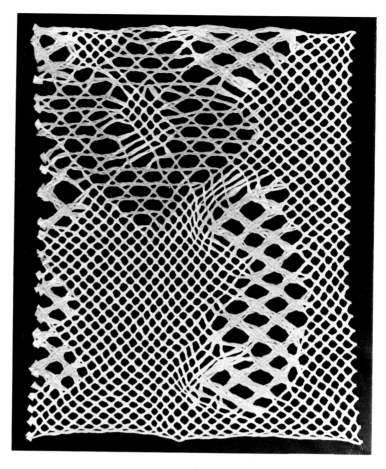

Ed Rossbach (1914)
Plastic Wallhanging, 1960-1970
Viscose ribbon, bobbin lace

Pierrette Bloch (1928)
Horsehair 9, 1980
Knotted and knitted horsehair
on glass rod
10¼″ × 7″

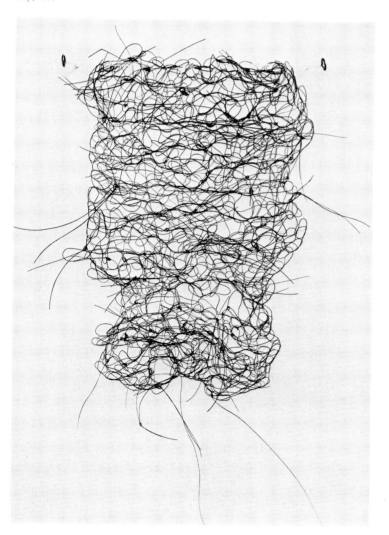

are perhaps most tellingly conveyed in works that embody raw, unprocessed fibre. The fashioning of paper pulp and of animal fibres in felt has afforded a means of recording the traces left by objects of everyday use. One may say that, for the past decade or so, paper has again been treated as a textile material and, like fabrics, it has lost its character as a mere ground or support and gained the status of an active element. Artists have always been fascinated by paper. Serge Clément writes in the magazine *Traverses*: "But for what we call Canson, Bristol, Japan, Ingres or backing sheets, we should be without our papers..." The blank white sheet, soft and appealing, with its smooth or rough surface, is to the mind like a priming and prompting. Most important of all is the fact that as in the case of the painted canvas, the materiality of the ground it offers has regained an enormous importance. "Paper has conveyed meaning in proportion to demographic and intellectual expansion. That it is meaningful in itself has passed unnoticed. And now at the threshold of the year 2000 artists are rediscovering in it a matter, or better a material, with its territory, body, texture, colours" (Bernard Gheerbrandt). Some painters have worked with coloured paper pulp: Sam Gilliam, Kenneth Noland, Ellsworth Kelly, Frank Stella and more recently David Hockney. But paper art of this kind has only been made possible by the revival of mills whose activity had declined or ceased since industrialization. A notable example in France is the Richard de Bas paper mill, purchased and restored in 1940 by Marius Peraudeau: it has attracted artists like Dali, Mathieu and Rauschenberg. In the United States several personalities have made their mark in this field:

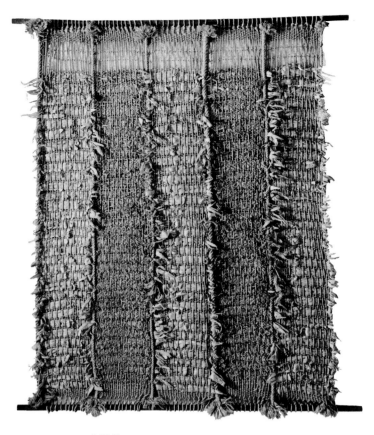

ELSI GIAUQUE (1900)
CORN, 1945
Rope, string, corn leaves
5'11" × 4'11"

Dard Hunter and especially Douglas Morse Howell, both poet and wood engraver, who after meeting Jackson Pollock in 1951 prepared papers for him "permitting colour to become an intimate part of the work."

Some artists versed in fabrics have taken to paper and shown that it can embody the same traditional or transactional values as textiles. Christian Tobas, Elisabeth Krotoff and Bernard Fabvre have woven newspapers, Pavlos has

ANNE FLATEN PIXLEY (1932)
POST AND PAPER, 1982
Handmade paper and wood
6' × 6' × 4"

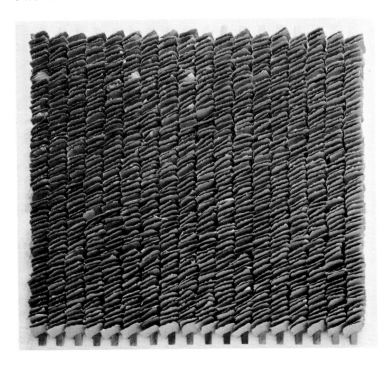

accumulated gift-wrapping papers, Marie-José Pillet has exploited the blotting effect. Ellie Vossen has dyed handkerchiefs made of cellulose wadding, Louise Holeman has built up the paper pulp over superimposed gratings, Francis Braun and Michèle Favenec have utilized its accidental shapes and buried textile elements in them, Joanne Mattera has drawn with thread over handmade papers, Anne Flaten Pixley has accumulated the coloured rhythms of small leaves all alike, Caroline Greenwald has built up frail paper sculptures according to Japanese and Korean techniques, Michelle Heon has wrought some large coats, sometimes mixed with felt. Though by no means complete, this enumeration gives some idea of the variety of approaches in this field, where paper provides the medium of an artistic transaction with others.

Paper also enables the artist to make play with transitional spaces, either concealing appearances or on the contrary retaining their imprint. For paper, even more than a fabric, is a second skin. Uncrossed, its fibres retain a pliancy comparable to that of collagen. As a second derm, overlaying the epidermis, distortable by water which makes it swell, it can be moulded over the body and

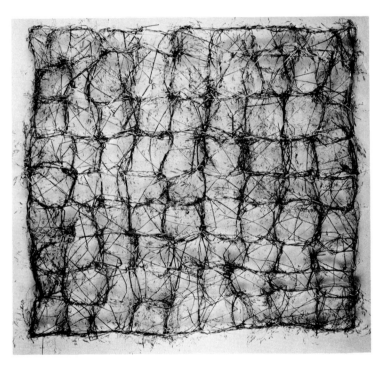

MARINETTE CUECO (1934)
GRASS, AGROSTIS I, 1980
Woven blades of grass
16" × 16"

act as a recording film—a substitute for the skin of objects, for the skin of fruit, for flesh. Here one thinks of the pure rag pulps of Michel Gérard, coloured by iron oxides and moulded over forms forged by himself; one thinks of the mouldings of Krasno and of Anne and Patrick Poirier.

In this field the work of Ritzi Jacobi and Bernadette Lambrecht is exemplary. The rice paper pieces done by Ritzi Jacobi form part of a coherent whole linked together by the different materials she employs with her husband Peter: marble, thread and paper. In *Transilvania I* (1972) the interconnection is even more fully worked out: a rough-surface textile, with the traces of weaving left deliberately conspicuous, stands out against a paper ground stretched over a frame. "One realizes that the tenuous de-

NANCE O'BANION (1949)
MIRAGE SERIES: TOO, 1984
Handmade abaca paper and bamboo
4′ × 8′

sign which runs over the paper and rises out of it in places like so many filaments, is not an ensemble of lines inscribed over a surface: it is the vibration of awakening matter. The graphite is in the paper, it belongs to the paper, just as the germ of the first mountain belonged to chaos... Then the filament becomes fabric, and the fabric volume, and as the fabric/volume expresses itself it teems with extensions which are something like a new germination, the exudation of a new seed. Thus the loop is looped, the creative process is cancelled out in order to begin anew, and the paper is seen to be the primordial matter from which all arises, and at the same time it acts as the threshold of reality, the screen between two states of being" (Claude Ritschard).

For Bernadette Lambrecht, nature is figured and no longer symbolized by paper. There the artist sets out her garden, and the architecture of leaves, vegetables and fruits goes to constitute the aligned rays of a life recommenced with each season. With her, one might speak of an archaeology of the senses. Her art testifies to the work of the gardener, to his alignments and planks, to his weeding, spading and watering. It is also a testimony to vegetable architecture, to the growth patterns of a natural morphogenesis. But there is an underlying uneasiness in this work of hers. It is like a banking up of one part of reality, of our reality, therefore of appearances. An uneasiness at the death of appearances, at the ephemeral, at our own frail being and our death.

Other artists have chosen paper for its ambiguous dialogue with painting. One of them is Anne Marie Milliot, a French artist who in Lyons in 1979 and in Lausanne in 1981 presented a work twenty-three feet high, made up of a hundred sheets of paper braced and assembled.

It was during the making of these sheets in the press that the threads, later to link them together, were incorporated

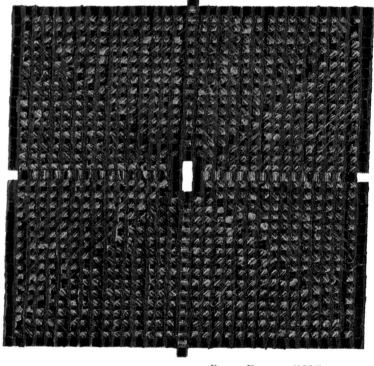

PIERRE DAQUIN (1936)
FRAMEWORK NO. 5, 1983
Wrapping paper, thread, painting
16½″ × 17″

in them. At that stage, then, in the press, it was a superimposed and simultaneous memory that was put into place, each sheet and its threads impressing their sunken mark on the previous sheet and the following one, and so on at every level. In other words, each sheet is a single object, but at the same time constitutes the memory imprint of the previous sheet and the memory mould of the following one. Once the sheets are set upright and knotted together, there comes the deployment of a global memory which can be read in space and demands a reading by the way. A double manipulation of space and time.

Since this work, Anne Marie Milliot has adopted a more painterly proceeding, inserting painted threads or fabrics in the paper, then pulling them out to leave their coloured mark, and joining industrial papers together with painting. For in the past few years painting has made a strong comeback into paper art, and not only by the use of paper pulp alone (which led David Hockney to say: "With this method, you just have to take the leap. Impossible to fool about with the line, there isn't any line."), but also by the combination of various manipulations which have reintegrated all the approaches of previous years.

If the notion of pattern, which is closely related to that of fabric, is very much present in the work of American artists, it is largely thanks to Nance O'Banion that this formal structure has found a major potentiality in connection with paper. Her work is described by Marie Frechette as follows: "First comes the contriving of a simple paper structure, out of abaca pulp with a twelve-inch mould, the sheets thus 'laid' partially overlapping each other according to a regular pattern until the desired sizes are obtained. Sometimes, already at this stage, there will be marks in the very skin of the paper by the watermark effect or else by the insertion of foreign elements in the pulp, usually cotton threads of all sorts of colours. Next, Nance O'Banion will enrich her work as a 'painter.' She will often use acrylic paints, varnishes and crumpled paper to 'play' straight onto the starting structure... By allowing certain places in the rigid structure of the pattern (the bodily frame of the work) to be seen through, she confronts transparency with the opacity and matness of the pink pulp of these winged, cloudy, ever shifting forms. There is a confronting (a contradicting?) of two real physical spaces: the cerebral space

CAROLINE GREENWALD (1938)
SUSPENDED MONUMENT, 1980-1981
Handmade paper, vegetable fibres,
white translucent silk
6'8" × 16'5" × 6'8"

of the pattern, out of which rises the dream space of these imaginary wings."

Patterns are equally present in Pierre Daquin, who since 1976 has been working with industrial paper braced with threads and backed with tar. With this material he has pursued his work of duplication, and has also gone on to tearing. After systematically tearing up a thin sheet of paper, square by square, Daquin proceeds to add colours which are absorbed by the underlying layers or are con-

centrated locally at the place where the threads come out. These works constitute a handwriting-painting in tracery, sometimes giving the illusion of weaving or basketry framing the blank space of the wall. At these subtle limits between painting and textile work (or soft-ground work), the material regains a fresh vigour from its specific reactions.

Here then is another way of renewing the forms and gestures originating in the old centres of textile art.

KAREN HANSEN (1946)
GLIDE, 1983
Metal, sprang
59″ × 51″ × 39″

Sculpture, space, architecture, the body

Kay Sekimachi (1926)
Amiyose III, 1971
Clear nylon monofilament, weaving
65" × 15" × 14"

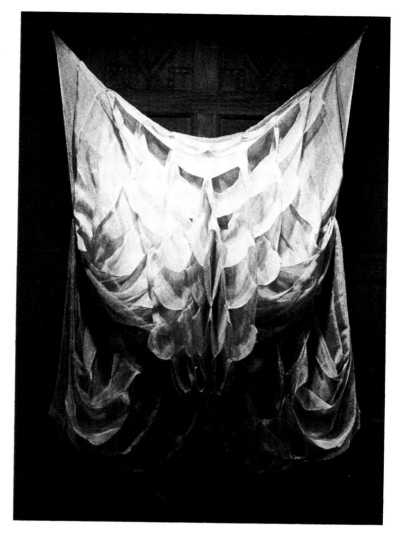

Sherri Smith (1943)
Sythia, 1975
Woven silver guimpe
7'4" × 4'

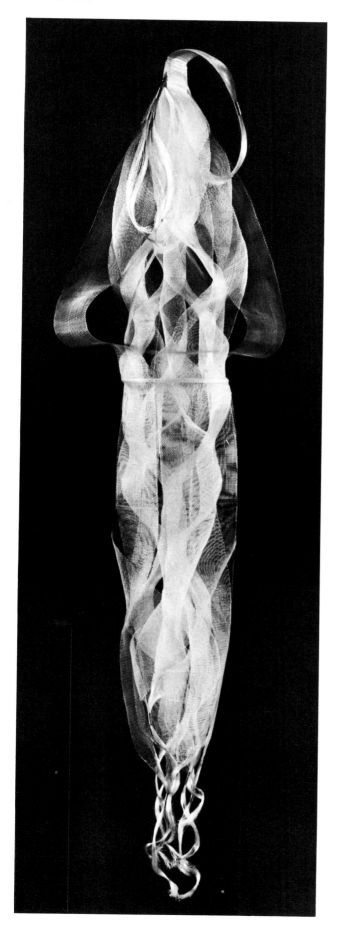

Rereading the writings of the 1960s about the new forms of textile expression, one sees at once that what critics and journalists were most impressed with was the notion of "space tapestry." For the painter-designers who, like Jean Lurçat, regarded tapestry as being and remaining a mural work of large size, this was heresy. For the many critics who took to "space tapestry," it was nothing short of a revolution.

The fact is that, already at that time, this notion of mural art had ceased to be a preoccupation for the plastic arts. The idea of relief dates from the beginning of the century, while the painted canvas has ceased, since the 1950s, to refer solely to the wall. Moreover, the notion of environmental art was well established, and land art had already laid its foundations. So that the true "revolution" for textile art was not the passage from wall to space, but the recognition of the fabric for its own sake.

From the moment that textile art no longer sought to imitate painting, it joined up again with all the qualities of the fabric. Many of the works already referred to here do not have to be looked at frontally: they develop technical and materialogical concepts which are independent of their position in relation to the wall. Indeed, on the contrary, they are meant to be looked through, being transparent, or to be looked at from both sides. Some, too, can just as well be laid out on the floor as placed on the wall. Many of them, through the very manipulation of the

MASAO YOSHIMURA (1946)
CUTTING CLOTH SERIES 80-6, 1980
Cotton cloth, cutting, piling, sewing
6'5½" × 9½" × 19"

AURELIA MUÑOZ (1926)
THREE PERSONAGES M8 M9 M10, 1971
Sisal and jute, macramé
67" × 33½"/65½" × 27½"/65" × 33½"

threads, possess an intrinsic doubleness which necessarily works out into reliefs and brings into play the relative weight of masses of fabrics depending on the way they are set up in space. Some relate explicitly to the carpet, others are intended to record external volumes. The fabric then, being soft and pliant, proposes a new sculptural notion, that of soft and pliant sculpture.

Some works illustrate this idea more tellingly than others. Such are Kay Sekimachi's *Amiyose III* (1971), woven in several sheets of nylon monofilaments, and Sherri Smith's *Sythia* (1975), done in silver threads. In both cases it is the mastery of the tool and the tension of the threads that create volume.

Sherri Smith has described the making of an earlier work *(Stalactites)*: "Several square pieces are woven on a sixteen-frame loom, then dyed in six shades. These varied layers of colour are then brought together by stitching. When this stratified construction is hung from the ceiling, the bottom of each cell structure falls down creating an important elongation." The working process itself goes to create the pliant sculpture.

Even if the fabric is laid out flat for weaving or knotting, it is the subsequent manipulation which enables the artist, on account of its thickness, to give it a sculptural aspect. Thus Sheila Hicks's *Cristobal Triangle* demonstrates the expressive power of a simple fold, while the *Three Personages* of Aurelia Muñoz are made up of very tight macramé knotting, coiled up and standing on the floor, a forcible presence.

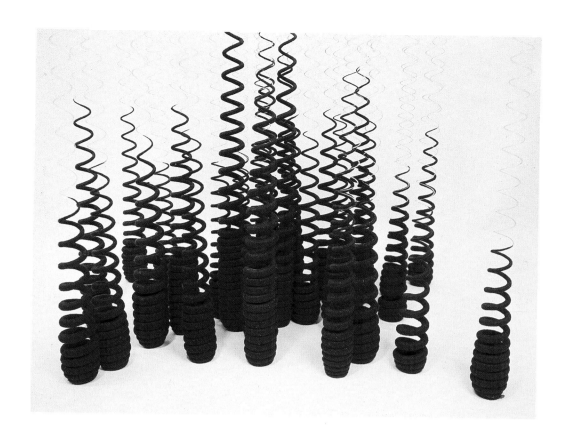

Many works by Jagoda Buic are deployed in space in the form of porticoes, of rounded, counterpointed masses, though they were woven on the same principle as traditional tapestry. Similarly, Josep Grau-Garriga has made play to telling effect with the installation of large woven masses in colour, set out in operational relation to each other. The knotted cotton ropes of Françoise Grossen (*Contact 1971*) are one example from an oeuvre in which knotting has often given birth to sculptures akin to the animal world.

Françoise Grossen's ten sphinxes entitled *Ahnen Galerie*, shown at the Lausanne Biennial in 1977 and at the Soft Art exhibition in Zurich in 1979, accordingly assume a forceful emblematic value. The textile seems to imitate stone, but does not thereby require any withdrawal of matter. The ropes fall into place naturally, evoking without constraint. They maintain their own tension.

It is undoubtedly the notion of dynamic tension which best characterizes these textile works done in a sculptural spirit. The tension may result from an accumulation which has a stiffening effect. Such as the *Cutting Cloths* of Masao Yoshimura. They belong to a series of works which the artist has pursued by accumulating, sewing and ripping piles of white linen. Released from the seam which held them together or ripped up in certain places, the layers of cloth regain their freedom and fall in cascades, offering a tangible demonstration of that revealed tension.

A similar concern for purity and accumulation has led Naomi Kobayashi to set up sculptures which bring Zen gardens to mind. White, black or red, made of serried threads which seem to sketch out a real skeleton, these works evoke the idea of a carefully hoed garden with its planted seeds. An identical tension appears in the small sculpture by Claire Zeisler, called *Chapter I*, where chamois leather edged with red thread goes to make up a kind of book with closed pages; or in the virtual cubes of the

Japanese artist Sachiko Morino, made up of stiffened ropes which envelope the absent space of an empty package.

In this field, as in those previously surveyed, some artists stand out as playing a leading role. Among these are Claire Zeisler and Daniel Graffin. The former is an American lady, now eighty-two years old. Together with Lenore Tawney, Ed Rossbach and Sheila Hicks, she belongs to a group of textile artists who were revealed to the public in the late 1950s and early 1960s.

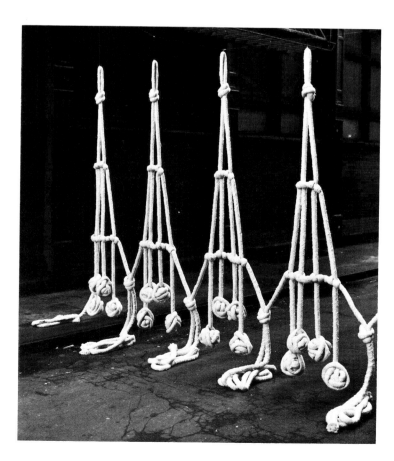

As with all the outstanding creators, Claire Zeisler's work has developed from simple principles. She employs natural tones of jute and wool contrasting with those of red, blue or green thread. She keeps strictly to knotting and wrapping. The tension results from the dynamics of gravity or helixes. With unfailing mastery she succeeds in evoking the highest tension by the use of the simplest materials, with no baroque excess, always stopping just in time, before overstepping the point at which the form appears natural, as if destined to be so from all eternity.

Daniel Graffin, a Frenchman, belongs to the generation of artists who came to the fore in the mid-1970s. Taking part in the great movement of rediscovery of textiles, he made a long stay in Egypt, working there with the architect Wissa Wassef. But while he is sensitive to the everyday textile images and architectural forms of the East, the Middle East and the countries of Eastern Europe, what really attracts him is space. He too bases his work on a few simple principles which he applies with aptness and exactitude, putting them to the service of the idea of tension.

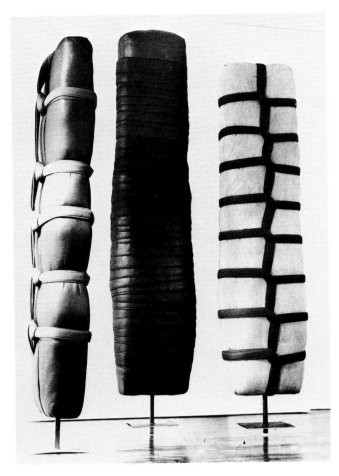

Daniel Graffin (1938)
Threefold Piece, 1976
Fibrane, linen strap
78¾″ × 23½″ × 11¾″

Masakazu Kobayashi (1944)
Meditation, 1979
Mixed media, silver thread
3′9″ × 18′4″ × 1′6″

Graffin began his work by stretching into space some large spreads of cotton, leather and fibrane, like so many unfurled sails, conspicuously textured and usually dyed with indigo. Of these he says: "For me, blue is the colour of death. It's the colour of life too. This blue is very neutral in space. It acts as a material and not as a colour. It is like bronze, a pliant textile bronze." From tension as imposed from the outside, Graffin has moved towards a tension exerted from within the objects. His large, air-inflated mummies are girdled with straps. Like his sails, they refer to ancestral and eternal architectural forms. "You know," he says, speaking of these, "what makes a movement beautiful is the body. It's the body of the mother or the woman. Here the body is air and it is the missing presence. What charges the objects with a presence is the fact that there is no armature. It is a mystery. The beautiful thing about a dress is its movement, what it suggests."

It is in *Mallarmé's Meteorites* (1979) that Graffin has followed up this search for tension with the most marked classicism. Made up of cotton straps suspended from a height of twenty-three feet and held taut by blocks of Carrara marble, this work plays on the concept of the sling. Its position in space brings to mind the image of an arrested ship. It only exists in terms of tension balanced to a nicety, and this tension appears as if stilled and eternal. Fascinated by tensed, airborne objects, Graffin has also made what he calls wind sculptures, cellular structures which live only through their deployment and an external breathing: "This sort of breathing is not mine. I would put into the object something else besides my own desire." Graffin was led to cultivate this strain of classicism, of peace and severity, in reaction against the excesses of ex-

SACHIKO MORINO (1943)
ROPE CONSTRUCTION, 1983
Synthetic fibre rope
20′9″ × 15′10″ × 12½″

DANIEL GRAFFIN (1938)
MALLARMÉ'S METEORITES, 1979
Carrara marble and cotton straps
23′ × 19½′ × 16½′

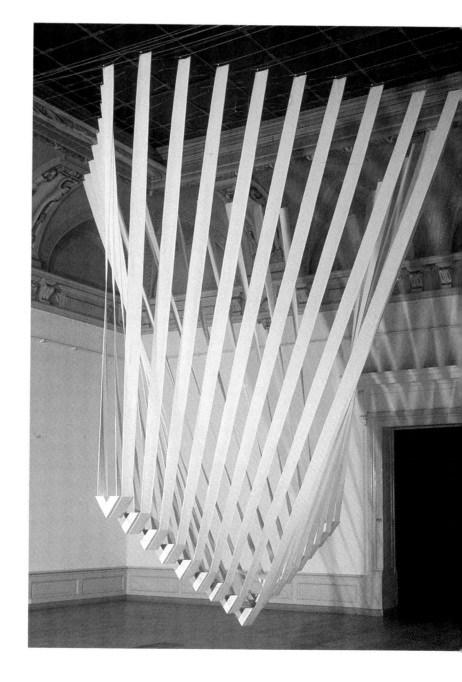

pressionism in the handling of fibres. Often referring back to the Bauhaus, to the Constructivists, to the severity practised by his elders in textile art, Sheila Hicks and Claire Zeisler, he adds: "Everyone puts the accent on the affect and the ego. I was irritated by everything I saw of so-called textiles. Owing to the apparent richness of this material, it inclines to obscenity. It is already extremely outspoken. This obscenity would be avoided by keeping to a very great strictness, a very great distance. I did not want it to be I myself telling my story in my relation to textiles and dyeing, I wanted it to be the textile and the dyeing which should relate to each other."

Certain it is that the rustling of the fabric and its extreme tension under the driving of the wind must attract artists who are sensitive to ephemeral constructions and spontaneous events. This is the case with Cindy Snodgrass, who in the last few years has peopled the space of American cities with works which the moving air sweeps up and swells out, giving their colours and forms a momentary life, like that of a parachute before it reaches the ground. The work is born of an external energy, it takes ever shifting shapes in contrast to the architectural rigidity around it. Such is the contrast which, at the Cloth Forms exhibition at the Dayton Art Institute, the artist set up with large bales of fabric held prisoner behind barred windows—the political symbol of all confinement. The artist has confided: "Sometimes I tell myself I've done nothing, because nothing is left of what I produced. And yet it's so beautiful. I could never make anything that moves like that, that puts me in a trance like that, that has so much to do with the brightness of daylight and sky, if I were only trying for permanence."

ELSI GIAUQUE (1900)
SPATIAL ELEMENT, 1970
Variable elements, high warp,
linen silk, terylene
11'6" × 14'9" × 3'3"

LENORE TAWNEY (1925)
CLOUD, 1984
Canvas and thread
79" × 47"

232

With textile forms, space has found a new element of dialogue, and it is chiefly thanks to its transparency that this dialogue has been established. The textile can draw in space and connect the walls that limit space.

What preoccupies Karen Hansen can be felt at once by comparing two works of hers: *Glide*, which takes support from both wall and floor, and effects what may be likened to a semantic glide, and *Diagonals*, which stands out at several points, causing the eye to measure space in a new light. Karen Hansen's pieces require to be described around and about. Their description cannot be enclosed in a format which is always subject to change. It cannot be limited to a particular place. Her sails and grilles are set playing between the walls. They describe both space and time, for in the constituent gesture which symmetrizes the meshes, the next time becomes the mirror of the fore-time. They are literally mixed with space. Much like the clouds of Lenore Tawney which vibrate from one thread to the other, or the grille-mirages of Rebecca Medel which offer a bewildering line of flight to the image, through the space which they pattern.

KAREN HANSEN (1946)
DIAGONALS, 1984
Wire, sprang

Through the textile, it has been said, space can be formulated. This idea could be applied to any form of sculpture, even the smallest, such as the basketwork of a new kind which Ed Rossbach has introduced into contemporary art, as what he calls the New Basketry. But the work of Sylvia Seventy, Lois Lancaster, Joanne Segal Brandford and Marijo Yagi belongs in fact to a new state of mind which has nothing to do with the notion of basketry, apart from the forms evoked. In it, the reality of utility has given place to the reality of an archetype. These works tell first of all of space contained and space traversed.

ED ROSSBACH (1914)
NEWSPAPER BASKET, 1980
Woven and assembled paper
6″ × 6″

NANCE O'BANION (1949)
SINGAPORE ROCK (LEFT), 1984
TEAHOUSE ROCK (RIGHT), 1984
Painted wood and thread
15¾″ × 22″ × 7″/22″ × 17″ × 7″

LOIS LANCASTER (1932)
CUT BALL, 1976
Handmade felt and cement
Diameter 19¾″

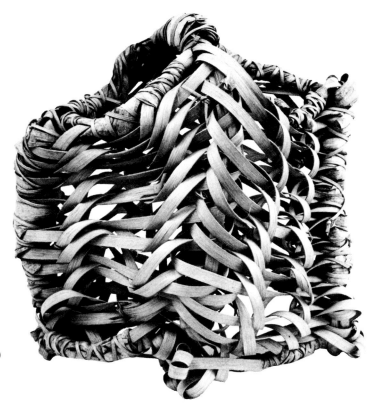

JOANNE SEGAL BRANDFORD (1933)
BASKET-TORSO, 1983
Rattan, pandanus, dye
Height 19¾″

235

Starting from these basket forms, which she makes no bigger than a man's hand, Gyongy Laky has demonstrated that one could equally well project them into a space of large dimensions and thereby obtain the idea of a work in process of growth, pausing for a moment over a formulation: the curving space of the basket. Marie Frechette has described this operation of transforming and continuously endangering the work, an operation carried out for a week in 1983 in the Fiberworks Gallery at Berkeley: "The first time, I saw some long brown plant stems hanging everywhere from the ceiling by invisible threads, filling the space forcibly and lightly. The reality of the stem coming out of the ground was merged in this spatial mutation into a dropping of stems from the sky. Then, three days later, expecting a continuance of this gesture, I entered the room and saw a huge magnificent basket, not touching the ground, it too hanging in the centre of the room." The state of mind of these young artists is like that of researchers intent on continually transforming space and making it fit to live in. What they are after is a keener perception of forms and volumes. They want architects to understand that if textiles and their formal elements are to be integrated into architecture, this cannot be done in the manner of an overlaid garment, but only by creating new spaces to explore, new transitional spaces. Two contrasting views of the matter are taken by Robert Wogensky, who represents the period when architects "integrated" a wall tapestry just as they would have done a fresco, and by Magdalena Abakanowicz, creator of an immense environment set up in the North Brabant House at Bois-le-Duc. Wogensky states: "For me tapestry is a skin. It is a skin of architecture and I think that materials have something to offer in their own right... I think wool is a marvellous material. It is warm and noble. It clings to the wall and

Rebecca Medel (1948)
Windowed Doors through
a Corridor of Infinity, 1983
Linen, cotton, *ikat* dyeing, knotting
8' × 5' × 19½'

236

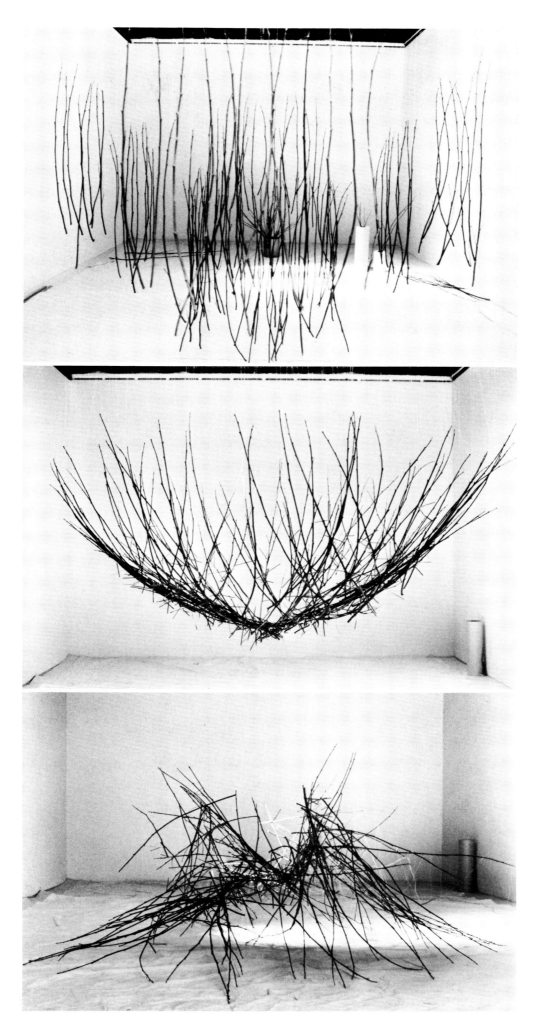

GYONGY LAKY (1944)
EPISODES IN TEXTILE THINKING:
EPISODE 1, DAYS 1, 3 AND 4
Sycomore twigs in space
Fiberworks Gallery, Berkeley, California, May 1983

hugs it, without merging with it." Magdalena Abakanowicz writes: "To understand the possibilities of the material and the diversity of its surface, this means that the woven object is not limited to the visual contact with the spectator, but that the contact is made by touch and that he who communicates with it can thus fulfil his desire to enter into the material and shut himself up in it."

The large walls of bolted rubber of the Belgian artist Tapta, which act as so many shadow-catching hollows; the cascades of bright fabrics which Gerhardt Knodel has set up in different cities of the United States; the showers of synthetic fibres created by Susan Watson for the Palais de Rumine in Lausanne and Exchange Tower II in Toronto–these answer to this projection of the body into the work, a projection which is peculiar to textile art.

Also worth considering is the fact that the architectural works which include fabrics among their components often answer to the notion of a shattered body whose parts go to describe space and inhabit it.

This situation is best illustrated by Vera Szekely, a Hungarian artist now living in the Paris area. Of her installations, each form results from the confrontation of three materials and their properties: canvas (solid–supple for stretching), thread (solid–soft for tensing), and wood (solid–hard for resisting). Everything starts from that, and from then on the memory of the materials allows itself to be unmasked. Forms at once evoke the nacelle, the cradle, the umbrella, the bellying sails of a boat, the soaring wing or the drooping wing. Consecutive forms, in which the creator's work consists in arresting an ephemeral image made up of respiration and flight.

The memory of the materials which Vera Szekely revives is a profound organic memory. Initially, it is the

TAPTA (1926)
ELASTIC STRUCTURE, 1981
Black rubber sheets 2 to 3 millimetres thick,
rusty iron bolts, assemblage, personal technique
14'9" × 18' × 10"

memory of the human organism, but in a larger sense it is the memory of the evolution of the forms of the living world. When she adds her modular units to each other, she inevitably retrieves the universality of metamerized bodies whose organization has passed from one scale to another during the geological ages, by imperceptible transformations which spatial geometry or physics would call torsion, shifting, stacking, symmetrization, vibration, repetition, translation. By integrating into this work the counterpoint of wooden bars and the white billows of felt, Vera Szekely now disposes of all the elements of a scattered body, and her fundamental search consists in retrieving it within the space proposed. Like a perpetually modified outflow from the body, each proposition may engender a new proposition. No one who penetrates into such a space can remain a mere spectator, because he finds himself present in the space. From the point where he stands, he is immediately projected into the work, he immediately sees the before and after of these forms. In fact he learns to see himself with new eyes.

The textile in architecture, then, is not a mere skin, but a mobile body, and it is no chance parallel that we find between the installations of Vera Szekely and the linkage of textile and body undertaken from 1970 by Debra Rappoport and more recently by Frederic Amat.

These works have actually been conceived as a series of imaginary forms: "These are textile constructions whose form flows from the shape and movement of the body which they contain. While the body and the textile answer to each other and influence each other by rhythmical movements, the textile becomes a form of space, moving, fluid, shifting."

Susan Watson (1949)
Cloudlight, 1981
Acrylic nylon fibres,
polyester resin, aluminium
37'9" × 28' × 28'

Vera Szekely (1922)
Structures-Tensions, 1978-1984
Cotton cloth, wood, felt
Installation
Kulturhuseet, Stockholm

240

One cannot evoke these close relations between body and textile without thinking of the work of Magdalena Abakanowicz. If the name of this Polish artist has turned up repeatedly in this survey of contemporary textile art, the reason is that she has contributed decisively to opening people's eyes to the realities of textile art, and to textile art as a power to be reckoned with, on a level with the other great currents which have traversed the contemporary arts.

From the abstract phase of her *Abakans*, those large monochrome sculptures of the 1960s, by way of *The Rope* which we have already referred to several times, to the series of *Alterations*, already more figurative, and on to the cycle of *Embryologies*, a single notion transpires: the close connection between vegetable fibres and the animal fibres of the human body. As Jean-Luc Daval aptly writes, "The fibre omnipresent in the organic world is at the origin of the art of Magdalena Abakanowicz. Simple or complex in her composition, delicate or harsh in her weaving, changeable or rigid in her progression, she weaves each living figure and each of her works. With her it is not a question of naturalizing life, but of reflecting it in the truth of its transformation and its movement."

The body of Magdalena Abakanowicz is a mother's body, a childless mother's body. She acknowledges the shreds of her flesh in the flesh of her sculptures; she acknowledges the pregnancy of her body in the mass of her fibres, in the bags of her *Embryologies*; she acknowledges the travail of her womb in her embryonic drawings. In her corporal laceration Magdalena acknowledges a past stretching back beyond ourselves, where biological evolution is made transparent in appearances. She acknowledges that the gestures of her body, knotting, combining, drawing, go to create a continued bodily existence. She reconstructs man, as child, adult, old man, in the nakedness of his bodily privacy.

MAGDALENA ABAKANOWICZ (1930)

△ THE SMALL OBJECT, 1975-1976
from the cycle "Alterations"
Knotted sisal
6″ × 4″ × 2¾″

◁ EMBRYOLOGY (DETAIL), 1978-1981
Sackcloth, cotton gauze,
hemp rope, nylon, sisal
Entire: from 1½″ to 8′

FREDERIC AMAT (1952)
ACCIO ZERO, 1974-1976
Clothes and performance textiles

HISTORY AND CONCEPTS

The evolution of contemporary textile art is more than a matter of reviving techniques and materials and reconquering architectural space. As many artists and critics see it, structural analysis lays too much stress on technologies and their workings, to the detriment of meaning.

The renaissance of textile art needs to be seen against a wider background. If textile artists have relearned their language and clearly signified its foundations by formalizing them in the work, they have also relearned how to speak.

This confrontation between workmanship and meaning is not peculiar to contemporary textile art. Everything arises from an encounter: that of the artist's desire with his will to self-expression, by way of painting, or lithography, or photography, or video, or the computer—or the textile. As that desire comes to grips with technical constraints, there arises a language of expression which becomes aware of the means at its disposal, of their limits and possible transgressions.

Textile art, quite as much as the other forms of contemporary art, has come to realize that the very notion of artistic creation has evolved and extended into hitherto unfamiliar realms. This is a historical extension, since the

PATRICE HUGUES (1930)
ANGELS, 1979.
Five voiles and thermo-printed cloth
7½' × 10½' × 10½'

243

artist reaches back into the past–into the pre-Renaissance past of Western civilization. It is a geographical extension, since he has come to recognize the wealth of primitive art. It is a scientific extension, since this annexation of the remote past and remote places also bears on the acquired knowledge of the exact sciences, both human and natural.

Artistic endeavour today reaches out and takes over the language of painter, photographer, archaeologist, physicist, investigator, and integrates the known facts about the myths and rituals of fixed societies. Artists are more responsive than ever to the ethnographic or medical records of past centuries, so that the issues at stake cross and recross the frontiers of art and science.

In textile art this appeal to history is particularly strong, because for so long textiles were dependent on painting: thread and fabric were a subordinate art form in the service of painting.

To revive textile language as it was in pre-tapestry times, in the hands of the Copts or Peruvians; to draw on the arts of Africa or Indonesia; to resituate embroidery, lace and basketry outside the context of utility–these are endeavours in which the historical past necessarily fuses with the meaning conveyed by the creations of today.

The entire work of Patrice Hugues stands in this intimate fusion. Each of his thermo-printed veils bears witness to a gesture taken over from the past.

The historical revival of meaning is full and complete, with all references adduced. Cashmere shawls are side by side with an Annunciation, the folds of a figured satin gown with those of an industrial velvet-folding machine. The draperies of Napoleon's bed accept the back view of some jeans pinned to the wall, and they fade away into an oilcloth design. Nature is never far away, with its innumerable features: thousands of leaves shaken by the wind, thousands of blades of grass, appear as so many printed textile designs.

An exquisitely keen response to the history of fabrics, in order to "paint" a history which has lost its linear evolution in the interests of a transparent sequence of periods. With Patrice Hugues, as with Ed Rossbach, the point is to embody everything, to follow up the search for all that connects the personal memory with the collective memory, with the itinerary of an art language–that of fabrics and their designs.

A similar contraction of the time-span characterizes the recent work of Gerhardt Knodel. His hangings are in the straight line of descent from those of the Middle Ages, however different the technical means employed. Having travelled all over the world in search of textile images, he contrives to integrate their combined powers in his work, whether intended for wall or space. This intent reconsideration of the past is one of Knodel's primary concerns:

VERENA SIEBER-FUCHS (1943)
OBJECTS, 1982
Iron and copper wire, gilt and
silvered metal beads, crochet
6¼" × 6¼" 1½"/6" × 6" × 1⅛"/5½" × 5½" × 1⅛"

By printing he transfers painted or photographic images, fabric or wallpaper designs, to light transparent fabrics set out in proximity, in perspective, in counterpoint.

Thus set in place, they permit the component elements to circulate from one panel to another. They play on the inclusion of an image in a design, on the contest between image and design, sometimes on the poetic inclusion of writing. But this writing deliberately departs from any linear directioning, to feature the interplay of the text in depth, or to feature a word, a word that escapes from a veil, as from a page, like a sound escaping from a tune and taking on a meaning of its own.

"I've had enough of those textiles that keep on saying: here's how it's made. That was important in the 1960s when a systemic approach was developed. But now that's been done... I love fifteenth-century tapestries. I was looking again lately at the *Hunt of the Unicorn* in the Cloisters in New York. These tapestries are like a garden in which every square inch appeals to the eye. Each time, I feed on this sight for a long while... I dream of those rooms where the tapestries hung in castles and I'm fascinated by the idea of such a place full of images telling the whole history of the Western world. These images stand on a level, hanging beside each other, in space. They stand there like stage sets

DOMINIC DI MARE (1932)
CURTAIN/OLIO/ACT ELEVEN, 1979
Handmade rag paper, spun gampi paper,
hawthorn wood, carved bone, silk,
coloured pencil, ink
14″ × 16″ × 5″

waiting to be brought down on the stage and come to life. That is one of the nomad aspects of textile. Never abandoned or stocked, but waiting... One may easily imagine that the inmates of the castles must have felt themselves surrounded by a crowd of figures. There is a great sensuality in feeling this living presence, like touching the material of the clothes worn by others."

This is history re-experienced, but also ethnographic rediscovery, sham archaeology, a private liturgy. The New Basketry, the braidings of Guy Houdouin, the ritual sculptures of Dominic Di Mare, the objects of Verena Sieber-Fuchs, are like reminders of distant places. They are works of today, and yet they evoke archetypes lost beyond recall.

Guy Houdouin has reconstructed a world, that of a king named Patak, whose emblems, garments and jewelry he rediscovers year after year. This Peruvian king enables us to measure the distance of a delusion: "People are terribly interested by someone who at last speaks out and says it's all a delusion because it's fun and, at the limit, it could exist." As exist in the realm of delusion the trophies of Dominic Di Mare, small works of wood, spun paper, silk thread or bone fragments, the felt balls of Lois Lancaster, the mummies of Magdalena Abakanowicz, the mini-textiles of Sheila Hicks, the dart of Wojciech Sadley, the artifacts of Harry Boom, the beads of Verena Sieber-Fuchs.

The young artist last named, who lives near Zurich, has accumulated what might be called the fossils of the present day. Objects made up of beads, flakes, films, threads, even bonbons, and no sooner are they created than they turn into relics. Evoking the past, born of the present, they bear from birth the stigma of the future.

GUY HOUDOUIN (1940)
PURPLE PATAK, 1983
Paper acrylic-painted and braided
Diameter 35½″

They assume an anonymous value by embodying a meaning which is not that of the ego, but of the world. They too delude, but their delusion is not a fault, it is an outspoken way of saying: don't forget the savage state, the primary state when knotting, knitting, assembling, weaving, were sacred gestures, essential to the cohesion of a community. The weaver, the needlewoman who made or mended the linen, the washerwoman who made it fresh and clean again, the peasant who cut the wheat and knotted the sheaf, the child who took up and fingered the yarn, were repeating necessary and at the same time sacred gestures.

To some, it may seem strange and artificial that the everydayness of fabric and fibre should be displayed in the exhibition halls of museums, which are places cut off from the real world. But they touch us. The declaratory value of these questing works touches us because they point to things that could disappear from human memory.

Today primitive art is no longer copied only in its modes of representation, but also in its manner of peopling the space of ritual, of marking out a territory, of recalling gestures and traditions. Nearly ten years ago, first at the Lausanne Biennial, than at Lund, Montreuil and Aix-en-Provence, Sheila Hicks made a deliberate break-away from the concept of textile work by borrowing some linen from a hospital and exhibiting it in a pile. Sheets, napkins, pillow cases, shirts, blouses, bust bodices, bands to wrap round the belly of newborn babes: the signifiers of body intimacy, in the sense meant by Roland Barthes, that every usage tends to turn into a sign of that usage. Instead

CHRISTINE AYMON (1953)
LOST SENSES, 1981
Repp, canvas, silk, cotton, linen
12′ × 5′

LISA REHSTEINER (1945)
ASHES-STARCH-BLUE, 1981
17 elements of linen and silk
Installation
10th Biennial, Lausanne, Switzerland
9′ × 26′ × 14½′

246

of trying to explain this step which may at first have come as a shock, Sheila Hicks preferred to append beside her works a quotation from Dominique Autié's fine essay *Mystique des Linges*: "Linens are *par excellence* objects of manipulation. Among the domestic or sacred furniture which they adorn, the consumable goods of the table, and the body which they assist to the point of sharing its decay, linens circulate from hand to hand. They negotiate the question of space and through the wear and tear of passing time they fraternize in death." Seven years ago the Hungarian art world was marked by the exhibition "Textile Without Textile," featuring the work of graphic designers, film-makers and plasticians who had gone in search of textile concepts adapted to their own usual means of expression. A musician constructed the course of a magnetic tape over the length of a warping. A video sculpture was set up with sixteen screens arranged like a canvas stitch.

Judit Kele, a young Hungarian artist now living in Paris, has in a photographic work set in place the body and the tool, superimposing the images of her naked body, standing and reclining, dimensioned in the size of a high-warp loom. Measurement of the working space, measurement of the gestures, crossing and superimposing of her body which is centred, as at the tie-point. At the Lausanne Biennial of 1981 two works also established a dialogue with the usage values of the fabric. Sixteen panels of white linen installed by Lisa Rehsteiner *(Ashes-Starch-Blue)* were like a big batch of washing, surfacing from the days of her Catalan childhood: they came as the offered reading of a

WOJCIECH SADLEY (1932)
THE DART, 1978
Sisal
16″ × 47″ × 12″

present-day tradition. These sheets, unwoven along the perpendiculars and re-embroidered in places, allowed the fragile structure of the fabric to express itself: "The days served as a geometric basis for me, because the fabric is made like that. And then the mendings came out like a random composition, as when one breaks or tears something. The design of the mendings depends on chance."

Christine Aymon exhibited a large weaving ten feet high, pierced in places, as if by wear and tear. "We stand in front of this hanging, facing a mirror which is not reserved for the weaver alone, though the tapestry is the first

to be questioned, but which is the mirror of our destiny. Inscribed in this fabric is not only history, an anonymous archaeological vestige, but also our own history which is only an extension of it. A threadbare shroud brandished like a banner, it acts as the stage on which we exchange our dialogue with time, life and death. In this room, poor and sumptuous at once, speaks the tapestry, and its slow passage of unbroken thread, and there are joined the perceptions of space and time to the point of the last insensibility" (Claude Ritschard).

Three dates which, in the art world, are the signs of a reappropriation: the fabric in one part of its history and destination; clothing, linen, the whole near the body. Three dates which of course are somewhat arbitrary, like all dates, and others could be added to them. At one extremity *The Wardrobe*, a work by Peter and Ritzi Jacobi, of 1971, made up of clothes woven in high warp and suspended in a suggested space. In the middle, Maria Teresa Codina's exhibition of 1978 at the Miró Foundation in Barcelona: *Sacs, Palles y Sargits*. It brought together a mended sheet, a frayed well-rope, Mexican gunny sacks which once contained corn or cotton, tufts of grass, bales of straw, wads of esparto fibres used by Spanish peasants to scrub the floor or scour saucepans. Objects displaying "a science of our present society, a science of receptivity, analysis and expression." Objects among which circulate an infinity of gestures linking the generations together.

MARIA TERESA CODINA (1926) ▽ THE FISHERMAN'S WIFE, 1981
Tarpaulin, needle for sewing
fishing nets, wooden sticks
8″ × 8″ × 10″

▷ STRAWS I, 1977
Straw and rope
23½″ × 15¾″ × 14″

Then, at the other extremity, *The Needlowoman*, an installation by Anne Veronica Jenssens. Here, in the midst of a space full of draped fabrics, a film projected the image of a woman plying her needle for eternity: eternal woman mending indefinitely the fabric of life.

Other works taken over a broader spectrum in which artists manipulate the signs of body communication by bogus self-portraits (Boltanski, Cindy Sherman, David Buchan), by make-up (Annette Messager), by ritual (Orlan, Gina Pane).

Starting from a fabric which tries to retrieve the gestures of the painter, the textile thus harks frantically back to its origins, and in doing so sets out theories, arguments and conclusions to lay a basis for its existence. It brings the creator down from an obsolete pedestal and compels him to grapple with the reality of his own textile appearance and the reality of the textiles surrounding him.

Whether he weaves his body in a mural rectangle where he projects himself, or whether he looks over the characteristics of his own body wrapped in fabrics, he learns to recognize the signs of his being in the world and the signs of his history.

SHEILA HICKS (1934)

▷ LAUNDRY, 1982
Dyed blouses
"Presence of Forms" exhibition,
Les Angles

▽ LAUNDRY, 1978
Hanging blouses
"Thread" exhibition,
Montreuil

New relations with painting

The wave of textile art that unfurled anew during the 1960s asserted its specific identity within the visual arts through its opposition to traditional tapestry. It also managed to become integrated into the evolution of the totality of contemporary art and take its place in wider movements in painting or sculpture.

In fact, if the work of Eva Hesse and Robert Morris or of Christo and Colette evolved in close step with the major arts, that of Claire Zeisler, Lenore Tawney, Sheila Hicks or Magdalena Abakanowicz, which stood in a dialectical relation to tapestry, was not thereby diminished in value vis-à-vis the first group named. All this work was of the same order, starting from distinctly separate fields, from different investigations, but winding up in closely related concepts.

There was, however, an area in which textile practice sparked off the rise of a new class of works based on thread or cloth, close to painting in spirit but with textile language enriching the work of artists even beyond the point reached by American and European painting.

It must be supposed, or hoped, that an attempt will be made to reinterpret the art of this century in another light than the still prevailing one of pictorial reality. The ex-pression "I am a painter first" undoubtedly has its importance; so, just as much, does the recognition of the reality of textile, reached by pictorial means. What matters most, however, are the meeting grounds, the convergences, the reciprocal recognitions.

In his approach to the work of Pierrette Bloch, Daniel Abadie writes: "The collages and the stitches assert the permanence of a pictorial reflection through non-pictorial means." He might say the same of Tápies and perhaps of Dubuffet; he might say, too, that in art the end dominates the means. But that is as much as to say that the means are elements conditioning the language: its vocabulary and development. Threads, fibres, fabrics have been adopted by artists in a thoroughly baffling historical turnabout.

It is possible to paint with thread if the thread possesses the desired syntactical elements. Pierrette Bloch, a painter first if you like, finds a calligraphic line that falls outside the pictorial; and her calligraphy is all the richer for being in thread and being granted by the horsehair a unique passage through space, a calligraphic space that overflows the page, breaking its boundary lines and spilling over into a space beyond that of traditional pictorial format. It is not a question here of taking a work further than it intends to go, but of recognizing its components when they do in fact go beyond pictoriality.

Several artists, while accepting cloth completely, without fear of its decorative connotations, and while living with it every day in their creations, have also suggested

EDWARD BARAN (1934)
BLUE MEMORANDUM, 1980
Wrapping paper, thread, glue, ink
39″ × 39″

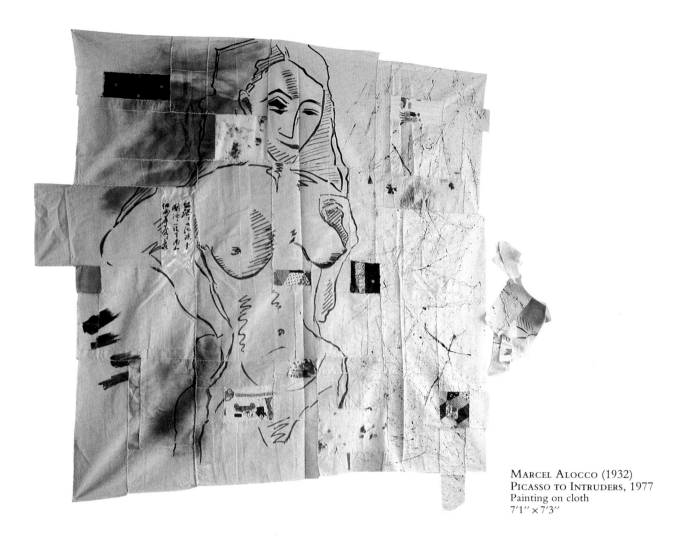

MARCEL ALOCCO (1932)
PICASSO TO INTRUDERS, 1977
Painting on cloth
7'1" × 7'3"

another questioning of painting by recognizing the age-old confrontation of cloth, dye, paint, image and motif.

Daniel Graffin's series of indigo *Traces*, based on the contemporary takeover of African techniques of dyeing *(plangi, tritik)*, has as the first of its components the use of chance as an analytical tool. Control is exercised in a limited form through stitching, the imprisonment of an area of canvas, the taking up of a pleat. Chance operates through the greater or lesser resistance of the barrier which opposes the penetration of the pigment. The result of the analysis is given both by the display of the space-trace of the trap and of the tool used to set it, the mark of which cannot and must not be concealed.

It seems, moreover, that this work replies to one line of questioning by contemporary painters on pictorial saturation and the breaking of the monochrome. This indigo-dyeing operation is a genuine breaking of the monochrome in a double sense, since it breaks open a uniform process, closed and secret–that of dyeing–and breaks up the result, the dyed canvas.

By a long manipulation, Edward Baran also proposes a new pictorial approach, in which his past as a weaver-creator cannot be overlooked. As a weaver, Baran wove blocked monochromatic forms, compacted into themselves; palpable expressions of a knotted body. As a painter, he followed the trail blazed by Barnett Newman: "The challenge of the painting is to destroy the wall."

To start with, a veil of airy cloth, a network of threads in precise order: parallel warp threads, parallel weft threads. Two mutually perpendicular directions. Above, several layers of paper: blank paper with no surface direction, like the kite membrane that fascinates the artist. Newsprint, covered by a set of rigid columns and precise parallel lines of type. Further above, the field of operations of ink or paint: imprinting, spreading, coating, trickles, accidental spatterings and blobs on twill areas. The path taken by painters since Pollock: chaos.

And yet actually there is nothing above or below. Everything is in the middle or in the interval between. Henceforth nothing matters but internal space, what works from within, drinks and dribbles, is switched from one level to the other, guided by the cloth or stopped by the paper; what binds the surfaces to each other, glues them together, takes the dye and goes through them. Then comes the search for all the strata of perceptible chromatography. Work done blindly with the brush, the moistened finger, the partial and scrappy rent which extract order from the inside of chaos. On the finished work rises a telescoped mass of what is visible (a meshwork heavy or faint as the case may be, but which forms the figure), what is rendered visible (the anti-meshwork of the wall, pierced by the meshes but including them), what opposes the visible (the blurred, broken, haphazard outline of stains), and lastly what disturbs the memory of the body (the imagination seeking what is removed from view by the complex interplay of the painter's personal exploration).

In the same way as Daniel Graffin's *Traces*, the work is matter, structure, act, colour. The process by which it is made is inseparable from it, just as it is inseparable from space. The same stimulating ambiguity appears in those paintings by Francis Wilson shown at the tenth Lausanne Biennial, which confess their fabric meshwork while at the same time swelling out in soft sculptures ready to leave the wall. Painted and hardened by the paint, they conserve their quality of envelope and skin, rubbed to the limit of wear; they are a testimony to work, revealing their dual textile origin: canvas on cloth, cloth on canvas; old clothes, perhaps. His latest works, *Giva, Nabadu, Soula*, present a kind of ideal model of the confrontation between the rhythms of the painter and those native to fabric. Riddled with the tension of the folds and the broken lines of the stitchings, they record the stroke of the brush in so many marks lightening from the centre towards the periphery.

Another meeting place is arranged by textile research using serigraphy, solarization or thermo-printing on cloth. In this regard a statement of Judith Reigl may be recalled apropos of a series of body canvases: "I paint cloths only to show what is on the other side." Only cloth can answer this will, this desire to step through the looking-glass, and it is indeed in that sense that we may regard the sensitive work of Patrice Hugues. The veils answering each other in space in as many figures and mingled motifs fixing shadow or light are responding in their author's own terms to a frantic quest to fuse painting, sculpture and textile memory: "Elements that present the problem in the heart's core, because they can reach a depth

Daniel Graffin (1938)
Cross Trace No. 2, 1978
Cotton, indigo, tritik
47¼″ × 39½″

of our being otherwise inaccessible by painting and even by the three-dimensional solid. I need the impalpable passage of space between the puffs of impression I have applied to the plane of the cloth in order to find a third force between the representation on the canvas support and, for example, sculpture."

The Nice painter Alocco plays on the same register of a tide of images and signs. But he also intervenes, by his stubborn quest for fabric, in a synthesis of Viallat and Pop Art. The name of one of his shows, "Painting Overflows," is significant. It meant both that painting was losing its traditional frame and stretcher by overflowing the canvas and that it was also overflowing the framework of a personal image and signature by reincorporating signs as diverse as the painting of Lascaux, Matisse or Picasso, normally linked with art history, and images from everyday life such as the abbreviation for post-telephone-telegraph (PTT) or the image of Mickey Mouse; and that, finally, it was concerned with the warp-weft assemblage of its support. Alocco's current patchwork paintings take the canvas apart and reassemble it, unravelling the threads, displaying the significant waste scraps alongside it, like a kind of *ikat* in reverse. An approach reincorporating history, the landmark image, the time of the journey.

Within these overlappings, in which the painter has as much to say about cloth as the weaver about painting, new ways are born affirming that if the renaissance of textile art has come about through excavation, its future lies in meetings and syntheses.

Francis Wilson (1935)
Soula, 1983
Acrylic on cotton cloth
8′6″ × 4′11″

PERSPECTIVES

Many times in the course of this work we have insisted on the fact that textiles are related to numbers. From the pre-Inca or Inca civilizations of South America which were able to count by means of knots tied in a cord, through Indonesian weavers who memorized the lengths of the threads to be dyed in preparing motifs for cloths treated by the *ikat* process, down to the hand loom and Jacquard loom which, in their programmed operation, may be considered the ancestors of the computer, all epochs and all civilizations have adopted, for the making of textiles, intuitive or mechanical coding schemes, contrivances of threads, rhythms and recurrent patterns.

Patrice Hugues stresses this point by affirming: "In civilization, fabrics are the earliest example, and no doubt the most important, of a concrete structure based on a binary coding scheme, like the working of the computer (+ or −, 1 or 0: the weft thread is taken up by the warp if it passes underneath, or 'left' by the warp thread if it passes above it)."

If these facts are important in helping to bring together the functioning of age-old tools and the latest contemporary tools—which according to Töffler is one of the characteristics of post-industrial society—and in allowing us to hope that the civilization of computer science will quite naturally once again take the importance of fabrics into account, they also help to throw light on the contradictory relations between tapestry and painting from a different angle.

"Painting is the analogical art *par excellence*. It is even the form in which analogy becomes language, finds a natural language in passing through diagram," writes Gilles Deleuze in commenting on the paintings of Francis Bacon. In the continuous line of the brush the painter is often actually seeking the mirror: "In Italy, Leonardo shows how much the mirror is the master of painters," observes René Huyghe.

For five centuries in the West, where pictorial art insisted in turn on the ideas of beauty, realism, symbolism, surrealism, impression and illusion, favouring form or matter, the plastic or the pictorial, organization or disorder, the question of coding systems was practically never raised in painting. An unshakable conviction made the soul or inspiration or the unconscious the driving force of artistic mediation. "A kind of soul that becomes sonorous," said Claudel.

In a parallel sense, the painters asked the handweavers to pursue, as their equals, an analogous approach, by reproducing, in a hyper-realistic manner, their own canvas, realm of the continuous, in the discontinuity of the track of the thread. However, with the advent of the photographic image, the video image and more recently the image of synthesis, painting has had to question its technical elements, the nature of its support and the influence exerted upon it by these new artistic media.

Art critics have stressed that for the painter, the canvas is never blank. On it he picks out figures, colours, preexisting perspectives which he must either sweep aside or use rationally in order to begin his work.

These beginnings are first of all material: ribbings of threads: "To paint is to let oneself be drawn by a confused surface, often that of a woven canvas, in the hope that images will arise from it," Marc Le Bot reminds us.

Today, more and more, these starting points are previously photo-engraved images. We know the influence of Marey's motion-analysis studies on Marcel Duchamp's *Nude Descending a Staircase*; that of the images of Marilyn Monroe or Elvis Presley, repeated in silkscreen

MARISA BANDIERA CERANTOLA (1934)
RESEARCH INTO HIDDEN VISUAL
STRUCTURES THROUGH ELEMENTARY
MATHEMATICAL LAWS, 1974-1976
Indian ink drawing on tracing paper
31½″ × 39″

MARISA BANDIERA CERANTOLA (1934)
THE CLOTH WEAVES ITSELF, 1982-1983
Cotton cloth and acrylic
7′10″ × 7′10″ × 32′10″

printing by Andy Warhol; or that of coloured photo-engravings in dots made from comic-strip drawings on Roy Lichtenstein.

In these new approaches an order already exists prior to the painting. It is no longer a matter merely of analogical translation, but of analysis. We do not speak so much of inspiration as of consciousness.

In abstract art itself, the systematizing of codified choices, the dissection of the constituent elements of the picture, have led to the plastic demonstration of the basic elements of painting.

But, as Gilles Deleuze further remarks, "The Abstractionists often turn out to be great painters; that is, they do not apply to painting a code that is external to it, but on the contrary elaborate a code that is intrinsically pictorial. The code is thus paradoxical, since instead of being opposed to analogy it takes analogy for its object; it is the digital expression of the analogical as such."

Stena Vasualka, another artist who uses video and information processing, is emphatic: "As soon as we had a computer, our preoccupation changed. Before, we were obsessed with perfecting the checking out of analogical effects. But by plunging into the digital we made a *de facto* entry into a sphere where everything produced can only be the product of checking out."

If contemporary artists are now looking at the importance of codes in their means of expression, textiles must obviously therefore constitute a model for this approach. Here textiles find total relevance as parallel model, solid foundation and all but universal memory.

"To weave is also to write the visual; a fabric is at once expressed in numbers, and its elaboration is achieved through a system of knotwork. At the crossroads of the digital and the analogical, it is that homely place, familiar from everyday life, the symbolic implications of which have been extremely powerful in civilizations other than our own," observes Rémy Prin. To which Patrice Hugues adds, "For a long time fabrics have been ready to receive assistance from the computer. They might be said to have been waiting for it." This specific textile character should also help to restore to its rightful place an art too long relegated to the sidelines, and make it possible to grasp one of the glaring contradictions that will always persist between the painted and the woven surface.

If painting "is the analogical art *par excellence*," textile is the digital art *par excellence*, and it is easy to understand that the transposition of a photographic image on a ruled screen or of the video image composed of multiple points and multiple lines may be achieved more easily in tapestry or weaving than by the stroke of the painter's brush.

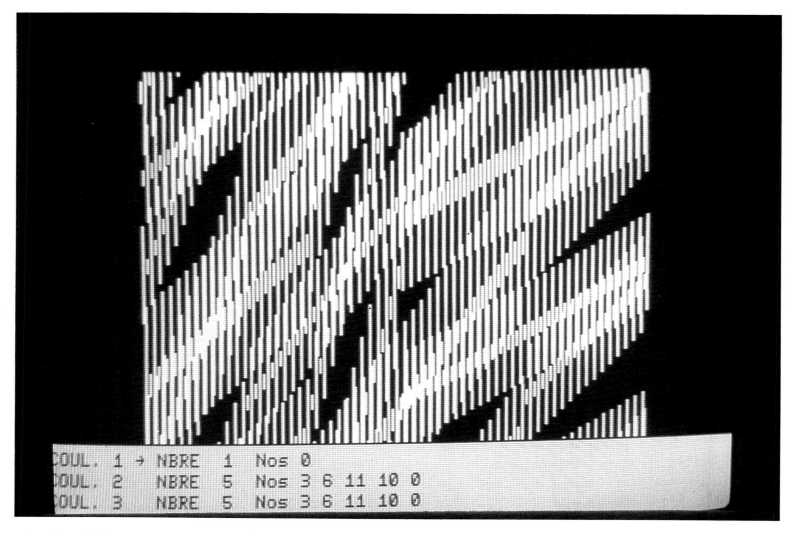

```
COUL. 1 → NBRE 1 Nos 0
COUL. 2   NBRE 5 Nos 3 6 11 10 0
COUL. 3   NBRE 5 Nos 3 6 11 10 0
```

RÉMY PRIN (1946)
COLOUR FRAGMENTATION, 1984
Textile research from software
for colour-fragmentation *ikat*

In the methods utilized by the American weaver Ancelevicius, the Frenchman Hocine Touhami, the Poles Ursula Plewka-Schmidt or Honorata Blicharska, photographic portraits are woven line by line, formed rib by rib, sometimes by playing on the length of the stitch taken or the interpenetration of hatchings; and it is the ensemble of these stitches that determine the image in a quest to establish coherence between the codes of two different media.

This methodology of weaving based on an operational logic has been illustrated in a fundamental way by the Italian artist Marisa Bandiera Cerantola. Since 1970 she has striven, both in two dimensions and in space, and by the use of very simple materials (bands of crisscrossing painted cloths or of knotted coloured threads) to make the spectator become aware, through a multitude of possibilities, of all the stages in the construction of textile objects. One of her first pieces of research "on the binary possibilities of fabrics," carried out with the help of a calculator, was displayed at the Stedelijk Museum of Amsterdam in 1976–1977.

With this formal grounding it may easily be understood that more and more creators have decided to use the tools of data processing in textile creation. Certain graphic palettes, starting either from the video capture of a pre-existing image or from a drawing produced on a digitizing board, enable rapid and infinite manipulations of parameters as different as form, colour, axes of symmetry and repetition. The transformed and recopied motifs can thus be placed in series and linked up to form the object of a textile impression. Along these lines Annick Top has prepared printed textile panels, but also cartoons for tapestries and carpets, some of which have been produced by the French national manufactories.

But, better still, software packages have been devised both in the United States and Japan as well as in England and France, which make possible the simulation of fabrics on a screen, after selection and manipulation of their characteristic parameters. Apart from the creation of textile weaves, some software, such as that perfected in France by Rémy Prin, makes it possible to select all the formal elements of an *ikat* fabric.

Textile creation thus has at its disposal up-to-date tools which, apart from their fashionable status in other fields, are here in perfect accord with the very nature of fabrics. This event is absolutely decisive in the rediscovery of textile memory which has seemed to us to characterize textile art in the West.

To a very large extent, this rediscovery is comparable to the formation of an important artistic data bank, which, by confrontation with the capacity for information processing possessed by the computer, should find an outlet in new visual structures and a new creative spirit.

Faced by these structures and these reminders of the past, the artist will fortunately always remain in charge. Indeed, it is for him to exercise his power of choice in the face of a dizzying sense of possibilities.

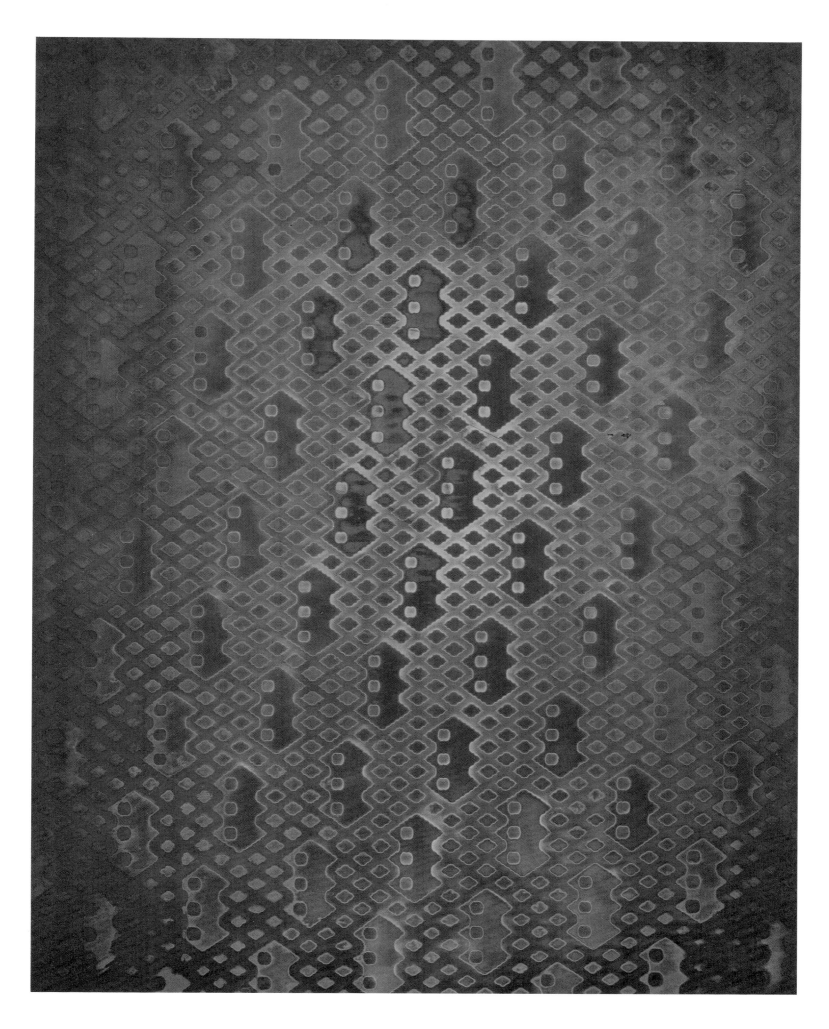

ANNICK TOP (1952)
TEXTILE DESIGN, 1984
Textile research from
data-processing software,
photograph worked over with paints
14″ × 11″

BIBLIOGRAPHY

LIST OF ILLUSTRATIONS

INDEX OF NAMES

Bibliography

General

ACKERMAN P., *Tapestry, the Mirror of Civilization*, New York, London, Toronto 1933.

ALBERS A., *On Designing*, New York 1959. *On Weaving*, Middletown 1965.

ANQUETIL J., *Le tissage*, Paris 1977.

BATTENFIELD J., *Ikat Technique*, New York, London 1978.

BEAULIEU M., *Les tissus d'art*, Paris 1965.

BERNATCHEZ M., HARVEY-PERRIER G., *La tapisserie*, Montreal 1977.

BRUNELLO F., *The Art of Dyeing in the History of Mankind*, Vicenza 1973.

CHERBLANC E., *Mémoire sur l'invention du tissu*, Paris 1935.

COFFINET J., *Arachné ou l'art de la tapisserie*, Geneva 1971. *Métamorphoses de la tapisserie*, Geneva 1977.

COLLINGWOOD P., *The Technique of Rug Weaving*, London 1968. *The Technique of Sprang*, London 1974. *The Technique of Tablet Weaving*, London 1982.

CONSTANTINE M., LARSEN J. L., *Beyond Craft: The Art Fabric*, New York 1973. *The Art Fabric: Mainstream*, New York, Cincinnati, London, Toronto, Melbourne 1980.

EMERY I., *The Primary Structures of Fabrics*, Washington D.C. 1980.

GEIJER A., *A History of Textile Art*, London 1979.

GRAND P. M., *La tapisserie*, Paris 1981.

D'HENNEZEL H., *Pour comprendre les tissus d'art*, Paris 1930.

HUGUES P., *Le tissu et ses motifs, un itinéraire concret du langage*, Rouen 1976. *Le langage du tissu*, Paris 1982.

JARRY M., *La tapisserie des origines à nos jours*, Paris 1968. *La tapisserie, art du XXᵉ siècle*, Lausanne 1974.

KUENZI A., *La nouvelle tapisserie*, Geneva 1974.

LARSEN J. L., *The Dyer's Art. Ikat, Batik, Plangi*, New York, London 1976.

LEROI-GOURHAN A., *L'homme et la matière*, Paris 1971.

LUBELL C., *Textile Collections of the World* (3 vols.), London 1976-1977.

MEILACH D. Z., *Le livre de la vannerie*, Montreal 1976.

MIGEON G., *Les arts du tissu*, Paris 1929.

PARRY L., *William Morris Textiles*, London 1983.

PIRSON J. F., *La structure et l'objet*, Brussels 1984.

RITCH D., WADA Y., *Ikat: An Introduction*, Berkeley 1975.

SANTINA L., *Lace, a History*, London 1983.

SEILER-BALDINGER A., *Systematik der Textilen Techniken*, Basel 1973. *Classification of Textile Techniques*, Ahmedabad 1979.

THOMSON F. P., *Tapestry, Mirror of History*, New York 1980.

VAN GELDER L., *Ikat*, 1980.

VERLET P., FLORISOONE M., HOFFMEISTER A., TABARD F., *La tapisserie, histoire et technique du XIVᵉ au XXᵉ siècle* (preface by Jean LURÇAT), Lausanne 1977.

VIALLET N., *Principes d'analyse scientifique. Tapisserie. Méthode et vocabulaire* (foreword by J. CAIN and A. CHASTEL), Paris 1971.

WILSON K., *A History of Textiles*, Boulder 1979.

Catalogues

AIX-EN-PROVENCE, Musée des tapisseries, *Approches de la tapisserie et des structures textiles*, 1979. Catalogue by M. KROTOFF; preface by M. JARRY.

BEAUVAIS, Galerie nationale de la tapisserie et d'art textile, *Chaîne, trame et mailles. Art et technique*, 1981.

Chapter I

World Centres of Textile Art

ARCHAEOLOGY

EMERY I., *Archaeological Textiles (Roundtable proceedings)*, Textile Museum, Washington 1975.

HALD M., *Ancient Danish Textiles from Bogs and Burials*, National Museum of Denmark, Copenhagen 1980.

ANCIENT PERU

ASCHER M.R., *Code of the Quipu*, Michigan 1981.

CASON M., CAHLANDER A., *The Art of Bolivian Highland Weaving*, USA 1976.

D'HARCOURT R., *Les textiles anciens du Pérou et leurs techniques*, Paris 1934. *Textiles of Ancient Peru and their Techniques*, Washington 1975.

DESROSIERS S., *Métier à tisser et vêtements andins. Le tissu comme être vivant*, Paris 1982.

NASS U., *Weaves of the Incas*, Flourtown 1980.

ROWE A.P., *Warp Patterned Weaves of the Andes*, Textile Museum, Washington 1977. *A Century of Change in Guatemalan Textiles*, 1981.

STIERLIN H., *Nazca, la clé du mystère*, Paris 1983.

Articles:

GIRAULT L., *Textiles boliviens, région de Charazani*, Objets et mondes T. IX supplément, Paris 1969.

D'HARCOURT R., *Les textiles dans l'Ancien Pérou*, Cahiers Ciba, Vol. VIII No. 86, Basel 1960.

MURRA J. V., *La Función del Tejido en varios contextos sociales y políticos*, Formaciones Económicas y Políticas del mundo andino, Lima 1975.

Catalogue:

LOS ANGELES, Craft and Folk Art Museum, *Weaving Tradition of Highland Bolivia*, Texts by L. ADELSON, B. TAKAMI 1978.

SYRIA

Articles:

PFISTER R., *Textiles de Palmyre découverts par le Service des Antiquités du Haut-Commissariat de la République française dans la nécropole de Palmyre*, Paris 1934. *Nouveaux textiles de Palmyre découverts par le Service des Antiquités du Haut-Commissariat de la République française dans la nécropole de Palmyre (Tour d'Elahbel)*, Paris 1937.

BYZANTIUM

DIEHL C., *Manuel d'art byzantin*, Paris 1910.

STERN H., *L'art byzantin*, Paris 1982.

Articles:

DE MICHEAUX R., *Le tissu de Mozac. Fragment du suaire de Saint Austremoine (VIIIᵉ siècle)*, Bulletin de liaison du CIETA No. 17, 1963.

HEICHELHEIM F. M., *Soieries byzantines*, Cahiers Ciba, No. 47, Basel 1953.

COPTIC ART

DU BOURGUET P., *Catalogue des étoffes coptes*, Musée du Louvre, Paris 1964. *L'art copte*, Paris 1968.

GERSPACH M., *Les tapisseries coptes*, Paris 1890.

KYBALOVA L., *L'art des bords du Nil. Les tissus coptes*, Paris 1967.

RUTSCHOWSCAYA M.-H., *Tissage et tissus coptes*, Musée du Louvre, Petits guides des grands musées No. 58, Paris.

SIMON E., *Meleager und Atlante*, Berne 1970.

Articles:

BECKWITH J., *Tissus coptes*, Cahiers Ciba No. 83, Basel 1959.
DU BOURGUET P., *Survivances pharaoniques dans quelques tissus coptes du musée du Louvre*, Bulletin de la Société française d'égyptologie No. 4, Paris 1950. *Du thème de saison à celui de Daphné dans des œuvres coptes*, La Revue du Louvre No. 1, Paris 1970. *De l'art copte païen à l'art copte chrétien*, La Revue du Louvre No. 3, Paris 1970. *Reliefs sur pierre et étoffes*, La Revue du Louvre No. 2, Paris 1971.
JOSPIN J.-P., *La tapisserie aux poissons d'Antinoé*, Archeologia No. 182, Paris 1983.
KUHNEL E., *La tradition copte dans les tissus musulmans*, Bulletin de la Société d'archéologie copte, Cairo 1938.
RUTSCHOWSCAYA M.-H., *Un ensemble de tapisseries coptes à décor mythologique*, La Revue du Louvre Nos. 5-6, Paris 1984.
TRILLING J., *The Roman Heritage. Textiles from Egyptian Art and the Eastern Mediterranean 300 to 600 A.D.*, Textile Museum, Washington 1982.

Catalogues:

ANGERS, Musée, Third Festival of Anjou, *Tissus coptes*. Texts by P. DU BOURGUET, P. GREMONT.
THE HAGUE, Haags Gemeentemuseum. *Koptische weefsels*, 1982.
PARIS, Petit Palais, *L'art copte*, 1964. Musée d'Art et d'Essai, *Un siècle de fouilles françaises en Egypte 1880-1980*. 1981.

ISLAM

DIMAND M., *A Handbook of Muhammadan Art*, New York 1944.
GUERARD M., EL HABIB M., *Art islamique au Maghreb*, Musée du Louvre, Petits guides des grands musées No. 28, Paris 1976.
LAFONTAINE-DOSOGNE J., *Textiles islamiques*, Vols. I and II, Musées Royaux d'Art et d'Histoire, Brussels 1981-1983.
LOMBARD M., *Les textiles dans le monde musulman VIIᵉ-XIIᵉs. Etudes d'économie médiévale*, Paris, The Hague, New York 1978.
MIGEON G., *Manuel d'art musulman*, Vol. II, *Les arts plastiques et industriels*, Paris 1927.
OTTO-DORN K., *L'art de l'Islam*, Paris 1967.

Articles:

BERNUS M., MARCHAL H., VIAL G., *Le suaire de Saint Josse. Dossier de recensement*, Bulletin de liaison du CIETA No. 33, Paris 1971.
GROHMANN A., *Tiraz*, Encyclopédie de l'Islam, Leyden 1924.
STEENSGAARD N., INALCIK H., GHARAIBEH A.K., SCHMIDT H.J., *Haru*, Encyclopédie de l'Islam, Leyden 1966.
WIET G., *Tissus et tapisseries du musée arabe du Caire*, Syria, Vol. XVI, 1935.

Catalogue:

SANTA BARBARA (USA), Museum of Art, *At the Edge of Asia: Five Centuries of Turkish Textiles*, 1983.

ITALY

SANT-ANGELO A., *Art italien, le tissu du XIIᵉ au XVIIIᵉ siècle*, Paris 1960.

Articles:

DAUJAT Y., *L'influence orientale sur les tissus italiens du Moyen Age*, Information culturelle et artistique No. I, Paris 1955.
EDLER DE ROOVER F., *Lucques, ville de la soie*, Cahiers Ciba No. 39, Basel 1952.
DE FRANCESCO G., *Soieries vénitiennes*, Cahiers Ciba No. 25, Basel 1949.
WARDWELL A.E., *Italian Gothic Silks in the Museum Collection*, County Museum of Art Bulletin No. 24, Los Angeles 1978.

CHINA

CAMMAN S., *China's Dragon Robes*, New York 1952.
SOAME J.R., *Arts de la Chine*, Vol. IV, Fribourg 1965.
SOUK-HI-LI, *Pour un retour au k'o-sseu* (Mémoire), Paris 1984.

Articles:

CAMMAN S., *Notes on the Origin of Chinese k'o-sseu*, Artibus Asiae Vol. 11, Ascona 1948. *Anciennes soieries chinoises*, Cahiers Ciba No. 2, Basel 1963.

Catalogue:

NEW YORK, The Metropolitan Museum, *Chinese Patterned Silks*. Text by P. SIMMONS, 1948.

JAPAN

BUISSON D. and S., *Kimono, art traditionnel du Japon*, Lausanne 1983.
NOMA S., *Japanese Costume and Textile Arts*, New York 1974.
TOMITA J. and N., *Japanese Ikat Weaving*, London 1982.

Articles:

ARSÈNE-HENRY C., *Tapisseries et soieries japonaises*, Bulletin de la Maison franco-japonaise Vol. XII, No. 1, Paris 1941.
TONOMURA K., *Méthodes de réserve japonaise*, Cahiers Ciba, Basel 1967.

INDIA
Articles:

HUGUES P., *A propos des châles cachemires*, Textile/Art No. 4, Paris 1982.
SCHWARTZ P.R., *La fabrication des toiles peintes aux Indes au XVIIIᵉ s.*, Bulletin de la société industrielle Vol. IV, Mulhouse 1957.
TUCHSCHERER J.M., *Les indiennes et impression des étoffes du XVIᵉ au XVIIIᵉ s.*, Bulletin de la société industrielle Vol. IV, Mulhouse 1975.

Catalogues:

LONDON, Victoria and Albert Museum, *The Kashmir Shawl*. Text by J. IRWIN, 1973. British Museum, *Textiles of Baluchistan*. Text by M.G. KONIECZNY 1979.
LYON, Musée Historique des Tissus, *Le châle cachemire en France au XIXᵉ s.* Text by M. LÉVI-STRAUSS 1983.
WASHINGTON, The Textile Museum, *Master Dyers to the World. Technique and Trade in Early Indian Dyed Cotton Textiles*. Text by M. GITTINGER 1982.

SOUTH-EAST ASIA

HAAKE A., *Javanische Batik*, Hanover 1984.
MAC CABE ELLIOTT I., *Batik, Fabled Cloth of Java*, New York 1984.
WARMING W., GAWORSKI M., *The World of Indonesian Textiles*, London 1981.

Article:

ADAMS M., *Tissus décorés de l'île de Sumba*, Objets et mondes Vol. VI, No. 1, Paris 1966.

Catalogues:

BERKELEY, R.H. Lowie Museum of Anthropology, *Threads of Tradition: Textiles of Indonesia and Sarawak*. Text by J. FISCHER 1979.
WASHINGTON, The Textile Museum, *Splendid Symbols*. Text by M. GITTINGER 1979.
OTAGO, Otago Museum, *Woven Images, Traditions in Weaving from Indonesia*. Text by M. BLACKMAN 1981.

CENTRAL ASIA

BACON E.E., *Central Asians under Russian Rule: A Study in Culture Change*, Ithaca 1966.

Articles:

DUPAIGNE B., *Un artisan d'Afghanistan, sa vie, ses problèmes, ses espoirs*, Objets et mondes Vol. XIX, Paris 1974. *Aperçus sur quelques techniques afghanes*, Objets et mondes Vol. VII, Paris 1968.
LEIX A., *Turkestan and its Textile Crafts*, Cahiers Ciba No. 40, Basel 1941.

AFRICA

BOSER SARIVAXEVANIS R., *Les tissus de l'Afrique occidentale*, Basel 1972.
FISKE P., *West African Strip Weaving*, Washington 1975.
LAMB V. and A., *Au Cameroun, Weaving-Tissage*, London 1981. *Sierra Leone Weaving*, Hartingsfordbury 1984.
LEIRIS M., DELANGE J., *Afrique noire, la création plastique*, Paris 1967.
PICTON J., MACK J., *African Textiles, Looms, Weaving and Design*, London 1979.
POLAKOFF C., *African Textiles and Dyeing Techniques*, London 1982.

Articles:

BOSER SARIVAXEVANIS R., *Aperçus sur la teinture de l'indigo en Afrique occidentale*, Naturforschende Gesellschaft, Basel 1969. *Les tissus de l'Afrique occidentale: méthode de classification et catalogue raisonné des étoffes tissées de l'Afrique de l'Ouest établi à partir de données techniques et historiques*, Basler Beiträge zur Ethnologie Vol. XIII, Basel 1972. *Textilhandwerk in West Afrika*, Bulletin of Museum für Völkerkunde, Basel 1972. *Recherches sur l'histoire des textiles traditionnels tissés et teints de l'Afrique occidentale*, Naturforschende Gesellschaft, Basel 1975.
BOSER R., MUTTER I., *Systematik der Sticheformen*, Bulletin of Museum für Völkerkunde, Basel 1968.
CLOUZOT H., LEVEL A., *La décoration des textiles au Congo belge. Les tissus veloutés Babuka*, L'Amour de l'Art No. 6, Paris 1923.

LAMB V. and A., *The Lamb Collection of West African Narrow Strip Weaving*, Bulletin of the Textile Museum, Washington 1975. *Traditional African Weaving and Textile*, Textile History Vol. 11, Washington 1980.

Catalogue:

MULHOUSE, Musée de l'Impression sur étoffes, *Teinture, expression de l'Afrique noire*, 1982.

Chapter II

EARLY TAPESTRY

AJALBERT J., *Beauvais, la Manufacture nationale de tapisserie*, Paris 1927.

ALEXANDER E. J., WOODWARD C. H., *The Flora of the Unicorn Tapestries*, New York 1974.

ASSELBERGHS J. P., *La tenture de l'Histoire de Jacob*, Brussels 1972.

AUZAS P. M., MAUPEOU C. de, MERINDOL C. de, MUEL F., RUAIS A., *L'Apocalypse d'Angers. Chef-d'œuvre de la tapisserie médiévale*, Fribourg 1985.

BADIN J., *La manufacture de tapisseries de Beauvais depuis ses origines jusqu'à nos jours*, foreword by J. GUIFFREY, Paris 1909.

BENNETT A. G., *Five Centuries of Tapestry from the Fine Arts Museum of San Francisco*, Rutland, Tokyo 1976.

BERTRAND S., *La tapisserie de Bayeux et la manière de vivre au XIᵉ siècle*, La Pierre-qui-Vire 1966.

BOCCARA D., *Les belles heures de la tapisserie*, Paris 1971.

BREL-BORDAZ O., *Broderies d'ornements liturgiques, XIIᵉ-XIVᵉ s.*, Paris 1982.

CALMETTES F., *Etat général des tapisseries de la manufacture des Gobelins depuis son origine jusqu'à nos jours*, Paris 1912.

COFFINET J., PIANZOLA M., *La tapisserie*, Geneva 1971.

COFFINET J., *Pratique de la tapisserie*, Geneva 1977.

CRICK-KUNTZIGER M., *La tenture de la Légende de Notre-Dame du Sablon*, Antwerp 1942. *Les tapisseries de l'hôtel de ville de Bruxelles*, Antwerp 1944. *La tenture de l'Histoire de Jacob d'après Bernard van Orley*, Antwerp 1954.

DARCEL A., *Les manufactures nationales de tapisseries des Gobelins et de tapis de la Savonnerie*, Paris, 1885.

DEMOTTE, *La tapisserie gothique*, Paris 1922-1924.

D'HULST R. A., *Tapisseries flamandes du XVIᵉ au XVIIIᵉ siècle*, Brussels 1960.

DIGBY G. W., *The Tapestry Collection. Medieval and Renaissance*, Victoria and Albert Museum, London 1980.

DIGBY G. W., HEFFORD W., *The Devonshire Hunting Tapestries*, Leicester, London 1971.

ERLANDE-BRANDENBURG A., *La dame à la licorne*, Paris 1978.

ESPINAS, *La draperie dans la Flandre française au Moyen Age*, Paris 1923.

FÉNAILLE M., *Etat général des tapisseries de la manufacture des Gobelins depuis son origine jusqu'à nos jours, 1600-1900*, 6 vols., Paris 1903-1923.

FREEMAN M. B., *La chasse à la licorne*, Lausanne, Paris 1983.

GILBERT P., *Les tapisseries de la Victoire des Vertus*, Brussels 1964.

GUIFFREY J., *Histoire de la tapisserie depuis le Moyen Age jusqu'à nos jours*, Paris 1886. *Histoire de la tapisserie*, Tours 1886. *Les manufactures nationales de tapisseries, Les Gobelins et Beauvais*, Paris 1908. *Les tapisseries du XIIᵉ siècle à la fin du XVIᵉ*. Histoire des arts appliqués d'Emile Molinier T. VI, Paris 1911.

GUIFFREY J., MUNTZ E., PINCHART A., *Histoire générale de la tapisserie*, 3 vols., Paris 1878-1885.

GUIMBAUD L., *La tapisserie de haute et basse lisse*, Paris 1964.

GOBEL H., *Wandteppiche*, 6 vols., Leipzig 1923-1934.

HAVARD H., *Les arts de l'ameublement. La tapisserie*, Paris 1893.

HAVARD H., VACHON M., *Les manufactures nationales*, Paris 1889.

HEINZ D., *Europäische Wandteppiche*, Braunschweig 1963.

HOUDOY J., *Les tapisseries de haute lisse. Histoire de la fabrication lilloise du XIVᵉ au XVIIIᵉ siècle*, Lille 1871.

HUNTER G. L., *Tapestries. Their History and Renaissance*, New York, London, Toronto 1912. *The Practical Book of Tapestries*, London, Philadelphia, 1925.

JANNEAU G., *Evolution de la tapisserie*, Paris 1947.

JANNEAU G., NICLAUSSE J., *Le musée des Gobelins*, 2 vols., Paris 1938-1939.

JANNEAU G., VERLET P., YVER G., WEIGERT R. A., FONTAINE G., NICLAUSSE J., *La tapisserie*, Paris 1942.

JUBINAL A., *Les anciennes tapisseries historiées ou collections des monuments les plus remarquables de ce genre qui soient restés du Moyen Age à partir du XIᵉ au XVIᵉ siècle inclusivement*, 2 vols., Paris 1818, 1820.

LASZLO, E., KIADO C., *Flemish and French Tapestries in Hungary*, Budapest 1981.

LAURENT H., *Un grand commerce d'exportation. La draperie des Pays-Bas, en France et dans les pays méditerranéens*, Paris 1935.

LESTOCQUOY J., *Deux siècles de l'histoire de la tapisserie, 1300-1500*, Arras 1978.

LEFÉBURE E., *Broderies et dentelles*, Paris 1887.

LÈVE A., *La tapisserie de la Reine Mathilde dite la tapisserie de Bayeux*, Paris 1919.

MARQUET DE VASSELOT J. J., WEIGERT R. A., *Bibliographie de la tapisserie, des tapis et de la broderie en France*, Paris 1969.

MEYER D., *L'Histoire du Roy*, Paris 1980.

MERINDOL C. de, MUEL F., RUAIS A., SALET F., *La tenture de l'Apocalypse d'Angers. Une nouvelle vision*, Nantes 1985.

PARISSE M., *La tapisserie de Bayeux: un documentaire du XIᵉ siècle*, Paris 1983.

PLANCHENAULT R., *Les tapisseries d'Angers*, Paris 1955. *L'Apocalypse d'Angers*, Paris 1966. *Petites notes sur les tapisseries d'Angers*, Paris 1973.

RORIMER J. J., *Medieval Tapestries. The Metropolitan Museum of Art*, New York 1949. *The Unicorn Tapestries at the Cloisters*, New York 1962.

RORIMER J. J., FREEMAN M. B., *The Nine Heroes Tapestries at the Cloisters*. New York 1953.

SALET F., *La tapisserie française du Moyen Age à nos jours*, Paris 1946. *David et Bethsabée*, Paris 1980.

SHEARMAN J., *Raphael's Cartoons in the Royal Collection and the Leonine Tapestries in the Sistine Chapel*, London 1972.

SOUCHAL G., *Etudes sur la tapisserie parisienne. Règlements et techniques des tapissiers sarrasinois, hautelisseurs et nostrez*, Paris, 1969. *Les tapisseries de l'Apocalypse d'Angers*, Paris, Geneva 1969.

SOIL DE MORIANE E. J., *Les tapisseries de Tournai, les tapissiers et les hautelisseurs de cette ville*, Tournai 1892.

SZABLOWSKI J., *Les tapisseries flamandes au Château de Wawel*, Antwerp 1972.

THOMSON W. G., *Tapestry Weaving in England*, London 1914. *A History of Tapestry from the Earliest Times until the Present Day*, London, 1930, 1973.

VAN YSSELSTEYN G. T., *Tapestry, the Most Expensive Industry of the XVth and XVIth centuries. A Renewed Research into Technique, Origin and Iconography*, The Hague 1969.

VERLET P., SALET F., *La Dame à la licorne*, Paris 1960.

WAUTERS A., *Essai historique sur les tapisseries et les tapissiers de haute et basse lice de Bruxelles*, Brussels 1878, reprinted 1973.

WEIGERT R. A., *Cinq siècles de tapisseries d'Aubusson*, Paris 1935. *Les belles tentures de la Manufacture royale des Gobelins, 1662-1792*, Paris 1937. *La tapisserie française*, Paris 1956. *La tapisserie et le tapis*, Paris 1964.

ZELLER A. P., *Tapisserie*, Paris 1976.

Articles

ACKERMAN P., *The Lady and the Unicorn*, Burlington Magazine, Vol. LXVI.

ASSELBERGHS J. P., *Les tapisseries tournaisiennes de la Guerre de Troie*, Revue belge d'archéologie et d'histoire de l'art, XXIX, 1970, and Artes Belgicae, Brussels 1972.

BIGWOOD, *Les financiers d'Arras, contribution à l'étude des origines du capitalisme moderne*, Revue belge de philologie et d'histoire, III, Nos. 3, 4; IV, Nos. 2, 3, Brussels 1925.

COURAL J., *Notes documentaires sur les ateliers parisiens de 1597 à 1662*, Catalogue Chefs-d'œuvre de la tapisserie parisienne 1597-1662, Orangerie de Versailles, 1967.

CRICK-KUNTZIGER M., *Les «compléments» de nos tapisseries gothiques*, Bulletin des musées royaux d'art et d'histoire, May, July, Nov. 1931 and March 1933 and Revue belge d'archéologie et d'histoire de l'art, VI, July, Sept., Brussels 1936. *Tapisseries*, Trésor de l'art flamand du Moyen Age au XVIIIᵉ siècle, Brussels 1932. *La tenture d'Achille d'après Rubens et les tapissiers Jean et François Raes*, Bulletin des musées royaux d'art et d'histoire, Brussels 1934. *Marques et signatures de tapissiers bruxellois*, Annales de la Société royale d'archéologie et d'histoire, XL, Brussels 1936. *Note sur les tapisseries de l'Histoire d'Alexandre du Palais Doria à Rome*, Bulletin de l'Institut historique belge de Rome, XIX, 1938. *Bernard van Orley et le décor mural en tapisserie*, Annales de la Société royale d'archéologie et d'histoire, Brussels 1943. *La tapisserie bruxelloise du XVᵉ siècle*. Bruxelles au XVᵉ siècle, Brussels 1953. *Un chef-d'œuvre inconnu du Maître de la Dame à la licorne*, Revue belge d'archéologie et d'histoire de l'art, XXIII, Brussels 1954.

DELMARCEL G., *La légende d'Herkenbald et la justice de Trajan.* Catalogue des tapisseries bruxelloises de la pré-Renaissance 1976.

DESHAINE, *La tapisserie de haute lisse à Arras avant le XV° siècle.* Réunion des sociétés savantes et des sociétés des Beaux-Arts des départements 1879–1880.

DE VAIVRE J. B., *A propos d'une tapisserie aux armes Beaufort-Comminges,* Bulletin monumental Vol. 132.

DHANENS E., *L'importance du peintre Jean van Roome, dit de Bruxelles,* Catalogue des tapisseries bruxelloises de la pré-Renaissance 1976. *La légende d'Herkenbald. Examen et traitement de l'Institut royal du patrimoine artistique,* Catalogue des tapisseries bruxelloises de la pré-Renaissance 1976.

DIMIER L., *La tenture de la Galerie de Fontainebleau à Vienne,* Gazette des Beaux-Arts Vol. XVI.

GUESNON, *Le hautelisseur Pierre Féré d'Arras,* Revue du Nord 1910.

JANNEAU G., *Les tapisseries de Tournai,* Archives de l'Art français, XXII, 1959.

JARRY M., *Les Indes, série triomphale de l'exotisme,* Connaissance des Arts, No. 87, 1959.

JESTAZ B., *La tenture de la Galerie de Fontainebleau et sa restauration à Vienne à la fin du XVII° siècle,* Revue de l'art, No. 22, 1973.

JOUBERT F., *L'Apocalypse d'Angers et les débuts de la tapisserie historiée,* Bulletin monumental, 1981.

KING D., *How Many Apocalypse Tapestries,* Miscellany Harold B. Burnham, Toronto.

LESTOCQUOY J., *Le rôle des artistes tournaisiens à Arras: Jacques Daret et Michel de Gand,* Revue belge d'archéologie et d'histoire de l'art, 1937. *Financiers, courtiers, hautelisseurs d'Arras aux XII° et XIV° siècles,* Revue belge de philologie et d'histoire, 1938. *L'atelier de Baudouin de Bailleul et la tapisserie de Gédéon,* Revue belge d'archéologie et d'histoire de l'art, April-June 1938. *Origine et décadence de la tapisserie à Arras,* Revue belge d'archéologie et d'histoire de l'art, X, 1940.

MARGERIN, *Les tapisseries de verdure, de leur origine au milieu du XVI° s. dans les ateliers d'Arras, de Tournai et d'Audenarde,* Bulletin des musées de France, 1932.

MORELOWSKI M., *L'histoire du Chevalier au cygne.* Actes du congrès de l'histoire de l'art, III, 1921.

OPPERMAN H. A., *Oudry aux Gobelins,* Revue de l'art, No. 22, 1973.

PANOFSKY E., *The Friedsam Annunciation and the Problem of the Ghent Altarpiece,* Art Bulletin, Vol. XVII, 1935.

REYNAUD N., *Un peintre français cartonnier de tapisseries au XV° siècle, Henri de Vulcop,* Revue de l'art, No. 22, 1973.

REYNOLDS, *Merchants of Arras and the Overland Trade with Genoa, Twelfth Century,* Revue belge de philologie et d'histoire, IX, 1930.

ROLAND P., CRICK-KUNTZIGER M., MORELOWSKI M., *Le tapissier Pasquier Grenier et l'Eglise Saint-Quentin de Tournai,* Revue belge d'archéologie et d'histoire de l'art, Vol. VI, 1936.

RORIMER J. J., *A Fifteenth Century Tapestry of the Seven Sacraments,* Metropolitan Museum of Art Bulletin, Vol. XXXV, 1940. *The Annunciation Tapestry,* Metropolitan Museum of Art Bulletin, Vol. XX, 1961.

RUAIS A., *Les tapisseries du trésor de la Cathédrale d'Angers au XIX° siècle,* Mémoires de l'Académie d'Angers, 1977–1978.

SALET F., *La tapisserie bruxelloise au XV° siècle,* Bulletin monumental, 124, 1966.

SCHNEEBALG-PERELMAN S., *La tenture armoriée de Philippe le Bon à Berne,* Jahrbuch des Bernischen Historischen Museums, XXXIX and XL, 1961. «Le retouchage» *dans la tapisserie bruxelloise ou les origines de l'édit impérial de 1544,* Annales de la Société royale d'archéologie de Bruxelles, I. *Les sources de la tapisserie bruxelloise et la tapisserie en tant que source,* Annales de la Société royale d'archéologie de Bruxelles, LI, 1966. *La Dame à la Licorne a été tissée à Bruxelles,* Gazette des Beaux-Arts, Nov. 1967. *A propos de la Dame à la licorne,* Gazette des Beaux-Arts, No. 1201, Febr. 1969. *Un grand tapissier bruxellois, Pierre d'Enghien dit Pierre van Aelst,* L'âge d'or de la tapisserie flamande, Brussels 1969. *Rôle de la Banque de Médicis dans l'expansion de la tapisserie flamande au XV° siècle,* Revue belge d'archéologie et d'histoire de l'art, XXXVIII. *Richesses du garde-meuble parisien de François I°*, Inventaires inédits de 1542 et 1551, Gazette des Beaux-Arts, Nov. 1971. *Peintres retoucheurs de tapisseries au XVII° siècle,* Cahiers bruxellois, V, fasc. IV. *Un nouveau regard sur les origines et le développement de la tapisserie bruxelloise du XIV° siècle à la pré-Renaissance,* Catalogue Tapisseries bruxelloises de la pré-Renaissance, Brussels 1976.

SOUCHAL G., *Charles VIII et la tenture de la Guerre de Troie,* Revue belge d'archéologie et d'histoire de l'art, XXXIX, 1970 and Artes Belgicae, Brussels 1972. *Un grand peintre français de la fin du XV° siècle: le maître de la Chasse à la licorne,* Revue de l'art, No. 22, 1973.

STEPPE J. K., *Inscriptions décoratives contenant des signatures et des mentions du lieu d'origine sur des tapisseries bruxelloises de la fin du XV° et du début du XVI° siècle,* Catalogue Tapisseries bruxelloises de la pré-Renaissance.

STEPPE J. K., DELMARCEL G., *Les tapisseries du Cardinal Erard de la Marck, prince-évêque de Liège,* Revue de l'art, No. 25, 1974.

VAISSE P., *La querelle de la tapisserie au début de la III° République,* Revue de l'art, No. 22.

WEIGERT R. A., *Les commencements de la manufacture royale de Beauvais, 1664–1705,* Gazette des Beaux-Arts, 1964.

Catalogues

AIX-EN-PROVENCE, Musée des tapisseries, *La tenture des Anciennes et Nouvelles Indes,* 1984. Catalogue compiled by Marie-Henriette KROTOFF; preface by Jean COURAL.

BRUSSELS, Musées royaux d'art et d'histoire, *Tapisseries du XIV° au XVIII° siècle,* 1956. Catalogue compiled by M. CRICK-KUNTZIGER.

BRUSSELS, Musées royaux d'art et d'histoire, *Tapisseries bruxelloises de la pré-Renaissance,* 1976. Studies by S. SCHNEEBALG-PERELMAN, J. K. STEPPE, E. DHANENS and G. DELMARCEL; preface by G. DELMARCEL and R. DE ROO.

MONS, *Tapisseries anciennes d'Enghien,* 1980. Catalogue compiled by G. DELMARCEL.

PARIS, Mobilier national, *Le XVI° siècle européen,* 1965–1966. Catalogue compiled by G. VIATTE. Mobilier national, *Chefs-d'œuvre de la tapisserie parisienne 1597–1662.* Introduction by Jacques THUILLIER. Grand Palais, *Chefs-d'œuvre de la tapisserie du XIV° au XVI° siècle.* Catalogue compiled by G. SOUCHAL; Preface by F. SALET. Musée Jacquemart-André, *Les fastes de la tapisserie du XV° au XVIII° siècle,* 1984. Catalogue compiled by L. HUYGHE, I. DENIS, J. BOCCARA and N. PAZZIS-CHEVALIER; preface by R. HUYGHE.

TOURNAI, *La tapisserie tournaisienne au XV° siècle,* 1967. Catalogue compiled by J. P. ASSELBERGHS. *Tapisseries héraldiques et de la vie quotidienne,* 1970. Catalogue compiled by J. P. ASSELBERGHS.

Chapter II

CONTEMPORARY TAPESTRY

BAZIN G., LURÇAT J., PICART LE DOUX J., SAINT-SAËNS M., DEGAND L., TABARD F., *Muraille et laine,* Paris 1946.

BEUTLICH T., *The Technique of Woven Tapestry,* London 1967.

CASSOU J., DAMAIN M., MOUTARD-ULDRY R., *La tapisserie française et les peintres cartonniers,* Paris 1957.

FAUX G., *Lurçat à haute voix,* Paris 1962.

FOUGÈRE V., *Tapisseries de notre temps,* Paris 1969.

JARRY M., COHEN H., BRENNAN A., HODGE M., *Master Weavers. Tapestry from the Dovecot Studios, 1912–1980.* Edinburgh 1980.

LURÇAT J., *Le travail dans la tapisserie du Moyen Age,* Preface by Louis Gillet, Geneva, Paris 1947. *Le bestiaire de la tapisserie du Moyen Age,* Geneva, Paris 1947.

LUXOVA V., TUCNA D., *Československá tapiséria, 1945–1975,* Bratislava 1978.

NICLAUSSE J., JANNEAU G., *Le musée des Gobelins. De la tapisserie décor à la tapisserie peinture,* Paris 1939.

ROY C., *Lurçat,* Geneva 1956.

VILLENEUVE C., *Tapisserie. Dentelle,* Paris 1976.

WISSA-WASSEF R., *Tapisserie de la jeune Egypte,* Paris 1972.

Article

VAISSE P., *Sur la tapisserie contemporaine,* L'information d'histoire de l'art, No. 2, 1965.

Catalogues

BERLIN, Kunstamt Charlottenburg, *Aubusson XX. Jh. Retrospektive der Tapisserien,* 1980.

BOURGES, Palais Jacques Cœur, *La matière et la couleur dans la tapisserie contemporaine,* 1978. Text by Y. DELABORDE.

BOULOGNE-BILLANCOURT, Centre culturel, *Tapisserie-création, 1928–1978,* 1978.

CHÂTEAUROUX, Les Cordeliers, *La tapisserie et l'espace,* 1980. Text by Y. DELABORDE.

ERMONT, Théâtre Pierre Fresnay, *Tapisserie art textile,* 1979. Text by J. BRACHET.

GENEVA, Musée d'Art et d'Histoire, PARIS, Musée des Arts Décoratifs, *Les tapisseries de Le Corbusier,* 1975. Texts by C. GOERG and F. MATHEY.

LE HAVRE, Maison de la culture, *Tapisseries de petits formats*, 1961. Texts by P. WALDBERG and B. PRIVAT.

MONTPELLIER, Galerie Frédéric Bazille, *Tapisseries nouvelles: Alain Dupuis et ses amis*, 1981.

PARIS, Musée des Arts Décoratifs, *Le chant du monde. Jean Lurçat*, 1964. Texts by M. FARÉ and J. LURÇAT. Musée d'art moderne de la ville de Paris, *Tapisseries finlandaises*, 1972–1973. Musée d'art moderne de la ville de Paris, *Lurçat, 10 ans après*, 1976. Texts by Jacques LASSAIGNE, Christian ZERVOS, Jean CASSOU. Bibliothèque Forney, *Tapisseries*. Association des créateurs de tapisserie, 1977. Grand Palais, *Vivante tapisserie française*, 1979. Musée d'art moderne de la ville de Paris, *Tapisseries de la Manufacture de Portalegre/Portugal*, 1981. Texts by B. CONTENSOU and J. SOMMER RIBEIRO. Musée-Galerie de la Seita, *Pierre Baudouin: 80 tapisseries de peintres tissées de 1947 à 1970*, 1985. Text by J. EDELMANN.

PRAGUE, Muzea v Praze, *Jan Hladik. Figurální tapiserie 1978*. Text by D. TUCNA.

SAINT-ÉTIENNE-DU-ROUVRAY, Centre municipal Jean Prévost, *Tapisserie art vivant*, 1980. Texts by C. SOLOY and M. THOMAS.

VEVEY, Musée Jenisch, *Exposition internationale de tapisserie. La vigne, le vin, le sacré et le carton numéroté illustré par Mario PRASSINOS*, 1977. Texts by J. P. MARTI.

Chapter III

CONTEMPORARY REVIVAL OF TEXTILE ART

BILLCLIFFE R., *Mackintosh. Textile Designs*, London 1982.

BONFANTI R., *Creatore nella tessitura*, Bologna 1982.

DELAUNAY S., *Nous irons jusqu'au soleil*, Paris 1978.

FAIRCLOUGH O., LEARY E., *Textiles by William Morris and Morris and Co., 1861–1940*, London 1981.

FRAYCENOT G., *Le volume dans la tapisserie contemporaine* (thesis, Paris VIII), Paris 1963.

FRECHETTE M., *La rénovation de la tapisserie de 1960 à 1975 à travers les Biennales de Lausanne* (thesis), Paris 1976. *Approche structurale de la tapisserie*, Document sur n° 5, *Textile/Art/Langage*, Paris 1985.

GINTZ C., *Regards sur l'art américain des années soixante*, Paris 1979.

HELLER J., *Paper-making*, New York 1978.

HUMBLET C., *Le Bauhaus*, Paris I 1980.

JALLAIS A., *La tapisserie et l'art textile, 1960–1983* (memoir, Paris I), Paris 1983.

KATO K. L., *Arts in Fiber. Who's Who in Japan*, Tokyo 1984.

LEONARD P., *Wolfgang Gäfgen. Drawings 1970–1976*, Hamburg 1976.

MONTICELLI R., *Alocco, peinture en patchwork*, Nice 1979.

NACHURY M. O., *Nouvelle tapisserie 1960–1977. La chaîne apparente* (memoir, Paris I), Paris 1977.

NAYLOR G., *The Arts and Crafts Movement*, London 1971.

PUIG A., *Grau Garriga*, Barcelona 1977.

ROSSBACH E., *The New Basketry*, New York, London 1980.

STANGOS N., *Piscines de papier. David Hockney*, Paris 1980.

TALLEY C. S., *Contemporary Textile Art. Scandinavia*, Stockholm 1982.

TAYLOR D., *The First Through the Tenth Biennales Internationales de la Tapisserie* (thesis), North Texas State University 1983.

TOALE B., *The Art of Papermaking*, Worcester 1983.

TURNER S., SKIOLD B., *Handmade Paper Today*, New York 1983.

VANDEWYNCLELE I., *Langage textile* (memoir), Paris 1980.

WATKINSON R., *William Morris as Designer*, London 1979.

WINGLER H. M., *Bauhaus*, Cambridge (USA), London 1976.

YASSINSKAÏA I., *Textiles révolutionnaires soviétiques*, Paris 1983.

Articles

BILLETER E., *L'utopie de l'environnement*, Catalogue Fibre-Espace, 11ᶜ Biennale internationale de la tapisserie, Musée cantonal des Beaux-Arts, Lausanne 1983.

CONSTANTINE M., *Art textile contemporain aux Etats-Unis*, Revue de l'art, No. 22, 1973.

Revues spécialisées d'art textile contemporain: *Textile/Art*, Paris. *Driadi*, Paris.

Catalogues

AMSTERDAM, Stedelijk Museum, *Perspectief in Textiel*, 1969. Stedelijk Museum, *Structuur in Textiel*, 1976. Text by L. CROMMELIN.

ANGERS, *Expressions textiles nordiques*, 1973. Musée Pincé, *Japon tradition vivante*, 1976.

ANNECY, Musée-château, *Textiles appliqués*, 1976. Texts by M. GOSTELOW and R. BERGER. Musée-château, *Broderies et dentelles contemporaines*, 1978. Text by S. DARGÈRE. Musée-château, *Papier, détournements volontaires*, 1983.

ARLES, Musée Réattu, *Papier-Papier*, 1980. Introduction by M. MOUTASHAR.

BRUSSELS, Palais des Beaux-Arts, *Art Nouveau Belgique*, 1981.

CHAMBÉRY, Maison de la culture, *Textile-informatique: un parcours*, 1984. Texts by M. THOMAS and R. PRIN.

COLOGNE, Belgisches Haus, *Antitapisseries. Artistes belges à Cologne*, 1980.

COURTRAI, Koninklyke Academie voor Schone Kunsten, *Textielstructuren*, 1980. Texts by Claude RITSCHARD, Michel THOMAS and Jan WALGRAVE.

DAYTON, Art Institute, *Cloth Forms*, 1982.

GENNEVILLIERS, Galerie municipale Edouard Manet, *Présence textile*, 1980. Text by Michel THOMAS.

HALBTURN, Schloss. *Textilkunst aus Österreich, 1900–1979*, 1979. Texts by A. VOLKER.

HANOVER, *Handwerksform, Minitextilkunst*, 1983.

KYOTO, National Museum of Modern Art, *America-Japan*, 1977.

LAUSANNE, Musée cantonal des Beaux-Arts, *Biennale internationale de la tapisserie*, since 1962. Musée des Arts décoratifs, *Papier, un nouveau langage artistique* I et II, 1983, 1985.

LÓDZ, *Triennale – Fiber Artists and Designers*, since 1972.

LONDON, British Crafts Centre, *International Exhibition of Miniature Textiles*, 1974, 1976, 1978, 1980. Craft Council Gallery, *Paper as Image*, 1983.

LYON. Musée historique des tissus, *Les folles années de la soie*, 1975. Texts by COLETTE, Jean-Michel TUCHSCHERER, François DUCHARNE, Ketty DUBOST. Espace lyonnais d'art contemporain, *Espace et matière*, 1979.

MONTREAL, Musée d'art contemporain, *Biennale de la nouvelle tapisserie québécoise*, 1979. *La tapisserie canadienne contemporaine*, 1979. Introduction by Gilles TOUPIN. Galerie de l'Université du Québec, *Biennale de la tapisserie, Petit format*, 1981. Musée d'art contemporain, *Troisième Biennale de la tapisserie, Grand format*, 1984.

NEW YORK, American Craft Museum, *Making Paper*, 1982. Texts by L. A. BELL, D. KIMBALL, D. FARNSWORTH, T. BARRETT, W. LUTZ. American Craft Museum, *Art to wear*, 1983. Texts by P. J. SMITH and K. NUGENT.

OUVILLE, Abbaye, *Première Biennale internationale de créations textiles*, 1983. Texts by G. DRISION and M. THOMAS.

PARIS, Musée des Arts Décoratifs, *Tapisseries nouvelles*, 1975. Foreword by F. MATHEY. Musée des Arts Décoratifs, *Broderie au passé et au présent*, 1977. Text by N. GASC. Introduction by F. MATHEY. Fondation nationale des arts graphiques et plastiques, *Nœuds et ligatures*, 1983. Texts by Gilbert LASCAULT and Pierre ROSENSTIEHL.

PHILADELPHIA, Philadelphia College of Art, *The Tenth Paradigm: Contemporary Art Fabric of the Netherlands*, 1984. Texts by L. CROMMELIN and W. SEELIG.

PRINCETON, Art Museum of Princeton University, *The Arts and Crafts Movement in America, 1876-1916*, 1972. Texts by R. JUDSON-CLARK, M. EIDELBERG, D. A. HAWKS, S. OTIS-THOMPSON.

SÃO PAULO, Museu de Arte Moderna, *Tapestry Triennial*, since 1976.

STUTTGART, Württembergisches Landesmuseum, *Art Nouveau. Textil-Dekor um 1900*. Texts by R. GRONWOLDT and S. HESSE.

SZOMBATHELY, Savaria Museum, *International Minitextile Biennial*, since 1976.

TARRASA, Museo Provincial Textil, *Exposición colectiva de tapiz español contemporáneo y experiencias textiles*, 1975. Preface by F. TORRELLA NIUBÓ.

TILBURG, Nederlands Textielmuseum, *Textiel Nu n° 1 to 12*, 1980–1982.

Triennial of the Nordic Countries, travelling exhibition in Finland, Sweden, Norway, Iceland, Denmark, 1976–1977, 1979–1980, 1982–1983, 1985–1986.

VICHTE, Oude Kerk, *Biennale Textielstructuren*, since 1982.

LIST OF ILLUSTRATIONS

Index of names

PRODUCED BY THE TECHNICAL STAFF OF
EDITIONS D'ART ALBERT SKIRA S.A., GENEVA

COLOUR AND BLACK AND WHITE,
FILMSETTING AND PRINTING BY
IRL IMPRIMERIES RÉUNIES LAUSANNE S.A.

BINDING BY H. + J. SCHUMACHER AG
SCHMITTEN (FRIBOURG)

Printed in Switzerland